Longman Pocket Companion Series

KU-257-449

Pocket Companion

Quotation Guide

Longman

Longman Group Limited,
Longman House, Burnt Mill, Harlow,
Essex CM20 2JE, England
and Associated Companies throughout the world.

© Longman Group Limited 1983
All rights reserved. No part of this publication
may be reproduced, stored in a retrieval system
or transmitted in any form or by any means, electronic,
mechanical, photocopying, recording or otherwise,
without the prior written permission of the Publishers.

First published 1983

British Library Cataloguing in Publication Data
    Lamb, G. F.
    Quotation guide.—(Longman pocket companion series)
    1. Quotations, English
    I. Title
    080   PN6081
    ISBN 0-582-55659-7

Set in 7½/8 pt Linotron 202 Palatino

Phototypeset by Tradespools Limited, Frome, Somerset
Printed in Great Britain
by Collins, Glasgow

Foreword

Some time ago I carelessly spilt some ink on a tablecloth. 'Accidents will happen in the best-regulated families,' I remarked sententiously (and not quite correctly), and then wondered how the saying first arose. A dictionary of quotations gave a little information: the source was Dickens's *David Copperfield*. A second quotation book added 'chapter 28 (Mr Micawber)'.

So far so good. But what was the occasion that drew this helpful comment from Wilkins Micawber? In due course I found a copy of the novel and examined the relevant chapter. . . . Ah, so that was what it was all about!

I could not help feeling that it would have been quite time-saving if one of the dictionaries of quotations had given me the information I needed instead of leaving me to ferret it out for myself. That is why this little book has been written. For each quotation it supplies the context as well as the author and title.

Not everyone possesses a huge collection of books, or has the opportunity, time, and inclination to burrow about in (say) the London Library. I believe, therefore, that this *Pocket Companion Quotation Guide* will be found both useful and interesting. New and sometimes surprising light can be thrown on a familiar quotation when its origin is explained, enabling us to see it in greater depth. I think that most of the sayings will be at least vaguely known to many readers, and I hope that those that are fresh will become familiar in time.

The *Quotation Guide* is ideal as a book for browsing through, and the entries are in alphabetical order. But for those looking for a specific quotation or for one about a particular topic, there is a list of authors and an index of key words to help you.

Shakespeare inevitably provides a problem to the compiler of such a book. It would be easy to fill it with quotations from (for example) *Hamlet* and *Macbeth* alone. Such a temptation must obviously be resisted, and I have tried to resist it. Forty Shakespearean quotes seems a reasonable number for a book of this size.

This is intended to be a handy pocket-book, so I have limited the number of quotations to about a thousand. There are many more that might well have been included. Some almost begged to be allowed entrance, but had to be left outside. Perhaps one day they will find their way into another volume.

G. F. Lamb

'About suffering they were never wrong, The old Masters'
W. H. Auden, *Musée des Beaux Arts* (1940)

Auden is approving the attitude adopted by the great classical painters towards suffering. He is concerned particularly with the *Icarus* of the Flemish painter, Pieter Brueghel (*c*1525–69), exhibited in the Musée des Beaux Arts, Brussels. His picture portrays the boy Icarus, who in classical legend flew too near the sun and lost his wings through the melting of the wax that held them. He fell into the sea and was drowned. What Auden admires is the way Brueghel shows everyday life going on casually, indifferent to the drowning boy. A ploughman takes no notice, and a ship just sails on its way despite the amazing sight of a boy falling out of the sky. That is just how it would be in everyday life, Auden maintains.

'Accidents will occur in the best-regulated families'
Charles Dickens, *David Copperfield*, ch. 28 (1849)

David was entertaining the Micawbers to a dinner party which became plagued by mishaps. The leg of mutton was badly cooked and appeared to have been dropped in the fireplace; the gravy was upset on the stairs; and the pigeon pie proved to be lacking in pigeon. Such accidents, the good-natured Micawber observed, are always liable to occur, particularly to anyone without a wife. 'They may be expected with confidence, and must be borne with philosophy.' The saying is often misquoted as 'accidents will *happen*'.

'Adding fuel to the flame'
John Milton, *Samson Agonistes* (1671)

Samson, a blinded captive of the Philistines, is commanded by an officer to appear at one of their feasts to entertain them with feats of strength. When Samson refuses, the officer warns him that his answer will give offence to the Philistine leaders. The Chorus (representing Samson's friends) gloomily observe that the officer may report the refusal in such a way as to make it appear even more defiant than it was. 'Who knows how he may report / Thy words by adding fuel to the flame?'

'Adding insult to injury'
Edward Moore, *The Foundling*, V, ii (1748)

Young Belmont, the hero, has rescued the heroine, Fidelia, from the hands of her supposed guardian, Villiard. In the presence of highly respectable witnesses Villiard accuses Belmont of assault and robbery. When the young man meets the accusation by threatening to draw his sword he is told that his action aggravates the injury he has already caused Villiard by taking away his ward. However, the true facts presently emerge, and Belmont duly marries a happy Fidelia.

'The age of chivalry is gone'
Edmund Burke, *Reflections on the Revolution in France* (1790)

Burke was a lover of liberty, which the French Revolution claimed to foster. But he was also a lover of law, order, and decency, and he saw these abused and stifled in the chaos and bloodshed brought about by the revolutionaries. He was also disturbed by the maltreatment of the French royal family, which no previous errors on their part could justify, and especially shocked at the rebels' gross behaviour towards the Queen, Marie Antoinette, which she endured with dignity. Burke said he would have expected ten thousand Frenchmen to have leapt to her defence with their swords, but 'the age of chivalry is gone'.

'Alas, regardless of their doom
The little victims play'
Thomas Gray, *Ode on a Distant Prospect of Eton College* (1742)

The little victims were young Etonians, heedless of the fact that they would one day suffer the fate of becoming grown-up. Subject to melancholia as he reached manhood, Gray grew to regard childhood as a blissful time, with little to do but play – to cleave the glassy waves of the Thames or 'chase the rolling circle's speed'. Incidentally, this circle was not, as many people suppose, a cricket ball or football, but merely a wooden hoop. Undignified as it may seem to modern Etonians, bowling hoops and spinning peg-tops were once the favourite activities of the College.

'Allah is the Lord of all men's ways'
F. L. Lucas, *The Destined Hour*

In this dramatic rendering of an old Arabian legend, a modern poet tells the story of a man who tries to flee from Death but in fact runs into Death's path. A chieftain's servant believes he is being chased by Death, and begs permission to go to his home at Samarra for a few days in order to escape. But Samarra, in fact, is the very place where Allah has ordered Death to lay his hand on the man, that same night. Each verse ends with the quoted words, which mean that God rules every person's life as He sees fit.

'All, all are gone, the old familiar faces'
Charles Lamb, *The Old Familiar Faces* (1798)

We might expect this to have been written by the essayist in the evening of his life, looking back at the far-distant past. It was in fact written when he was twenty-three – about the age when Wordsworth was finding it bliss to be alive. With its strain of gentle dejection the poem looks back to the girl, Ann Simmons, with whom Lamb had fallen in love as a youth; to his friends Charles Lloyd and Coleridge, from whom he was for a short while estranged; and to his sister Mary, temporarily removed to a mental asylum.

> For some they have died, and some they have left me . . .
> All, all are gone, the old familiar faces.

'All animals are equal, but some animals are more equal than others'
George Orwell, *Animal Farm*, ch. 10 (1945)

In Orwell's pungent satire on Soviet Russia the animals on Manor Farm expel their human owner and take over the running of the farm. But the pigs, leaders of the rebellion, gradually become more and more like humans, and their tyranny over the other animals grows just like the human tyranny. At first one of the rules of the animals is, 'All animals are equal'. But in due course this rule is altered to the quoted sentence, with 'equal' undergoing a subtle change of meaning.

'All availed no more than the whistling of the wind'
Benjamin Franklin, *An Account of Negociations in London* (1775)

Benjamin Franklin, the distinguished American writer and politician, was sent to England in 1764 to negotiate with the Government on the question of taxation of the American colonies (as they then were). He returned to America in 1775, the lengthy mission having failed. Just before returning, he was able to hear the great speech of William Pitt, Earl of Chatham, urging the House of Lords to show reason and a spirit of conciliation. Franklin was delighted with Chatham's speech, but noted that their lordships voted against him. This mechanical voting for the Government, Franklin considered, made political debates pointless and ridiculous.

'All for one, one for all'
Alexandre Dumas, *The Three Musketeers*, ch. 9 (1844)

This is the motto of the four heroes of the famous Dumas story – the three musketeers (Athos, Porthos, and Aramis) plus the swashbuckling apprentice musketeer, D'Artagnan. It is D'Artagnan, the young novice, who proposes the motto, and they hold out their hands and swear to follow it. 'From this moment we are at feud with the Cardinal,' D'Artagnan declares importantly, though in fact the King's Musketeers and Cardinal Richelieu's Guards have long been at feud with each other. However, D'Artagnan is clearly the novelist's favourite character, so he must be allowed a little licence.

'All hell broke loose'
John Milton, *Paradise Lost*, Bk IV (1668)

Satan, engaged in the task of tempting Eve, is made prisoner by two guardian angels and taken before the archangel Gabriel, who rather unfairly taunts him with deserting his colleagues in order to escape the pains of Hell. 'Wherefore with thee / Came not all hell broke loose,' Gabriel asks. ('Why didn't the other rebels also break out of hell?'). The quoted phrase has lost its original sense and has come to imply a terrible and noisy upheaval.

'All her shining keys will be took from her, and her cupboards opened, and little things 'a didn't wish seen, anybody will see, and her wishes and ways will all be as nothing'
Thomas Hardy, *The Mayor of Casterbridge*, ch. 18 (1886)

The speaker is Mother Cuxsom, an old countrywoman of Casterbridge (Dorchester), talking of a lady who has just died. Mother Cuxsom is all but illiterate, but the words she utters form a little elegy that is truly poetic in language and spirit. The dead woman is the wife of the Mayor, Michael Henchard, who many years earlier had sold her at a Fair when he was drunk, though they were later reunited.

'All hope abandon, ye who enter here'
Dante Alighieri, *The Vision of Hell*, III, trans. H. F. Cary (1805)

Dante follows his guide, Virgil, to the gate of Hell, where he sees written over the arch these grim words. Through this gate lost souls passed 'into eternal pain'. The only way to keep out of this terrible place, it seemed, was to be very actively virtuous, for it was not only outright evildoers who were brought within the portal. The wretched inmates included (as the prose summary puts it) 'those who had passed their time in a state of apathy and indifference both to good and evil'.

'All is grand, and all appalling and horrible in the last degree'
Charles Dickens, *American Notes*, ch. 2 (1842)

In January 1842 Dickens visited America. The sea voyage across the Atlantic in an American paddle steamer was an essential preliminary. It also proved a devastating experience. A violent storm threw the ship on her side, then over on the other side, 'until a heavy sea strikes her with the noise of a hundred great guns, and hurls her back – she stops, and staggers, and shivers, as though stunned.' After later running aground in the mist at midnight, the ship at last docked safely in Halifax harbour, sixteen days after setting out.

*'All love, all liking, all delight
Lies drowned with us in endless night'*
Robert Herrick, *Corinna's Going a-Maying* (1648)

A typical expression of the 'fleeting time' theme, which impresses many people besides poets. Herrick found it particularly powerful and turned to it more than once. Here he invites the imaginary Corinna to enjoy the maytime festivities while the two of them are young enough to do so.
  We shall grow old apace, and die
  Before we know our liberty.

'All the live murmur of a summer's day'
Matthew Arnold, *The Scholar Gipsy* (1853)

The poem is based on an old legend of an Oxford scholar who joined the gipsies to learn their lore, and whose shade still haunts the Oxford countryside. Arnold begins by setting the scene – a field near Oxford where he sits at rest with the book which tells the story of the Scholar-Gipsy *The Vanity of Dogmatizing*, by Joseph Glanvill (1661). The sheep are bleating, the reaper has been at work in the cornfield, as Arnold lets his eyes travel to the distant towers of Oxford, listening to 'the live murmur of a summer's day'.

'All went merry as a marriage bell'
Lord Byron, *Childe Harold's Pilgrimage*, III, xxi (1816)

On the eve of the battle of Waterloo a ball was held in Brussels. The Duke of Wellington thought it best to leave people in ignorance of the coming conflict, so the dance was not cancelled. Officers attending it were instructed to slip away quietly. But to those with ears to hear there were more disquieting sounds than waltz music or marriage bells. 'Nearer, nearer, deadlier than before ... it is – the cannon's opening roar.' The third canto of the poem was written not very long after the battle, and has the ring of truth.

'Alone I did it!'
William Shakespeare, *Coriolanus*, V, vi (*c* 1608)

The former Roman general Coriolanus is brashly reminding the Volscians (Rome's enemies, whom he has now joined) that he once led the Romans to ransack the Volscian town Corioli. Although he has now changed sides, the reminder is hardly tactful. Moreover, his claim that this was a solo performance overlooks the fact that an army helped him to achieve the victory. In the end Coriolanus meets the fate that might be expected. The Volscians slay him.

'America is God's Crucible, the great Melting-Pot'
Israel Zangwill, *The Melting-Pot*, Act I (1908)

David Quixano, a young Russian Jew, had always dreamed of going to America. To him it is the place 'where all the races of Europe are melting and reforming'. Many of his family were victims of a cruel pogrom in Russia, and he revels in the freedom he finds in America.

Zangwill, London-born son of a Russian Jewish refugee, was a prominent author and playwright for many years, writing mostly on Jewish themes. In an appendix to the English edition of the play (1914) he gives figures showing that about one and a half million aliens of forty different races were admitted to America in 1913.

'And French she spake ful fayre and fetisly,
After the scole of Stratford-atte-Bowe'
Geoffrey Chaucer, *The Canterbury Tales – Prologue* (c 1387)

Chaucer is giving an amused but not unkindly look at a Prioress making the pilgrimage to Canterbury. She conducted herself very much in the manner of a refined Court lady, very dainty in her eating habits, and sensitive to animal suffering. Her French was the Anglo-French often taught in England, not highly regarded by experienced travellers such as Chaucer. Stratford-atte-Bowe, not to be confused with Shakespeare's home town, was in Chaucer's time an Essex village three or four miles from London where there was a nunnery. The Prioress had doubtless been educated there.

'And how can man die better
Than facing fearful odds?'
T. B. Macaulay, *Lays of Ancient Rome* –'*Horatius* (1842)

When the powerful Etruscan army was approaching to attack Rome, the Roman Consul gloomily observed that there would be no time to destroy the one bridge over the River Tiber before the Etruscan vanguard reached the city. The legendary hero, Horatius Cocles, Captain of the Gate, thereupon invited two other men to stand with him at the front of the bridge to keep the foe at bay while the structure was demolished behind them. Although he was quite ready to meet death in the enterprise, in fact he escaped by swimming the river, as the legend goes on to relate.

'And gladly wolde he lerne and gladly teche'
Geoffrey Chaucer, *The Canterbury Tales – Prologue* (c 1387)

There is a tinge of amusement in Chaucer's picture of the Oxford clerk's asceticism, but the poet also has respect for a scholar, who thus devotes his life to learning. He spends the little money he has on books, and is too busy studying philosophy to enjoy the living to which his qualifications entitle him

For he hadde geten him yet no benefice,

Ne was so worldly for to have office.

The teaching he undertakes would not be school teaching but tutoring. Oxford in the fourteenth century had a system whereby older fellows of the university helped to support themselves by coaching younger members.

'And that's the long and the short of it'
W. S. Gilbert, *Princess Ida*, Act II (1884)

Prince Hilarion is a captive in the castle of Princess Ida. His father, King Hildebrand, has invaded Ida's land to demand that the Prince be released, and to insist that the Princess carries out the vow she made (by proxy) at the age of one, to marry the prince. Hildebrand, as he himself puts it, is 'a peppery kind of King'. He threatens to smash the castle to smithereens unless his demands are met – 'and that's the long and the short of it!' Perhaps the King was a keen Shakespearean, unconsciously adapting Mistress Quickly's 'the short and the long of it' in *The Merry Wives of Windsor*.

> *'And was Jerusalem builded here,*
> *Among these dark Satanic mills?'*
> William Blake, *Milton – Preface* (1804)

The poem from which these lines come is sometimes, especially when sung, known as *Jerusalem*. It is, however, the Preface to Blake's long poem, *Milton*, in which the blind poet returns from eternity with a message. The lines appear to suggest that Blake foresaw the coming industrialization of England. But there was doubtless a further meaning, and the Satanic mills were those of the mind and soul. The opening lines of the poem ('And did those feet in ancient time / Walk upon England's mountains green') may refer to a legend that Christ visited England.

> *'And when they get to feeling old,*
> *They up and shoot themselves, I'm told'*
> Rupert Brooke, *The Old Vicarage, Grantchester* (1912)

Brooke, on a temporary visit to Germany, is thinking in humorous nostalgic vein of his English dwelling – the Old Vicarage at Grantchester, a village just outside Cambridge. With lively exaggeration he describes its inhabitants as perfect.

> The women there do all they ought;
> The men observe the Rules of Thought.

Finally, when age prevents them from serving the community any longer, they politely do away with themselves. Brooke was twenty-five when he wrote *Grantchester*, and old age no doubt seemed to his humorous eye as remote as it was undesirable.

> *'And whispering "I will ne'er consent" – consented'*
> Lord Byron, *Don Juan*, I, cxvii (1818)

Julia, the young wife of a much older husband, has known Juan (seven years younger than herself) since his early childhood. When he reaches the age of sixteen her interest in him becomes rather more than friendly. They sit together one summer evening, hand in hand. Juan is rapidly overcome by the new experience of love, while Julia attempts to keep the association piatonic – and fails.

> *'Annihilating all that's made*
> *To a green thought in a green shade'*
> Andrew Marvell, *The Garden* (1681)

Marvell revels in the 'Quiet . . . and Innocence' to be found among plants and trees. He reproves the desire to compete for wreaths of laurel, bay, and palm – the traditional prizes in classical times for intellectual and athletic prowess. Far more satisfaction, he suggests, can be gained from the living tree than from garlands stripped from its branches. Moreover, no female Beauty whose name is carved by a lover on a tree trunk can equal the beauty of the tree itself. Strangely enough, the author of this delightful poem of pastoral peace was also a vigorous and vituperative anti-Royalist political writer.

'Annual income twenty pounds, annual expenditure nineteen nineteen six, result happiness. Annual income twenty pounds, annual expenditure twenty ought and six, result misery'
Charles Dickens, *David Copperfield*, ch. 12 (1849–50)

This is the parting advice given by Mr Micawber to his young friend David, when the Micawber family are about to leave London. The advice is prompted by Micawber's own experiences, which should have caused him misery for he was ever in debt. But his invariable confidence that something would turn up left him remarkably cheerful in spite of everything. Dickens's own father is said to have been the model for this improvident but likeable personality. Readers whose education began after February 1971 may need to have it explained that Micawber's recipe for happy expenditure was £19.19s.6d – £19.97½p in less glamorous currency.

'Anyone who has been to an English public school will always feel comparatively at home in prison'
Evelyn Waugh, *Decline and Fall*, Pt 2, ch. 4 (1928)

Paul Pennyfeather, engaged to the lovely and wealthy widow, Margot Beste-Chetwynde, is arrested just before the wedding can take place, and later charged with running a white slave business. He has in fact been engaged in work for his fiancée, the source of whose wealth he is unaware; but he gallantly accepts the blame, and is sent to gaol. It is impossible, he feels, to think of so radiant and feminine a person as Margot in prison, but he is a male with grim experience of boarding school.

'April, April,
Laugh thy girlish laughter'
William Watson, *Song* (1896)

This brief poem personifies the notoriously changeable month of April with sun and rain following each other in quick succession. The poet's relationship with April is almost like that of a lover with his mistress. In spite of the uncertainties, he loves the variety that April brings.
  Laugh thy golden laughter,
  But, the moment after,
  Weep thy golden tears!
T. S. Eliot, however, had a much less favourable opinion of this deceptive month.

'April is the cruellest month, breeding Lilacs out of the dead land'
T. S. Eliot, *The Waste Land*, I (1922)

These are the cryptic opening lines of a strange but influential poem, much of which was composed in a Swiss sanatorium. A friendly critic (Robert Sencourt) has called it 'the poem of a man working his way through a nervous breakdown and dealing partly with his own memories and partly with a mass of material – both classic and contemporary – too vast for him to digest'. The rather pretentious notes that Eliot added to the poem contribute little of value. None the less *The Waste Land* played an important part in showing the direction in which a good deal of contemporary poetry would travel.

'Apt alliteration's artful aid'
Charles Churchill, *The Prophecy of Famine* (1763)

Rather surprisingly Churchill, not renowned for modesty, claims no heavenly inspiration for his lively verse. He claims only 'a mere knack of rhyme' and 'short gleams of sense'. However, he is really priding himself on saying what he means without frills, for he goes on to own allegiance to Nature, and expresses his scorn for 'those vile tricks which mar fair Nature's hue'. One of these tricks is alliteration, and his mention of it is not a tribute to a useful literary device but a satiric reference to the work of William Mason (1724–97), friend and editor of Thomas Gray, and a minor poet with a liking for alliterative phrases.

'Honest men are the soft easy cushions on which knaves repose'
Thomas Otway, *Venice Preserved*, I, i (1682)

Pierre, the speaker, and his friend Jaffier are both angry with the corrupt senators of Venice. Pierre declaims bitterly against honesty for enabling fools and cowards to take advantage of decent men. He even questions his own honesty, for although he pays his debts, scorns flattery, and shuns evil behaviour, he has tolerated the cheating of the people by the senators and taken no action. 'I am a villain,' he declares modestly. But he and Jaffier now decide to remedy this state of affairs, and a plot against the evil senators is hatched.

'Arguments out of a pretty mouth are unanswerable'
Joseph Addison, *The Freeholder*, no. 4 (2 January 1716)

The essayist is dealing with the important part played by women in politics (some two hundred years before they received the vote). Lovers had been estimated as 'at least the third part of the sensible men of the British nation', and lovers were always devoted to their mistresses. Women could thus have a vital influence in persuasive argument. No man of breeding would attempt to refute them. Addison was anxious that this feminine influence should be used in favour of the new Protestant King (George I) as opposed to his Catholic rival, James (The Old Pretender). *The Freeholder* (1715–16) was hastily established and written for this purpose.

'As busie as a bee'
John Lyly, *Euphues and his England* (1580)

Euphues, a young Athenian, visits England with a friend. Not far from Canterbury they pass a house with a pleasant garden, in which they see 'a comely old man as busie as a bee'. The simile is apt, for the old man is cultivating bees. These remarkable insects (their owner says) have organized themselves into a regular kingdom. They choose a king, and carry out his behests, and if any bee disobeys, he promptly commits suicide. They also have a parliament to conduct their affairs. Shakespeare made fun of Euphues, but he was not above filching the idea of the bees' commonwealth for *Henry V*.

'As Ded as a dore-nayl'
William Langland, *Piers Plowman*, I, 183 (*c* 1395)

A lovely lady, representing Holy Church, is telling the
narrator that love is essential. The Biblical *Epistle of James*,
she reminds him, says that faith without good deeds is
dead (James, ii, 26), just as the body without the spirit is
dead. Although the poem was long ascribed to Lang-
land, a Malvern cleric, its authorship is doubtful. The
unusual simile is no doubt due to the alliteration which is
essential to the poem.

'As idle as a painted ship
Upon a painted ocean'
S. T. Coleridge, *The Rime of the Ancient Mariner*, Pt II (1798)

During a voyage to distant seas a seaman (the narrator of
the story) shot an albatross, a bird of good omen. The
slaughter of the bird was avenged when the ship became
completely becalmed at the Equator. The seamen suffered agonies of thirst under the hot sun, without a
breeze.

> Day after day, day after day,
> We stuck, nor breath nor motion.

The whole sky seemed to be ablaze, and to make things
worse, the very sea appeared to grow rotten in the heat,
with strange, slimy reptiles crawling on its surface.

Periodically the old mariner is impelled to tell his
story, and those to whom he begins to tell it find
themselves impelled to listen.

'Ask me no questions, and I'll tell you no fibs'
Oliver Goldsmith, *She Stoops to Conquer*, III, i (1774)

Young Tony Lumpkin has agreed to help his cousin,
Constance, to elope with her lover, Hastings. But Tony's
mother wants Tony to marry Constance, and is keeping
her jewellery under lock and key. Tony has a key to his
mother's bureau, and gets possession of the jewel-box
which he passes on to Hastings. The latter wonders how
the lad managed to get hold of it, but Tony puts him off
with the quoted line. Most people who borrow his words
switch 'fibs' to 'lies'.

'Ask yourself whether you are happy, and you cease to be so'
J. S. Mill, *Autobiography*, ch. 5 (1873)

Mill had for some time been suffering from an unac-
countable depression. Fortunately his reading of a
French autobiography helped him to realize that it is a
mistake to seek happiness. 'This end was only to be
attained by not making it the direct end. Those only are
happy (I thought) who have their minds fixed on some
object other than their own happiness.' The object might
be the good of others, or the following of some art or
other pursuit. Happiness might then follow as a kind of
by-product. It would never be found by being sought.
Perhaps it was strange that a profound philosopher had
to reach so commonplace a conclusion by so roundabout
a route.

'As large as life, and twice as natural!'
Lewis Carroll, *Through the Looking-Glass*, ch. 7 (1871)

The unicorn is always regarded as a fabulous beast. In Looking-Glass land, however, when Alice meets a unicorn (resting during its fight with the lion) the legendary creature regards Alice as a fabulous monster instead of the other way round. It is told that she is a newly discovered creature called a child, 'as large as life, and twice as natural!'. 'Now that we *have* seen each other,' the unicorn observes, 'if you'll believe in me, I'll believe in you.'

'As savage as a bear with a sore head'
Capt. Frederick Marryatt, *The King's Own* (1830)

This tale, one of Marryatt's lesser-known sea stories, has a good many typical digressions, one of which is a yarn related by the coxswain. He describes how one of his previous captains had ordered the ship's cat to be killed. The action gave great offence to the crew, and the captain became so disturbed by the spirit aboard that he grew 'as savage as a bear with a sore head, and did nothing but growl for three days afterwards'.

'The Assyrian came down like a wolf on the fold'
Lord Byron, *The Destruction of Sennacherib* (1815)

According to the Biblical story (2 Kings, xviii, 32–6; 2 Chronicles, xxxii, 19–22) Sennacherib, King of Assyria from 705–680 B.C., launched a successful campaign against the land of Judah. But when he came to attack Jerusalem his army was afflicted by plague, and thus defeated 'unsmote by the sword'. Sennacherib was subsequently slain by his own sons.

'As unto the bow the cord is,
So unto the man is woman'
H. W. Longfellow, *The Song of Hiawatha*, Pt X (1855)

This rather cryptic simile is Hiawatha's own view of marriage, not really as slighting to women as it may at first seem. Although she obeys the man, she also bends him to do what she wants. Though she follows him, she also draws him to follow her. Honour is really even, and they are 'Useless each without the other!' Hiawatha's personal choice, at any rate, could not be faulted, for Minnehaha (Laughing Water), 'handsomest of all the women', belonged to a rival tribe, and the marriage meant the peaceful union of the two peoples.

'At our time of life, to be alone is sometimes as needful as sleep'
Charles Lamb, *Popular Fallacies*, XII (1833)

The essayist is putting forward the view that there are some homes which are no homes. Among such is 'the house of the man that is infested with many visitors'. Lamb does not refer to invited guests but to casual callers who constantly interrupt whatever occupation he is engaged in – reading, eating, or whatever it may be. They are, he thinks, like flies, 'that flap in at your window, and out again, leaving nothing but a sense of disturbance'. As age creeps on he resents their disturbances the more, for he has fewer years in which to enjoy his own activities.

'At the going down of the sun and in the morning We will remember them'
Laurence Binyon, *For the Fallen* (1914)

Written not, as is often thought, at the end of the First World War but in its early months, the poem mourns for the 'dead across the sea' who had fallen in the desperate Autumn battles. Though an elegy, it has a note of subdued and patient optimism.

There is music in the midst of desolation
And a glory that shines upon our tears.

The poet finds consolation, too, in the thought that 'They shall not grow old, as we that are left grow old'. The poem is often recited at war memorial services.

'Barkis is willin'. That's the message'
Charles Dickens, *David Copperfield*, ch. 5 (1849)

The carrier who took young David to London had a fancy for the Copperfields' servant (always known by her surname Peggotty) especially when he discovered that she was responsible for all the cooking in the household. Too shy to ask her openly to marry him, he got David to add the three-word message to the letter he was writing home to his mother. Although the message was cryptic and delivered so indirectly, Peggotty took the hint and she and Barkis were duly married.

'Beauty in distress'
Lord Byron, *To Florence* (1809)

Byron rightly claimed to be 'What man should ever be / The friend to Beauty in distress'. The distressed beauty was Mrs Spencer Smith, whom Byron in a letter described as 'very pretty, very accomplished, and extremely eccentric'. While in Malta he spent much of his time with her in what seems to have been a platonic friendship. She had excited the enmity of Napoleon by taking part in some conspiracy, and her distress – not immediate – was the danger that on the journey to England her ship might be captured by the French, in which case her life would perhaps have been in danger.

'Beauty is the lover's gift'
William Congreve, *The Way of the World*, II, v (1700)

Mirabell is trying to persuade Millamant, his hard-to-get mistress, that a woman loses her beauty when she has no lover to praise it. Even the plain can see fine features in their looking glass when they are complimented. Millamant utterly repudiates the suggestion. She avers that unless a woman is handsome she will not be praised, and she speaks disdainfully of lovers. 'Why, one makes lovers as fast as one pleases.' They can be made and discarded at will. 'One no more owes one's beauty to a lover, than one's wit to an echo.' Neither Millamant nor Mirabell should be taken too literally. They are verbally fencing with each other.

'Beauty unadorned'
Aphra Behn, *The Rover*, III, 1 (1681)

Most people would apply the phrase admiringly to female nudity (e.g. the Venus of Rubens or Botticelli). But it was originally used in a different and indeed disparaging sense. In Mrs Behn's popular Restoration comedy an old bawd is endeavouring to persuade a young courtesan that the ugliest woman decked out in finery will be more successful in attracting a lover than a handsome one without such adornment. 'Do you not daily see fine Clothes ... are more inviting than Beauty unadorn'd?'

'Because it is there'
George Mallory, quoted in David Robertson's *George Mallory* (1969)

Mallory gave this famous reply to a New York newspaper reporter who asked him why he wanted to climb Mount Everest. The question is really almost unanswerable, but in a later lecture Mallory tried to explain that a mountaineer wants to climb every available mountain, whatever the difficulties, for the same kind of reason that a composer wants to write music. He experiences an urge to do what his gift enables him to do. Mallory was the outstanding mountaineer of his day and the leading Everest climber. He and a companion disappeared on the mountain in 1924.

'Begin at the beginning, and go on till you come to the end; then stop'
Lewis Carroll, *Alice's Adventures in Wonderland*, ch. 12 (1865)

This is the instruction given by the King of Hearts to the White Rabbit at the trial of the Knave of Hearts for the theft of some tarts. The Rabbit has just picked up a piece of paper which proves to be a set of verses. He is commanded by the King to read them, and asks where to begin. In this instance the King's advice (admirable for any short-story writer or after-dinner speaker) is less pertinent than usual, for the verses have no beginning, no end – and no meaning.

'Being in a ship is being in a jail, with the chance of being drowned'
Samuel Johnson, in Boswell's *Journal of a Tour to the Hebrides* (1785)

This was a comparison which Johnson put forward more than once. The particular occasion here was that one of their Highland guides had formerly been press-ganged aboard a warship, but had managed to get out of the navy after nine months of service. Boswell naively expressed surprise at his wanting to leave the sea. Johnson offered a more realistic opinion. Enlarging upon this on a later occasion, Johnson asserted that a man in jail has more room, better food, and often better company than a man in a ship, and moreover is much safer.

'Be it ever so humble, there's no place like home'
John Howard Payne, *Clari, the Maid of Milan* (1823)

This very English sentiment comes from a song in an opera written by an American actor. However, he lived for a while in London, and wrote *Clari* for London's Covent Garden Theatre. Sir Henry Bishop composed the music, and the song *Home, Sweet Home* (sung more than once in the opera) became a popular song in its own right. Mme Patti (1843–1919), the most celebrated soprano of her period, loved it and sang it at every recital she gave.

'The best laid schemes o' mice an' men Gang aft a-gley'
Robert Burns, *To a Mouse* (1785)

A farm servant was pulling the plough which Burns was holding when a mouse ran out from under a clod. The poet restrained the man from killing it, and made the incident into a poem, sympathizing with the 'cow'rin, tim'rous beastie' that has suddenly had its dwelling destroyed, and reflecting that man also is pitifully liable to have his cherished plans upset. Burns, the son of a farmer, was a good ploughman but an unsuccessful farmer. His own plans too often went 'a-gley' (awry), and at one stage he was on the point of emigrating to Jamaica to try and better his fortune.

'The best things carried to excess are wrong'
Charles Churchill, *The Rosciad* (1761)

The adage has a general application, but Churchill is referring specifically to acting technique. Some critics had condemned David Garrick's 'unnatural Start, affected Pause'. While agreeing that if these were too freely used they were mere tricks which deserved to be laughed at, Churchill insisted that Garrick used them in such a way that they were absolutely natural. 'Each start is Nature; and each pause is Thought.' The poem ends with Shakespeare inviting Garrick to be enthroned as the king of actors. Charles Churchill, an unenthusiastic clergyman, was a keen follower of the theatre, and a lively satirist.

'A better farmer ne'er brushed dew from lawn,
A worse king never left a realm undone'
Lord Byron, *The Vision of Judgment*, VIII (1822)

The subject of this acid comment was George III, often known as 'Farmer George' because of his interest in agriculture and the domestic life of his subjects. Though his kingship, even allowing for his periods of insanity, was far from ideal, Byron's stricture was hardly an historical judgment. His poem, in fact, was basically an attack on Robert Southey, Poet Laureate, who had not only written a poem in praise of George after his death, but also dared to criticize Byron. Southey gave excellent counsel when he advised the noble lord to put his criticism into rhyme because this helped to curb his temper. The quarrel with Southey is dead, but *The Vision of Judgment* still has some vitality.

'A bird came down the walk,
He did not know I saw'
Emily Dickinson, *A Bird Came Down the Walk* (1862?)

A strangely simple poem by this very original American poetess. It merely describes a bird eating a worm, having a drink, and looking round with eyes that 'looked like frightened beads'. When she offered him a piece of bread,

He unrolled his feathers
And rowed him softer home
Than oars divide the ocean.

This is Emily Dickinson's delightful way of saying that he opened his wings and flew away as easily and smoothly as a boat skimming the waves.

'Bliss was it in that dawn to be alive,
But to be young was very Heaven!'
William Wordsworth, *The Prelude*, Bk XI (1850)

The 'dawn' was the age of liberty, equality, and fraternity. Wordsworth in his early twenties, like many other young liberals, believed such an age was being ushered in by the French Revolution of 1792. By the time he wrote *The Prelude* he knew that the dawn was a false one and that the society it had introduced was a tyranny ruled by bloodthirsty bigots.

'The bloom is gone, and with the bloom go I'
Matthew Arnold, *Thyrsis* (1867)

This is 'the cuckoo's parting cry' when June is wet and stormy. Imagining that summer is over he departs early for his winter quarters, not understanding that July will bring 'the high midsummer pomps' – a profusion of flowers and scents. Arnold comforts himself with the reflection that the bird will return next year, unlike the friend with whom he used to roam the countryside around Oxford, for death has claimed him. The dead friend was A. H. Clough, the poet, who died in Florence in 1861. In the poem he is portrayed as Thyrsis, who in classical poetry was a shepherd.

'Blow your pipe there till you burst!'
Robert Browning, *The Pied Piper of Hamelin* (1845)

After the Pied Piper had rid Hamelin town of rats, its Mayor rudely (in the quoted words) refused to pay the promised fee. The Piper thereupon played a tune which drew the town's children after him to a mysterious cavern in Koppelberg Hill. It closed after them, and they were never seen again. And the moral of this delightful children's poem is: 'If we've promised (them) aught, let us keep our promise.' The poem was written to amuse young William, the son of the great nineteenth-century actor, W. C. Macready.

'The boy stood on the burning deck
Whence all but he had fled'
F. D. Hemans *Casabianca* (1829)

The poem is based on fact. The ten-year-old son of Louis de Casabianca, captain of the French flagship at the battle of the Nile (1798), refused to leave the vessel when she was set on fire. There is perhaps some poetic licence in Mrs Hemans's version of the story. She avers that the father was dead and that his son died because he kept calling in vain for permission to leave the ship. It is believed that in fact the boy's reluctance to leave was because his father was badly wounded. Both were blown up when the vessel exploded.

'Boys who shine at school do not make the greatest figure when they grow up and come out into the world'
William Hazlitt, *Table Talk – On the Ignorance of the Learned* (1821)

Hazlitt was, of course, thinking of the kind of education received by boys at a public or grammar school at the beginning of the nineteenth century and earlier. It was predominantly classical and mainly a matter of memory. Such lessons did not exercise a boy's highest faculties, and were best learnt by a pupil with no very active mind. An idler at school would be more likely to want 'to feel the open air in his face ... than doze over a musty spelling-book'. Ironically, Hazlitt perhaps forgot that he himself, at the age of ten, was the brightest boy in his private school. He loved Latin and Greek, could teach arithmetic to a boy six years older than himself, and was always top of the school at spelling.

'A boy's will is the wind's will,
And the thoughts of youth are long, long thoughts'
H. W. Longfellow, *My Lost Youth* (1855)

The two lines, which conclude each stanza of the poem, are from an old Lapland song. They perhaps mean that a boy's imagination is as free and unrestricted as the wind, and roams far and wide in time and place. Now Longfellow looks back to his boyhood days, recalling some of the incidents and emotions that stirred him then. When he revisits the town where he used to live (Portland, Maine, U.S.A.) he finds the people strangers. However, 'Among the dreams of the days that were/I find my lost youth again.'

'A brave man struggling in the storms of fate'
Alexander Pope, *Prologue to Addison's 'Cato'* (1713)

Pope is supporting Addison's belief that virtue and innocence should not always be presented as triumphing on the stage, for they did not do so in life. In *Cato* the main theme is a good man struggling against adversity. The tears of the audience will be shed not through pity for human weakness but through admiration of human strength enduring the blows of fate.

> Here tears shall flow from a more generous cause,
> Such tears as patriots shed for dying laws.

There is, in fact, no record of damp handkerchiefs, but political references drew hearty applause from the political parties, both of which took favourable speeches to apply to themselves.

'Breathes there the man, with soul so dead,
Who never to himself hath said,
This is my own, my native land!'
Sir Walter Scott, *The Lay of the Last Minstrel* (1805)

An old Scottish minstrel is telling the romantic story of a medieval Border feud. Minstrelsy was dying out in Scotland, and he is asked why he remains there instead of going to England, where his skill as a harpist would be better rewarded. Scottish to the backbone, he declares that he will sing nothing but the ballads of his native land. Scott himself had a wide knowledge of the old ballads and songs of the Border country, and was largely responsible for the revival of interest in Scottish folklore.

'Brevity is the soul of wit'
William Shakespeare, *Hamlet*, II, ii (*c* 1601)

Polonius, Lord Chamberlain at the court of King Claudius of Denmark, is portrayed as a tedious old windbag. In the course of a long-winded statement to the King and Queen about Hamlet's supposed madness, Shakespeare ironically causes him to praise the virtue of brevity, which he declares is the essence of wisdom ('wit').

'Brightly dawns our wedding day'
W. S. Gilbert, *The Mikado*, Act II (1885)

On the morning of their intended wedding day Nanki-Poo and his bride-to-be, Yum-Yum, with a couple of friends, sing this madrigal to cheer themselves up as they try to look on the bright side of a somewhat unusual situation. The two lovers will be given a sumptuous wedding and will live happily together for a month. At the end of that time the bridegroom will be beheaded, according to a compact entered into with the Executioner. The verses begin brightly, but the madrigal ends in tears. In the end, however, Nanki-Poo's threatened fate is averted.

'Bright star, would I were steadfast as thou art'
John Keats, *Bright Star* (1820)

While in the Lake District in 1818 Keats felt that the lovely scenery 'refines one's sensual vision into a sort of north star'. The thought was developed into a sonnet which he handed to a friend not long before his death. It was the last poem he wrote, and remained unpublished until 1846. Though he desires to be steadfast, he does not wish to be alone. 'Not in lone splendour hung aloft the night.' He wishes rather to have his head 'Pillow'd upon my fair love's ripening breast.' Tragically, he died at the early age of twenty-five in 1821.

'A broken heart is a very pleasant complaint for a man in London if he has a comfortable income'
George Bernard Shaw, *Man and Superman* (1903)

Octavius Robinson ('Ricky-ticky-tavy'), poetic, romantic, and sentimental, believes himself to be desperately in love with Ann Whitefield, whom he wants to marry. But Ann not only has her eye on someone else but is also shrewd enough to realize that marriage would ultimately disillusion Octavius, and that she could never live up to his unreal idealization of her. She persuades him that if his love for her is to last he must lose her, and remain 'a sentimental old bachelor for my sake'.

'The bubbling and loud hissing urn
Throws up a steamy column, and the cups,
That cheer but not inebriate, wait on each'
William Cowper, *The Task*, Bk IV (1785)

It is time for tea. The window shutters are closed, the curtains are drawn, and the sofa is wheeled round to face the fire. The tea urn is boiling and the teacups are ready and waiting for each person present. Introduced into England in the seventeenth century, tea became a universal drink in the eighteenth and nineteenth, 'as well known and highly valued in the labourer's cottage as in the poet Cowper's parlour' (G. M. Trevelyan). Cobbett might later scoff at slavery to the teapot, but the tea habit was firmly established.

'But at my back I always hear
Time's wingèd chariot hurrying near'
Andrew Marvell, *To His Coy Mistress* (1681)

If there were time enough, this poet would be happy to devote countless years to his mistress in just praising her. But time is fleeting, and death will come all too soon, so 'let us sport us while we may'.

The grave's a fine and private place,

But none I think do there embrace.

A philosophical awareness that life is all too short is a frequent theme in the poetry of the seventeenth century, the Age of Philosophy.

'Butcher'd to make a Roman holiday'
Lord Byron, *Childe Harold's Pilgrimage*, IV, cxli (1817)

Among the places visited by Childe Harold (who closely resembles Byron) was Rome. The Roman holiday often involved Death and suffering in a great arena, and at the ruined Coliseum Harold sees in imagination a dying Roman gladiator, sacrificed to amuse the spectators. He might well be a foreign captive, his dying thoughts not with 'the inhuman shout which hail'd the wretch who won', but with his own home, perhaps 'a rude hut by the Danube', where his wife and children were.

'But now I only hear
Its melancholy long withdrawing roar'
Matthew Arnold, *Dover Beach* (1867)

The withdrawing roar is that of religious faith. Arnold, brought up in early life by a deeply religious father (the famous Dr Arnold of Rugby School) later became sceptical towards orthodox Christianity. In *Dover Beach*, probably written soon after his marriage, the sound of the sea at Dover, with the waves noisily drawing the shingle back as they recede, suggests to him the withdrawal of his religious belief. In the last stanza of the poem he stresses the need for human love in a universe that is blindly indifferent to man.

'By it and with it and on it and in it'
Kenneth Grahame, *The Wind in the Willows* (1908)

In this classic children's animal story Mole has just seen a river for the first time. He asks Rat if he really lives beside it. Rat explains that the river is his whole life. 'It's brother and sister to me. . . . It's my world, and I don't want any other.' The river always has its fun and excitements, whatever the season. 'There is *nothing* – absolutely nothing – half so much worth doing as simply messing about in boats.' In a boat it doesn't really matter where you go to, or even whether you get there. 'Nothing really seems to matter, that's the charm of it.'

'Call back yesterday, bid time return'
William Shakespeare, *Richard II*, III, ii (1597)

King Richard has just returned from an expedition to Ireland, landing in Wales. His rival, the Earl of Bolingbroke (later Henry IV), is already in open opposition, but at this stage Richard is reasonably confident. He cheerfully asks the Earl of Salisbury about the Welsh forces gathered to fight for their king. But Salisbury can 'speak of nothing but despair', and laments that Richard is just one day too late. Twelve thousand Welsh fighting men, discouraged by ill omens and false rumours, had dispersed the previous day, either returning to their homes or even joining Bolingbroke.

'Call for the robin-red-breast and the wren'
John Webster, *The White Devil*, V, iv (1608)

This famous dirge is recited by a woman who has
become distracted because one of her sons has been
murdered by the other. Webster had obviously been
watching *Hamlet* (written a few years earlier), for, like
Ophelia, the unhappy mother begins her mad scene by
offering flowers all round ('There's rosemary for you;
and rue for you.') The robin and the wren are called
upon because they cover with leaves the bodies of
unburied men, and Cornelia's son is not buried by the
Church because he died in a quarrel.

'Can I do you now, sir?'
Ted Kavanagh, *ITMA*, BBC radio comedy series (1939–49)

The outstanding radio series of the Second World War,
and perhaps of all time, was *ITMA* ('It's That Man
Again'), with the genial Lancashire comedian, Tommy
Handley, as the central figure. There was little, if any,
story or plot – merely a succession of odd and easily
distinguished characters coming and going in a way not
dissimilar from the later Theatre of the Absurd. Catch-
phrases were innumerable, some of which became absorbed into the common language of the day. One of
these was the line delivered by Mrs Mopp, the bedrag-
gled charlady always anxious to find an opportunity to
clean out Mr Handley's office. She was played by
Dorothy Summers.

'A cap by night – a stocking all the day'
Oliver Goldsmith, *The Citizen of the World*, XXX (1760)

Goldsmith is allowing a shabby poet to describe in verse
his own situation, living in a drab room with a patched
window, a fireless grate, and a row of cracked cups on
the mantelpiece. The poet is still in bed, and economi-
cally wearing his stocking as a nightcap. There is little
doubt that Goldsmith was turning a typically humorous
eye on his own privations. He had recently been eking
out existence in a garret in Green Arbour Court – which,
contradicting the name, was a slum near the Old Bailey.

'The captains and the kings depart'
Rudyard Kipling, *Recessional* (1897)

Kipling is often regarded as a passionate imperialist, but
this famous poem is a warning against imperial pride.
('Lest we forget.') It was written at the time of Queen
Victoria's Diamond Jubilee when imperialist feeling in
Britain was at its strongest, and the lines were a reminder
that national glory was ephemeral.

Lo, all our pomp of yesterday

Is one with Nineveh and Tyre!

It is true that Kipling thought so little of the poem that he
threw it in the waste-paper basket, from which a friend
rescued it. The poem subsequently exchanged the ignominy of the waste-paper basket for the glory of *The
Times*.

'Care-charming sleep, thou easer of all woes'
John Fletcher, *The Tragedy of Valentinian*, V, ii (*c* 1614)

This is the first line of a song offered to the Emperor
Valentinian. Unfortunately for him it does not ease his
woes, for he has been poisoned with a drug for which
there is no known antidote. Perhaps it serves him right,
for he had raped the beautiful wife of one of his finest
generals; and she, according to the dramatic conventions
of the time, had promptly committed suicide. The song
continues charmingly:

Pass by his troubled senses, sing his pain,
Like hollow murmuring wind, or silver rain.

But this does not prevent the Emperor from dying in
agony. Some historical truth underlies the play. Valentinian III was an undistinguished Roman emperor
(*c* A.D. 419-55).

'A cat may look at a king'
Lewis Carroll, *Alice's Adventures in Wonderland*, ch. 8 (1865)

The statement has been made famous by Alice, who was
introducing the Cheshire Cat to the King of Hearts. The
King objected to the way the cat looked at him, as no part
of it was visible but the head, and most of that consisted
of a broad grin. Alice defended the cat, mentioning that
she had read the quoted statement 'in some book, but I
don't remember where'. Perhaps she had somehow
come across a copy of John Heywood's sixteenth-century
Proverbes, which includes the aphorism 'A cat may looke
on a king'. The inference is that a very humble person
may reasonably be allowed to observe the actions of
anyone of high rank or importance.

'Cease this detestable boohooing instantly!'
George Bernard Shaw, *Pygmalion* (1912)

Professor Higgins, expert phonetician, is addressing the
flower-girl, Eliza Doolittle, at Covent Garden. She has
seen him taking phonetic notes of her remarks, and
mistaking him for a detective preparing to charge her
with soliciting, has been steadily murmuring Cockney
complaints, protesting that she is 'a good girl'. Higgins at
last tells her to keep quiet, reminding her that she is 'a
human being with a soul and the divine gift of articulate
speech'. He goes on to assert that he could train her to
speak so well that in three months he could pass her off
as a duchess.

'Certain women should be struck regularly, like gongs'
Noel Coward, *Private Lives*, Act III (1930)

Elyot and Amanda, divorced after a stormy marriage,
have come together again and are staying in Amanda's
Paris flat. But their early habit of bickering is still there.
After an evening row, in which he slaps her face, she is
being very icy in her manner next morning. Elyot is
trying to carry the situation off with his usual flippancy.
Amanda has just observed coldly that she has been
brought up to believe that for a man to strike a woman is
beyond the pale. His facetious reply is intended to annoy
her – and does.

'Chapter of accidents'
Lord Chesterfield, *Letters to his Friends* (1777)

The phrase is commonly used nowadays to describe a series of mishaps. Its earlier use, however, was in an opposite sense. At the age of sixty Chesterfield was suffering from deafness. No known cure had been found to help him, so (he wrote to a friend in 1753) he could do nothing but hope for some happy accident to cure him. He consoled himself with the thought that although the chapter of Knowledge is short, 'the chapter of accidents is a very long one, and I will keep dipping in it'.

'Charlie is my darling, the young Chevalier'
Carolina Nairne, *Charlie is My Darling* (1846)

Charlie is Charles Edward Stuart, the Young Pretender (Bonnie Prince Charlie), whose attempt to seize the throne from George II in 1745 (the Forty-five Rebellion) resulted in a disastrous defeat at Culloden. But the Prince was still very much alive when Carolina was born to an ardent Stuart supporter, who named her after the Prince. Her songs, published anonymously in her lifetime, are often full of Stuart or Jacobite sentiments. This one commemorates the arrival of Prince Charles in Scotland in 1745 to lead his ill-fated expedition.

'A child is afraid of being whipped, and gets his task, and there's an end on't'
Samuel Johnson, in Boswell's *Journal of a Tour to the Hebrides* (1785)

The great Doctor was so often right in his judgments that it is rather satisfying to find him for once on the wrong side of the fence. The occasion of his comment was a reference to Lady Errol, who, it was said, did not use force or fear in educating her children. 'Sir, she is wrong,' Johnson boomed; and having uttered the quoted sentence he went on to express the view that 'by exciting emulation ... you make brothers and sisters hate each other'. Johnson's belief that force is the best way to educate children has long been disproved by experience, and is as unjustified as his idea that competition necessarily breeds hatred.

'The Child is father of the Man'
William Wordsworth, *My Heart Leaps Up* (1807)

The rather startling paradox put forward by the quoted line, though seemingly absurd, reveals an interesting truth. The experiences of childhood have a powerful influence on a person's development, and in that sense father it. When he was young Wordsworth delighted in the appearance of a rainbow, and now that he is a grown man a rainbow still fills his heart with pleasure. The love of nature that characterized his youth has remained strong, and he hopes that this reverence for natural beauty will always thus link childhood with adult life.

'Christmas comes but once a year'
Thomas Tusser, *500 Points of Good Husbandry* (1557)

Tusser was a well-educated but not very successful farmer who wrote freely (in verse) about farming. His verses, though not ranking very highly as poetry, offer valuable information to present-day researchers into sixteenth-century farming practice. In Chapter 12 (*The Farmer's Daily Diet*) he runs through suitable food for different seasons. Christmas leaves him bereft of detail, for his only advice is to 'play and make good cheer' on account of the annual occurrence of this festival. Strangely enough it did not seem to strike him that other festivals, such as Easter and Whitsun, also appear only once a year.

'Church bells at best but ring us to the door, But go not in to mass'
H. W. Longfellow, *Tales of a Wayside Inn: The Bell of Atri* (1872)

In this tale of medieval Italy the King of Atri has hung a bell in the little town of Abruzzo, to be rung by anyone with a grievance. The Syndic (chief official) would thereupon come forward to judge the rights and wrongs of the case. An old horse turned out of its stable by a miserly knight plucks at the bryony strands which have been used to mend the rope, and rings the bell. The Syndic duly judges the case (details being supplied by interested neighbours), and orders the knight to take proper care of his horse. When the King of Atri hears about it he exclaims that his bell is even better than a church bell.

It cometh into court and pleads the cause
Of creatures dumb and unknown to the laws.

'A circulating library in a town is an evergreen tree of diabolical knowledge'
R. B. Sheridan, *The Rivals*, I, ii (1775)

Sir Anthony Absolute has discovered that Lydia Languish, to whom he is planning to marry his son, is in the habit of borrowing romances from a library. He expresses disapproval to her aunt, Mrs Malaprop, on the ground that such stories encourage lewd behaviour. 'They who are fond of handling the leaves will long for the fruit at last.' In his prejudiced and peppery way, he is even against allowing girls to read. 'I'd as soon have them taught the black art as the alphabet!'

'Claps his dish at the wrong man's door'
Ben Jonson, *Every Man in His Humour*, II, i (1598)

Squire Downright (whose name indicates his bluff, hot-tempered character) is talking about his half brother, Wellbred. Without real cause, Downright considers his brother a bit of a scapegrace, who will sooner or later get arrested for his goings on. If he does, Downright will not part with a halfpenny to bail him out, and if Wellbred expects him to, then he's 'clapping his dish at the wrong man's door'. In the sixteenth century beggars who were infected with a disease had to ask for alms holding out a dish with a cover, and by clapping this noisily they indicated their infectious condition.

'A clear fire, a clean hearth, and the rigour of the game'
Charles Lamb, *Mrs Battle's Opinions on Whist* (1821)

This opening sentence of one of Lamb's best-known essays quotes the wish of old Sarah Battle, 'who, next to her devotions, loved a good game of whist'. Mrs Battle (the name was deliberately chosen) treated the game seriously, and detested the type of player who was lukewarm, not minding whether he won or lost. She took, and gave, no concessions, and gave the game undivided attention. 'She unbent her mind afterwards, over a book.' This amusing, affectionate portrait of an ardent card-player was based on an actual friend, Mrs Sarah Burney, the wife of Captain (later Admiral) Burney, brother of the celebrated Fanny.

'The cold charities of man to man'
George Crabbe, *The Village*, Bk I (1783)

Goldsmith pictured his Auburn as a 'sweet smiling village', but there are no smiles in the picture of village life drawn by Crabbe. The people are as grim as their East Anglian landscape. One of the grimmest places is the poorhouse, where the cold charities are dispensed. Mud walls, broken thatch, a small patched window, and a dirty mattress on a filthy floor form its comforts. Its inhabitants are heartbroken widows, abandoned wives and children, unmarried mothers, old people in their dotage, together with the lame, the blind, and the half-witted. Such is 'the House that holds the parish poor'.

'A cold coming we had of it,
Just the worst time of the year
For a journey'
T. S. Eliot, *Journey of the Magi* (1927)

The Bible tells of three wise men who came from the East to offer gifts to the infant Jesus (Matthew, ii, 1). Eliot imagines one of these men recalling the journey in his old age, and the account is given from that point of view. He has been left unhappy, for the journey has caused a loss of faith in his old religion. The quoted lines are taken almost word for word from a sermon by Lancelot Andrewes, Bishop of Winchester (1618–26).

'Come down, O maid, from yonder mountain height'
Alfred Tennyson, *The Princess*, vii (1847)

Theocritus (*c* 270 B.C.) wrote an idyll in which a nymph is invited to leave her chilly mountain residence and share her shepherd suitor's pastoral home in the valley, a more suitable place for love-making. Tennyson adapted the Greek idyll to make a love poem for Princess Ida to read to the Prince to whom she had been affianced since childhood, but whose love she had rejected. There was a certain personal application in the lyric. Ida, in effect, was inviting herself to abandon her lofty opposition to man and to accept the warming influence of love.

'Come into the garden, Maud,
For the black bat, night, has flown'
Alfred Tennyson, *Maud*, I, xxii (1855)

The well-known song (music by M. W. Balfe) was once in every tenor's repertoire. However, it was not written as a song. The lines introduce an eleven-stanza section of a long dramatic monologue, telling a tragic story. Maud is a lovely and wealthy girl loved by an impecunious and rather unstable young man, the narrator. Maud comes to love him, but when she secretly accepts the invitation to the garden she is followed by her angry brother. He attacks her lover, and is killed in the ensuing fight. The lovers are parted and there is no happy ending.

'Come listen to me, you gallants so free,
All you that love mirth for to hear'
Ballad, *Robin Hood and Alan-a-Dale*

It was common for a ballad-singer in medieval England to invite people to gather round and listen to a tale. Listeners to this ballad would have heard about a young man, Alan-a-Dale, whose intended bride was about to be led into a forced marriage with an elderly lord for the sake of his money. Robin Hood, traditional helper of poor against rich, agreed to scotch this unromantic wedding. He boldly interrupted the church ceremony, and Little John (wearing the Bishop's cope) then conducted the wedding service, with Alan substituted for the elderly lord.

'Come live with me and be my love,
And we will all the pleasures prove'
Christopher Marlowe, *The Passionate Shepherd to his Love*
(c 1599)

The shepherd endeavours to entice his mistress to live with him by offering several not very practical inducements. They will sit watching other shepherds working, she will lie on a bed of roses, wearing flowers for a cap, a woollen gown, and slippers with gold buckles, not to mention a straw belt decorated with coral and amber. The remaining attraction is a May Day song and dance by shepherds. Sir Walter Raleigh later wrote *The Nymph's Reply to the Shepherd* in which the nymph pointed out that flowers fade and wither, and that only if youth were permanent would his appeal to her be acceptable.

'Come, my Corinna, come, let's go a-Maying'
Robert Herrick, *Corinna's Going a-Maying* (1648)

May was traditionally a time for celebrating the rites of Spring, and Herrick was too fond of such pursuits not to celebrate them in his own poetical way. Corinna was no genuine rural maiden. She was simply the feminine version of Corin, the pastoral type-name for a shepherd. In 1618 Charles I issued a 'Declaration to His Subjects Concerning Lawful Sports' which directed that spoil-sports were not to hinder less inhibited people from 'May-games ... the setting up of Maypoles and other sports therewith used'.

Let's obey

The proclamation made for May,

Herrick exclaimed enthusiastically.

'Come, take the bodies up'
John Suckling, *Aglaura*, V, i (1694)

A feature of a good many seventeenth-century tragedies was the sound of falling bodies. Even Shakespeare often welcomed death. More than half the main characters have disappeared from life by the end of *Hamlet*; and Webster is an even greater lover of the mortuary. Right at the end of the century Sir John Suckling (best known as a writer of light, graceful lyrics) kept up the tragic tradition with a will. In *Aglaura* Ziriff kills first the King, then the King's brother, and finally a lord. He himself is killed by the Queen, who is stabbed by Pasithas, who is about to be executed by one of the few survivors. Aglaura has by this time killed her lover by mistake, and has then fallen dead. Suckling himself seems to have been so horrified by this slaughter that he wrote an alternative Fifth Act in which the death rate was considerably reduced.

'Coming events cast their shadows before'
Thomas Campbell, *Lochiel's Warning* (1802)

Lochiel, head of the Cameron Clan, is conversing with a wizard who is warning him of ill events to come. He foresees trouble 'when the Lowlands shall meet thee in battle array'. He is not far wrong, for the Battle of Culloden (1746) looms ahead. Lochiel was a supporter of Bonnie Prince Charlie, the Stuart Pretender to the throne in the reign of George II, and shared in the defeat of that unfortunate would-be monarch by the Scottish Lowland and English forces.

'A common murderer, possibly, but a very uncommon cook'
Saki, *Beasts and Super-Beasts* – The Blind Spot (1914)

Sebastien is a cook of such uncommon skill that his present employer, Sir Lulworth, a gourmet of gourmets, values his talent above everything. The cook has a hot temper, to be sure, but what is that in comparison with a superb hot dinner? Sir Lulworth's nephew, Egbert, comes across a letter that proves almost certainly that Sebastien murdered his previous employer, a worthy Canon of the Church, after an altercation. Sir Lulworth receives the news with interest. Then he deals with the letter in a manner befitting a connoisseur of good food. He flings it into the fire!

'Conciliation failing, force remains; but force failing, no further hope of reconciliation is left'
Edmund Burke, *Speech for Conciliation with the Colonies* (22 March 1775)

Burke was arguing strongly in the House of Commons against the use of force in endeavouring to subdue the American colonies, who were strongly opposed to being taxed by Britain whilst not represented in the British Parliament. Force, he maintained, even if successful, was only temporary in its effect. It was an untried method of dealing with these colonies, and it ran counter to the liberty-loving spirit of the American people, most of whom were descended from the British. Burke's views were not heeded by the Government of the day, and Britain lost her American colonies for ever.

'Consent, if mutual, saves the lawyer's fee.
Consent is law enough to set you free'
George Farquhar, *The Beaux' Stratagem*, V, iv (1707)

The closing couplet of a play otherwise written in lively prose. Divorce laws have eased considerably during the last few years, but divorce by simple consent still remains at the wishful thinking stage. In this case the couple concerned are boorish Squire Sullen and his charming and pleasure-loving wife. It is hard to understand why she ever married him, though there were ten thousand good reasons why he married *her*, all of them gold. However, Farquhar's system of easy divorce enables Mrs Sullen to marry the handsome, dashing, but impoverished hero who has lost his heart to her in that best of meeting-places – church.

'Consider now, if they asked us, Will you give up your Indian Empire, or your Shakespeare, you English?'
Thomas Carlyle, *Heroes and Hero-Worship* (1840)

Carlyle was asking (rhetorically) whether it would be better for the English never to have had an Indian Empire or never to have had any Shakespeare. He put his money on the poet rather than the Punjab. 'Indian Empire will go, at any rate, some day; but this Shakespeare does not go, he lasts forever with us.' Carlyle's judgment was sound, for the Indian Empire nearly did go seventeen years later (Indian Mutiny 1857), and went completely ninety years after that. But Carlyle rather marred his championship of Shakespeare by trying to make out that the Man of Stratford was not merely a great dramatist, but was something between a great prophet and a god.

'The cook was a good cook, as cooks go; and as cooks go, she went'
Saki, *Reginald on Besetting Sins* (1904)

The besetting sin on this occasion was an addiction to the truth. The cook's employer (she is not named), having no children, got into the habit of telling the truth on all occasions. She was truthful about her age – to the annoyance of her elder sister – and she told her friends how they really looked when they asked for her candid opinion. Finally, 'one raw Wednesday morning, in a few ill-chosen words, she told the cook that she drank'. The result was what the familiar quotation indicates.

'Could I but teach the hundredth part
Of what from thee I learn'
William Wordsworth, *Anecdote for Fathers* (1798)

Wordsworth was mentally addressing a five-year-old boy, the son of a friend. One day Wordsworth asked him whether he preferred 'Kilve by the green sea' or 'sweet Liswyn farm'. The boy answered, 'Kilve'. On being constantly pressed to say why, and catching sight of a weather vane, he said desperately that he liked Kilve because there was no weathercock there. Wordsworth rightly blamed himself for forcing a reply out of a child who had no formulated opinion thus inviting him to utter a falsehood. The child had taught him a lesson.

'Courage never to submit or yield'
John Milton, *Paradise Lost*, Bk I (1667)

This admirable sentiment is expressed by Satan who, unfortunately for Milton's intention, turned out to be the most heroic figure in his epic. After being ejected from Heaven by the Almighty, Satan, bold rebel that he is, contemplates an attempt to recover the position of which he has been deprived, claiming that 'all is not lost' and bravely refusing 'to bow and sue for grace'.

'Cover her face; mine eyes dazzle: she died young'
John Webster, *The Duchess of Malfi*, IV, ii (1614)

The violent but inadequately motivated actions in this grim horror-tragedy have resulted in the death of the young widowed duchess. Her evil brother Ferdinand, who has engineered her mental torture and murder for no sufficient reason, comes to make sure that his orders have been carried out. When he sees her strangled body he suffers a remorse even more unexplained than the murder. The quoted line that he utters has been extravagantly praised by some critics, but others have seen it as a good line inappropriately used. Much of the unreality of the play may arise from the drawing of the story from Painter's *Palace of Pleasure* (1566–7), translated from Italian and classical sources.

'Cowardly dogs bark loudest'
John Webster, *The White Devil*, III, i (1608)

Vittoria the 'White Devil' – not to modern eyes all that devilish – has just been accused of being Count Brachiano's mistress. The charge is justified, but the attitude of Cardinal Monticelso is so abusively censorious that the audience's sympathies must lie with Vittoria. Brachiano himself is not reluctant in self-defence against the Cardinal's accusation of lust, and, after calling him a cowardly dog, warns 'sirrah priest' that he is likely to find himself with a sword through his bowels. This very violent play is said to have been grounded on events that took place in Italy some twenty-odd years previously.

'The Creator made Italy from designs by Michael Angelo'
Mark Twain, *The Innocents Abroad* (1869)

The quotation is Twain's ironic suggestion as to what the Italian guide ought to say to save mentioning Michelangelo on every occasion in every town. In his guided tour of Europe, Twain has grown tired of hearing the great sculptor/painter (1475–1564) constantly praised. Genoa, Milan, Lake Como, Padua, Venice – all these seemed to have owed their existence, or at least their success, to Michelangelo. 'I never felt so fervently thankful . . . so filled with a blessed peace, as I did when I learnt that Michael Angelo was dead.' We should not, of course, need to be reminded that Twain was a humorist.

'Crossing the road without due care'
A. P. Herbert, *Without Due Care* (1936)

The famous *Punch* humorist takes a sentence freely used by coroners in road accident cases, using it as a chorus line for a satirical verse stressing that the driver of such a lethal weapon as a car ought to be the one to exercise the greatest care. An old lady stood for a long time waiting to get across the road, and at length thought she saw a chance. But she misjudged the speed of a powerful car. And everyone agreed, Herbert observes ironically,

'Twas not the car that went too fast,
But she who went too slow.

'Cricket thickens the biceps, enlarges the bust, and makes for very large hands and feet'
John Dighton, *The Happiest Days of Your Life*, Act I (1948)

Budding Bothams need not worry, for the reference is to cricket as a game for girls. Miss Whitchurch, Principal of St Swithin's School for Girls, is opposed to it, to the regret of the games mistress, Miss Gossage. Even Miss Gossage is a little shaken, however, when a pair of large cricket boots is discovered in the Common Room of what they believe to be the girls' school to which they have been evacuated. The solution, in fact, is that owing to a mistake on the part of the Ministry, they have been sent to a boys' school – a farcical situation which produced a lot of runs at the Apollo Theatre, London.

'Curfew must not ring tonight'
Rose. H. Thorpe, *Curfew Must Not Ring Tonight* (1870)

This once-popular verse for recitation, tells the story of a girl's brave effort to save her lover from execution by Cromwell during the Civil War. He is due to die at the ringing of the curfew. The girl, Bessie, tries unsuccessfully to persuade the sexton not to ring it. Then she ascends the tower, and as the great bell is about to sound she grasps the clapper and clings to it. When the battered girl staggers down to the ground and comes face to face with Cromwell, he is so impressed by her action that he gives orders for her lover to be spared. This very English ballad was written by an American for an American newspaper.

'"The curse has come upon me," cried The Lady of Shalott'
Alfred Tennyson, *The Lady of Shalott* (1852)

The lady was weaving a magic tapestry, using as a pattern the sights she saw through a mirror. She had to watch everything through a mirror, for if she were to look directly down the river towards Camelot a curse would fall upon her, so the legend said. One day she left her mirror to gaze directly on Sir Lancelot as he rode towards Camelot. At once the tapestry drifted away into the river, while the mirror cracked from side to side. She knew then that the curse had come upon her. She found herself compelled to find a boat and drift downriver to Camelot. But before the boat reached it she was dead. Malory says Camelot is Winchester, but others have placed it in Somerset.

'Cut is the branch that might have grown full straight'
Christopher Marlowe, *Doctor Faustus – Epilogue* (1604)

The Chorus sums up the moral of the Faustus story (probably written 1588). Having sold himself to the Devil in exchange for twenty-four years of unlimited power – power of which he has made little use – Faustus has at last been claimed and dragged away to Hell. The Chorus exhorts the onlookers to regard his fate as a warning not to dabble in such unlawful things as Black Magic. Marlowe himself probably dabbled a bit in magic when he was at Cambridge. He certainly knew how to draw a magic circle for the purpose of conjuring up devils.

'Damn with faint praise'
Alexander Pope, *Epistle to Dr Arbuthnot* (1735)

Pope's *Epistle* cleverly satirizes various contemporary writers, in the form of a supposed dialogue between himself and his friend Dr Arbuthnot, physician, author, and wit. The figure guilty of damning with faint praise was 'Atticus', a thin disguise for the distinguished essayist and man of letters, Joseph Addison. His offence was to have given less praise to Pope (especially his translations of Homer) than Pope felt he deserved.

'Danger is a good teacher, and makes apt scholars'
William Hazlitt, *Table-Talk – The Indian Jugglers* (1821)

Hazlitt is referring to the perfection attained by such people as jugglers and rope-walkers. If an Indian juggler made a mistake in performing with three knives, 'which keep their positions like the leaves of a crocus in the air', he would cut his fingers. Similarly, if a rope-dancer performed on a tightrope with as many mistakes as an artist makes in a painting, he would soon break his neck. The sheer technical excellence of these people, enabling them to do seemingly impossible things with ease and grace, makes the essayist ashamed of his own blundering attempts to write.

'A Daniel come to judgment!'
William Shakespeare, *The Merchant of Venice*, IV, i (1600)

The Jewish money-lender, Shylock, demanding legal satisfaction against Antonio, a Venetian merchant, at first believes Portia (disguised as a lawyer) to be on his side. Shylock delightedly proclaims him/her a splendid advocate – the equal of Daniel, whose skill in advocacy saved Susanna, wife of a wealthy Babylonian, from a false accusation of adultery. In due course, however, Portia turns the tables on Shylock, and his phrase 'a Daniel come to judgment' is mockingly repeated by one of Antonio's friends. The story of Daniel and Susanna is not told in the Bible but is to be found in the Apocryphal *History of Susanna*.

'A dark horse'
Benjamin Disraeli, *The Young Duke*, II, ch.5 (1831)

Nowadays a 'dark horse' is anyone who conceals his abilities until the time when he can produce them to the best advantage. As originally used in Disraeli's novel, the phrase applied literally to a particular horse which unexpectedly won a race. 'A dark horse which had never been thought of ... rushed past the grandstand in sweeping triumph.'

'Dead men don't bite'
R. L. Stevenson, *Treasure Island*, ch.26 (1883)

Israel Hands, the rascally coxswain of the *Hispaniola*, has killed a fellow mutineer during a quarrel. He tells young Jim Hawkins, who is trying to capture the injured coxswain, that he has never seen any good come of kindness. Once you've killed a man he can't fight back. He puts his opinion into practice again and flings a concealed dagger at the boy, causing Jim to fire at him inadvertently. Hands is struck and falls overboard – a dead man who can no longer bite.

'Death, be not proud'
John Donne, *Holy Sonnets* (1633)

By personifying Death, Donne feels able to defy it, maintaining that this scourge of man is not as powerful as people think. Men derive pleasure from sleep, which is Death's copy or 'picture'. How much more pleasure, then, should they derive from the real thing – Death itself. This argument, more ingenious than convincing, is bolstered up by Donne's confident expectation of ever-lasting life.

One short sleep past, we wake eternally,
And Death shall be no more: Death, thou shalt die.

'A decent provision for the poor is the true test of civilization'
Samuel Johnson, in Boswell's *Life of Johnson* (1791)

Johnson was maintaining that 'where a great proportion of the people are suffered to languish in helpless misery, that country must be wretchedly governed'. Gentlemen of rank and education were much the same in all countries. It was the condition of the poor that was the true test. Johnson's belief was that the poor in England were better looked after than in any other great nation. This record of Johnson's views came not from Boswell, who was not in London during this time (1770), but from another friend of Johnson, Dr Maxwell.

> *'Delightful task! to rear the tender thought,*
> *And teach the young idea how to shoot'*
> James Thomson, *The Seasons – Spring* (1728)

Thomson was not engaging in rifle practice with a bunch of school cadets. He was thinking of the young child as a 'human blossom'; and to teach the young idea to shoot is to encourage the young mind to develop, as a plant sends forth its shoots. It is perhaps exaggerating a little to say that 'nothing strikes your eye but sights of bliss' when you contemplate the duties of parenthood. The nursery holds pains as well as pleasures. But then Thomson had never changed a nappy in his life. He lived and died a happy bachelor.

> *'Detested sport, that owes its pleasure to another's pain'*
> William Cowper, *The Task*, Bk III (1785)

The idea of animal welfare is comparatively recent. Not until the early nineteenth century was there any attempt to organize restraint upon human beastliness towards other animals. But a humane attitude was sometimes shown by individuals, and Cowper was a notable example. Both here and in Book VI he strongly attacks hunting for sport: 'the persecution and the pain / That man inflicts on all inferior kinds'.

He goes on to contrast the misery of the hunted hare to the sheltered existence of the hare that was one of his own pets, and about which he wrote so freely and so delightfully.

> *'Did Helen's breast though ne'er so soft,*
> *Do Greece or Ilium any good?'*
> George Darley, *It Is Not Beauty I Demand* (1828)

The poem, seventeenth century in spirit, is by a nineteenth century poet and critic, who wrote for two of the leading literary journals, the *London Magazine* and the *Athenaeum*. Here he is putting forward the very sensible theme that 'a tender heart, a loyal mind' are more important than beauty. 'It is not beauty I demand,' he begins; and he goes on to point out that Helen, whose beauty was the indirect cause of the ten-year war between Greece and Troy (Ilium), was no benefactor to either nation.

> *'Did you once see Shelley plain,*
> *And did he stop and speak to you?'*
> Robert Browning, *Memorabilia* (1855)

Browning recorded that when he was a boy he had come across a poem of Shelley's in a box of secondhand books. He had never heard of the dead poet, but henceforth his life was transformed. Shelley remained his poetic idol, and *Memorabilia* (things worth remembering) is a record of an incident that occurred some years later. 'I was one day in the shop of Hodgson, the well-known London bookseller, when a stranger . . . spoke of something that Shelley had once said to him. Suddenly the stranger paused and burst into laughter as he observed me staring at him with blanched face.'

'Dirty British coaster with a salt-caked smoke stack'
John Masefield, *Cargoes* (1902)

This famous poem portrays three types of merchant vessel, widely spaced in time, carrying very different kinds of cargo. The first stanza depicts the ancient Assyrian galley, with five benches of oars, bearing rare goods. Next there is the stately Spanish galleon carrying precious stones. Finally, in complete contrast, comes a tramp steamer with a very unglamorous cargo of cheap metals and coal. The three vessels perhaps typify different types of Empire, the first two concerned with opulence and ostentation, the third practical and down to earth.

'The dirty little secret is most difficult to kill'
D. H. Lawrence, *Pornography and Obscenity* (1929)

'The dirty little secret' is the attitude to sex of almost everyone except Lawrence. This pamphlet – issued after some of his work had been banned – hit out in every direction. The guilty parties were not only the Puritans and 'the mob of people today'. Even the carefree young, the sex-liberated Bohemians, the readers of Dr Marie Stopes (the birth-control expert), of Proust, and still more of Charlotte Brontë, or George Eliot, or Tolstoy – all were marked in some degree by 'the dirty little secret'. The phrase became almost an obsession.

'Discontented or hungry jurymen, my dear sir, always find for the plaintiff'
Charles Dickens, *The Pickwick Papers*, ch.34 (1837)

Mr Perker, Pickwick's solicitor, is talking to his client on the morning of the breach of promise case – Bardell v Pickwick. Mrs Bardell, Pickwick's landlady, mistakenly believed that her employer had proposed to her and was suing him, through her crafty lawyers Dodson and Fogg, for breach of promise. Dickens took the opportunity to satirize the law courts of the day in the persons of Serjeant Buzzfuzz, the browbeating counsel for the plaintiff, and Mr Justice Stareleigh, the prejudiced and sharp-tempered judge. Whether the jurymen were hungry or not was not made plain, but they took no more than fifteen minutes to find for the plaintiff, with damages against Mr Pickwick in the sum of £750.

'Disgusting! The porridge is burnt again!'
Charlotte Brontë, *Jane Eyre* (1847)

Jane's first morning at Lowood School for girls, where the aim of its egregious governor was to instil humility, was marked typically by a breakfast that nobody could eat. Less typically, the kindly headmistress supplemented it by a meal of bread and cheese, for which she was sternly reproved by the governor, Mr Brocklehurst. 'When you put bread and cheese, instead of burnt porridge, into these children's mouths, you may indeed feed their vile bodies, but you little think how you starve their immortal souls!' The quoted words are whispered by the senior girls.

'A distinction without a difference'
Henry Fielding, *Tom Jones*, Bk VI, ch.13 (1749)

Black George, a gamekeeper supposedly friendly with
Tom Jones, has robbed him by secretly finding and
keeping a packet containing £500. Later he is openly
entrusted with £16 to convey to Tom. His conscience and
his avarice are now in conflict. Conscience tells him that
although he cheerfully stole £500 by finding it, he ought
not to steal the £16 that has actually been entrusted to
him. But avarice tells him that this is 'a distinction
without a difference'. Fortunately fear of discovery
comes to the aid of conscience, and he duly hands over
the money.

'Doctors never see through their patients. It's not what
they're paid for, and it's contrary to professional etiquette'
St John Hankin, *The Return of the Prodigal*, Act II (1905)

This caustic commentary on the medical profession is
made by Eustace, the ne'er-do-well but agreeable elder
son of Mr Jackson. Eustace, down on his luck after being
sent away to Australia with £1,000, returns home and lies
on the doorstep in a pretended faint of exhaustion. The
local doctor is completely taken in, and prescribes rest
and wine as a tonic. Eustace frankly faces the fact that he
is no good at anything, and genially blackmails his father
into giving him a regular allowance by threatening to
ruin Mr Jackson's prospects in the election for which he
is a candidate. The play is one of the wittiest and most
intelligent of its period.

'Does a boy get a chance to whitewash a fence every day?'
Mark Twain, *The Adventures of Tom Sawyer* (1876)

A classic episode in American fiction, and an equally
classic example of psychological subtlety. Tom has been
ordered by his aunt to spend Saturday morning whitewashing thirty yards of fence instead of amusing himself
in his own way. He is struck by a sudden inspiration. As
each of his friends comes by, prepared to jeer at Tom for
having to work on a Saturday, Tom pretends that he is
whitewashing the fence for fun. Those who come to scoff
find themselves insidiously persuaded to *want* to share in
the task. In the end Tom not only sits watching his
victims doing his work for him but has them paying (in
kind) for the privilege.

'A dog can be happy on a chain – a cat's far too fine'
Eden Phillpotts, *The Farmer's Wife*, Act I (1916)

Churdles Ash, a sour and cynical old countryman, has
expressed the opinion that women are poor things
compared with men. The difference between a man and
a woman, he declares, is the difference between a dog
and a cat, implying that a dog is the nobler beast. But
Araminta, the farmer's housekeeper, points out that cats
are superior to dogs, for man has never learnt to tame
them.

*'A dog is the only creature that, leaving his fellows, attempts
to cultivate the friendship of man'*
Oliver Goldsmith, *The Citizen of the World*, LXIX (1760–61)

The author begins this essay by pouring gentle scorn on
the English tendency to let rumour create a terror of
mad-dog epidemics, with a mild incident being steadily
exaggerated into a disaster. Goldsmith then considers
the service given by dogs to man, such as keeping
robbers at a distance, and encouraging exercise. The dog
is always eager to please, and faithful even when ill-
treated. 'In him alone fawning is not flattery.'

'Do memories plague their ears like flies?'
Philip Larkin, *At Grass* (1955)

Former racehorses put out to grass are now almost
motionless in the field they graze in. Once famous
names, watched eagerly by thousands of cheering spectators, now they just stand about, unknown, with an
occasional gallop round the field for fun. The poet
wonders if they sometimes remember their great days,
and are bothered by the recollection of what is now past.

'Do not go gentle into that Goodnight'
Dylan Thomas, *Do Not Go Gentle* (1951)

The poet is deeply concerned at the idea of his father's
life being snuffed out, and the poem urges him to rage
against death and not accept meekly the cutting short of
his life. Although the lines are addressed to his father, in
fact (as Dylan wrote to a friend) he was the one person to
whom they could not be shown, as the father did not
realize that he was dying.

*'Don't expose me! Just this once!
This was the first and only time, I'll swear'*
Robert Browning, *Mr Sludge, 'The Medium'* (1864)

One of Browning's most powerful poems, though overlong, is this psychological study of a spiritualist medium
caught cheating, and attempting (ultimately with success) to justify and excuse himself. It has often been said
to be based on D. D. Home, the famous medium of the
mid-Victorian era, who successfully deceived Elizabeth
Browning and thereby incurred her husband's detesta-
tion. That *Mr Sludge* was inspired by Home is almost
certain, but Sludge is a representative figure and not a
personal portrait.

'Do or die'
Beaumont and Fletcher, *The Island Princess*, II, ii (1621)

The brother of Princess Quisara has been imprisoned by the wicked Governor of a neighbouring island. She insists that the man who wishes to be her suitor must first rescue the brother. A stranger, Armusia, overhears her demand and resolves 'either to do, or die'. He is as good as his word and brings the brother safely home. He gains his reward in the end, but only after three more Acts.

'Do other men, for they would do you'
Charles Dickens, *Martin Chuzzlewit*, ch.11 (1843–4)

This was the motto of Jonas Chuzzlewit, a cousin of the hero, Martin, and a deep-dyed villain. He is offering his father a rule for getting the best from a bargain; and his father, Anthony, who is as grasping as his son, is delighted with it. He is less delighted when Jonas carries the rule of doing other people to its extreme: he attempts to do for Anthony by poisoning him. Strangely enough, even this does not kill parental feeling, and his father forgives him. But in the end Jonas does for himself. After murdering a fraudulent company director, Jonas poisons himself in order to avoid the gallows.

'Do you believe in fairies?'
J. M. Barrie, *Peter Pan*, Act IV (1904)

Tinker Bell, a fairy (indicated only by a moving spotlight), is an assistant to Peter Pan, the boy who never grows up. An enemy, the Pirate Captain, slips some poison in Peter's medicine. Tinker Bell knows this but is unable to stop Peter from drinking it; so she drinks it herself to save him. As she begins to die Peter tells the audience that she can recover if children believe in fairies. And Barrie thereupon blackmails the children in the audience (and even some of the grown-ups fall for it) to applaud to prove that they *do* believe. They always respond favourably, so Tinker Bell recovers.

'"Do you know where the wicked go after death?" "They go to hell," was my ready and orthodox answer'
Charlotte Brontë, *Jane Eyre* (1847)

Jane, at the age of ten, is being catechized by the unpleasant clergyman, Mr Brocklehurst, manager and governor of Lowood charity school for girls. He follows up his first question by asking what is hell, and receives the orthodox reply, 'A pit full of fire.' Having got Jane to agree that she would hate to go there, he asks her what she must do to avoid being sent there. But instead of giving him the expected and orthodox answer about being virtuous and obedient, she tells him, with the practical good sense characteristic of her: 'I must keep in good health, and not die!'

'The drama's laws, the drama's patrons give
For we that live to please, must please to live'
Samuel Johnson, Prologue to *The Merchant of Venice* (15
September 1747)

The occasion of this prologue was the opening of Drury
Lane Theatre under new management. Garrick was co-
patentee – his introduction to management, and a very
successful one. Johnson's Prologue was a neat summary
of the actor's position. It stressed his dependence on his
audience, and the difficulties arising from capricious
changes of taste. It asked for the audience's support for
good sense and natural performances.

'Tis yours, this night, to bid the reign commence
Of rescu'd nature, and reviving sense.

'Drink, pretty creature, drink'
William Wordsworth, *The Pet Lamb* (1800)

The pretty creature is a snow-white lamb which Wordsworth saw one evening in the Lake District being fed by a
little girl. In the poem Wordsworth wrote several verses
in which she talks lovingly to her pet. He did not know
who the child was, so he gave her the name of a little girl
he knew and whose prettiness he admired. It was not
altogether a happy idea. The girl (Barbara Lewthwaite)
became very vain about figuring in a poem. Still worse,
she lost all sense of truthfulness, and used to assert that
she remembered the occasion quite well.

'Driven into a desperate strait'
Philip Massinger, *The Great Duke of Florence*, III, i (acted 1627)

The Duke has heard such reports concerning the beauty
of Lidia, daughter of a country scholar, that he sends his
court favourite, Sanazarro, to check up on these accounts. Sanazarro himself finds her charms so over-
whelming that he is at a loss what to do. If he reports
truthfully, the Duke will probably marry the girl. If he
gives a false report decrying the girl's beauty, and the
Duke subsequently discovers the truth, he will almost
certainly lose all the honours the Duke has showered on
him. 'I am driven into a desperate strait,' he laments,
'and cannot steer a middle course.'

'Ducks are comical things'
F. W. Harvey, *Ducks* (1919)

Harvey finds relief from trouble by looking at or thinking
about ducks. On shore they arouse amusement with
their clumsy waddling, but in the water they are lovely.
They are brave, too, when they defend their young
angrily against weasel and fox. But above all they are
comical. God must have smiled on the day he created the
duck. 'And he's probably laughing still at the sound that
came out of its bill!'

'During twenty-six years' experience of the ocean in all its moods I had not encountered a wave so gigantic'
Ernest Shackleton, *South*, ch.9 (1919)

Shackleton was in a small twenty-foot boat with five other men. He was attempting to sail across 800 miles of dangerous Antarctic seas to reach a whaling station to obtain help for the rest of his party, marooned on a desolate island. On the tenth night Shackleton observed what he thought was a patch of clear sky behind him. Then he realized that the whiteness was not sky but the crest of an immense wave about to crash down on them – 'a mighty upheaval of the ocean'. Somehow the little boat managed to survive, and the whaling station was at length reached.

'Duty is what one expects from others, it is not what one does oneself'
Oscar Wilde, *A Woman of No Importance*, Act II (1893)

Some of cynical Lord Illingworth's witticisms merely contradict an accepted view. The quotation, however, has an underlying sting of truth, perhaps because it touches himself quite closely. Twenty years earlier he had seduced a young girl, making her pregnant. His father insisted that it was young Illingworth's duty to marry her, but Illingworth refused because of his youth and lack of expectations. Now he and the woman have met again, and it is when she refers to his father's views that Illingworth utters his pungent words on duty.

'Duty to your calling outweighs duty to friend or client'
John Galsworthy, *Loyalties*, III, ii (1922)

Ronald Dancy has been openly accused of stealing by a fellow member of a London club. Dancy is persuaded to bring an action for slander, and he engages a highly respected solicitor, Mr Twisden. While the case is in progress information reaches Twisden clearly indicating Dancy's guilt, which Dancy himself now admits. As an honourable lawyer Twisden is unable to continue with a case that he now knows is based on false evidence. A friend of Dancy accuses Twisden of not playing the game, but he is firmly told that a lawyer's first duty is to serve the Law honestly.

'Earth has not anything to show more fair'
William Wordsworth, *Sonnet Composed upon Westminster Bridge* (1802)

The bridge upon which Wordsworth stood was not the present one, which was erected 1854–62. Nor would he have recognized the scene from the bridge today, with gaunt architectural monsters dominating the skyline. In 1802 London was still almost a country town; its rapid development occurred during the nineteenth century. When he wrote his sonnet, 'ships, towers, domes, theatres, and temples' truly lay 'open unto the fields, and to the sky'. To the west were the graceful towers of the Abbey, to the east, more distant, was the splendid dome of St Paul's Cathedral in solitary majesty, flanked only by the humbler spires and towers of Wren's city churches.

'East is East, and West is West, and never the twain shall meet'
Rudyard Kipling, *Ballad of East and West* (1892)

An Indian rebel, Kamal, has stolen the horse of a British colonel. The Colonel's son boldly chases the thief into Kamal's own territory, where the youth might easily have been killed had Kamal cared to risk retaliation by the British. But the rebel is so impressed by the young man's courage and riding ability that he greets him as a friend, and freely returns the horse. The quoted line is often wrongly used to indicate that Kipling was asserting the utter incompatibility of Asians and Europeans. The last two lines of the stanza make it clear that his message was exactly the opposite:

> But there is neither East nor West, Border, nor
> Breed, nor Birth,
> When two strong men stand face to face, tho' they
> come from the ends of the earth!

'Everybody in the world speaks well of him'
R. B. Sheridan, *The School for Scandal*, II, iii (1777)

Sir Oliver Surface, who has just returned from abroad, is discussing the characters of his two nephews with his friend, Sir Peter Teazle. Sir Peter is endeavouring to persuade Oliver that the younger brother, Charles, is wild and dissolute, but that the elder, Joseph, is a model young man, approved of by everybody. Sir Oliver is not as impressed as his friend expects. He suspects praise that is too universal, and considers that a man who is really worthy will not be popular with knaves and fools. His doubts concerning Joseph are justified, as Sir Peter soon finds out.

'Everybody says I'm such a disagreeable man'
W. S. Gilbert, *Princess Ida*, Act I (1884)

King Gama finds it difficult to understand why he is not more popular, despite his many virtues. He is always eager to correct the faults and weaknesses of people he meets. He is prompt to expose flattery and vanity, and ready to show that charitable actions are really inspired by self interest. He is good at sneering, snubbing, and sniggering. He is clever at finding out a woman's age, and unhesitating in revealing it. Yet in spite of all these merits he is regarded as disagreeable!

'Every dog has his day'
George Borrow, *Lavengro*, ch.92 (1851)

Borrow has gained something of a reputation for boxing by knocking out a quarrelsome tinker known as the Flaming Tinman. The landlord of an inn that he frequents was formerly a boxer, and loves to talk about the ring. He is tempted to enter it again himself, but decides that his time for boxing is past. 'Youth will be served, every dog has his day, and mine has been a fine one – let me be content.'

'Every man meets his Waterloo at last'
Wendell Phillips, Talk at Brooklyn (1 November 1859)

Waterloo was, of course, the scene of Napoleon's defeat (1815), and to meet one's Waterloo is to fail. Wendell Phillips was an American lawyer and a vigorous opponent of slavery. His speech was occasioned by the capture, two weeks earlier, of another abolitionist, John Brown, after an abortive attack on a Virginian arsenal. Phillips was maintaining that all men are liable to fail, and that Brown's failure to capture the arsenal was not vitally significant.

'Everyone's a walking farce and a walking tragedy at the same time'
Aldous Huxley, *Antic Hay*, ch.29 (1923)

Huxley's brilliant satiric novel puts a section of the intelligentsia under a revealing microscope. The quoted words are expressed by Lypiatt, an unsuccessful artist-poet-musician, who for years has seen himself as a great but unrecognized Michelango. He is now writing a long letter preparatory to shooting himself. Despair has seized him after hearing indirectly of a scornful gibe about his work made by the woman he is desperately in love with. But his intended suicide becomes farce rather than tragedy, for at the very moment when he intends (or thinks he intends) to pull the trigger, he is interrupted by a knock at the door, and the impulse for death is lost.

'Every schoolboy knows who imprisoned Montezuma'
T. B. Macaulay, *Essay on Clive* (1840)

Macaulay was attempting to underline the ignorance of the general public on Indian affairs, contrasting this with the detailed knowledge he supposed people to possess on matters pertaining to the West. One suspects that he rated the nineteenth-century schoolboy's omniscience more highly than it deserved, for education at that time dealt almost exclusively with Greece and Rome. For the benefit of schoolboys (and indeed school teachers) who cannot rattle off the name of Montezuma's conqueror, even if they have heard of Montezuma, the answer is Hernando Cortes, or Cortez (1485–1547).

'Everything by starts and nothing long'
John Dryden, *Absalom and Achitophel*, Pt I (1681)

The line epitomizes the character of George Villiers, Second Duke of Buckingham, a talented, witty, charming, wealthy, intelligent courtier who achieved remarkably little. His literary fame now rests only on his contribution (probably the chief part) to the satirical burlesque *The Rehearsal* (1671), which made fun of the writers of heroic plays, particularly Dryden. Ten years later, Dryden returned the blow with a shrewd and pungent portrait of a gifted but unstable character who wasted his talents by inability to focus them on anything in particular, and

> In the course of one revolving moon,
> Was chemist, fiddler, statesman, and buffoon.

'Everything did banish moan
Save the Nightingale alone'
Richard Barnfield, *As it fell upon a Day* (c 1594)

Many people find the nightingale's song sweet rather than sad, but in times past the nightingale tended to be synonymous with melancholy. Traditionally she pressed herself against a sharp thorn, partly to give herself pain, partly to keep herself awake for her long-drawn-out song recital. Barnfield, an Oxford graduate and pastoral poet, tells us that 'As it fell upon a day / In the merry month of May' all nature displayed happiness except the nightingale, who 'lean'd her breast upon a thorn / And there sung the dolefull'st ditty'. The bird's woes put him in mind of his own.

'The evil that men do lives after them'
William Shakespeare, *Julius Caesar*, III, ll (c 1599)

Caesar has been murdered by Brutus and fellow conspirators for fear lest his ambition should make him a tyrant. His friend, Mark Antony, is allowed by Brutus to make a speech over the dead body on condition that he does not condemn the murderers. Antony pretends to agree, and he tells the crowd that whatever evil Caesar has done will be remembered, and that his virtues must be forgotten. In spite of his promise, Antony subtly succeeds in arousing the anger of the crowd against the conspirators, beginning his speech with the famous words, 'Friends, Romans, countrymen, lend me your ears.'

'Eyeless in Gaza at the mill with slaves'
John Milton, *Samson Agonistes* (1671)

This poem in dialogue form begins with Samson, in a long monologue, lamenting his present condition: blind, a captive in prison, and labouring like a slave. Why had he been created for great exploits if he was fated merely to suffer his present degradation? It had been promised that his great strength would deliver Israel from the Philistines, yet here he is blinded in Gaza (one of the chief cities of the Philistines) by his captors. Far from delivering his people from the Philistines, he has been forced by them to work at the treadmill with other slaves. Aldous Huxley used *Eyeless in Gaza* as the title of a novel (1936).

'Fair daffodils, we weep to see
You haste away so soon'
Robert Herrick, *To Daffodils* (1648)

The poet laments that daffodils die so quickly. He likens their brief existence to the brevity of human life.

We have short time to stay, as you,
We have as short a spring

Though a clergyman, he concludes with the pagan reflection that after death plants and people are 'ne'er to be found again'. No hint here of resurrection. Daffodils always seemed to turn his thoughts to melancholy. In another brief poem he tells us that when he sees a daffodil 'hanging down its head towards me' it reminds him that he too will soon be dead.

'Fair, fat, and forty'
Sir Walter Scott, *St Ronan's Well*, ch.7 (1824)

The phrase is applied to Mrs Margaret Blower, a ship-owner's widow who has been left with a comfortable fortune. The local doctor at the spa, Dr Quentin Quackle-ben, is soon charmed into marriage with her. Scott may have borrowed the words of the quotation from the less familiar 'fat, fair, and forty' which occurs in John O'Keefe's play *The Irish Mimic* (1797). He, in turn, could have taken the thought from Dryden, one of whose characters exclaims, 'I am resolved to grow fat, and look young till forty' (*The Maiden Queen*, 1668).

'Farewell, farewell, a long and last farewell'
Nathaniel Lee, *The Rival Queens*, III, i (1677)

This is not, as might be thought, the prelude to a typical heroic-tragedy suicide. Statira, Alexander the Great's second and much-loved wife, is so upset by her husband's temporary return to his first wife, Roxana, that she vows to withdraw to a lonely cell and never see him again. She relents enough to meet and pardon him, but then dismays him by announcing that her decision to withdraw from the world still stands. Not until the whole court, including Alexander, have gone down on their knees does she change her mind.

'Farewell the tranquil mind'
William Shakespeare, *Othello*, III, iii (*c* 1605)

After being easily tricked by the villainous Iago into the unjustified belief that his wife, Desdemona, is unfaithful to him, the gullible Moor, Othello, laments having been told about her (supposed) infidelity. If he had not known about it, he exclaims, he would have remained happy. However, instead of throttling Iago for abusing his peace of mind, he proceeds to murder Desdemona.

'Far from the madding crowd's ignoble strife, Their sober wishes never learned to stray'
Thomas Gray, *Elegy Written in a Country Churchyard* (1751)

Unlike Sherlock Holmes, who saw sin lurking in the smiling countryside (*The Copper Beeches*), Gray saw only innocence and simplicity. The rural community he knew was that of Stoke Poges in Buckinghamshire, where he stayed from time to time with relatives. It was the churchyard here whose gravestones almost certainly inspired his splendid Elegy. Beautifully though Gray's thoughts are expressed, it may be considered a moot point whether townspeople are really more sinful than country folk. Thomas Hardy used the phrase *Far from the Madding Crowd* (1874) as the title of one of his best-known novels.

'Fallen from his high estate'
John Dryden, *Alexander's Feast* (1697)

After defeating the Persians, Alexander held a great feast at which Timotheus, a notable poet and musician, was engaged to entertain the company. His songs, especially his drinking songs ('Drinking is the soldier's pleasure') so excite Alexander – he starts telling the story of his great victories – that Timotheus hastily changes the tune. He now dwells on the fall of Darius, the Persian king defeated by Alexander, showing how easily fortune can change. Alexander takes the hint, 'and tears began to flow'.

'Fallen on evil days'
John Milton, *Paradise Lost*, Bk VII (1668)

Half way through his great epic Milton calls upon Urania (the Muse of Astronomy) to guide and inspire him in telling the story of the creation of the world and the fall of Man. He himself, he laments, has 'fallen on evil days ... in darkness, and with dangers compassed round'. At this time, not many years after the Restoration of Charles II, Milton was suffering from blindness, and being a Cromwellian who had supported the illegal execution of Charles I he was naturally uneasy. In fact he survived with far less hardship than might have been expected.

'"Falsely, falsely have ye done,
O mother," she said, "if this be true"'
Alfred Tennyson, *Lady Clare*

This simple but romantic tale is in the style of an old ballad. Lady Clare, the young owner of a rich estate, is about to wed her cousin, Lord Ronald. On the eve of the wedding her nurse tells her that she is not Lady Clare but the nurse's own daughter. When the Earl's baby daughter died she had secretly substituted her own child. She begs Clare to keep her mouth shut, at least till after the wedding. But the girl refuses to deceive her lover, and tells him the truth. Lord Ronald remains true to her, and they live happily ever after.

> We two will wed tomorrow morn,
> And you shall still be Lady Clare.

'Fame is the spur that the clear spirit doth raise ...
To scorn delights, and live laborious days'
John Milton, *Lycidas* (1638)

The desire for fame makes us toil away at study and verse-writing. But before we achieve fame, Milton goes on regretfully to suggest, our life is cut short by one of the Fates, who 'slits the thin spun life' with her dread scissors. He is reminded by Phoebus, the god of Poetry, that praise and fame will continue after death.

> Fame is no plant that grows on mortal soil ...
> But lives and spreads aloft by those pure eyes,
> And perfect witness of all-judging Jove.

Though he calls it 'that last infirmity of noble mind', Milton by no means despised fame, and (as Phoebus indicates) he no doubt looked forward to receiving a prize for poetry when he reached Heaven.

'The fat of the land'
Bible, Genesis, xlv, 18

A happy and expressive phrase used by the Pharaoh of
Egypt to indicate the best and richest food. He was
kindly inviting Joseph to send for his father and brothers
so that they could enjoy plenty in Egypt during a famine
in their own land, Canaan. The term 'fat' was no doubt
suggested to Pharaoh by his dreams of fat cattle and fat
ears of corn – dreams which Joseph was fortunately able
to interpret correctly.

'A favourite has no friend'
Thomas Gray, *Ode on the Death of a Favourite Cat* (1748)

The poem, in mock-heroic style, tells the story of a cat
(belonging to Gray's friend Horace Walpole) that was
drowned through falling into a large goldfish bowl in
which she was trying to catch a fish. The servants failed
to heed her cries: 'No cruel Tom nor Susan heard', and
the poet adds ironically: 'A fav'rite has no friend'. The
poem has been praised by some writers for its elegance;
others have found it a rather unpleasant little piece,
devoid of the sensitivity that a poet such as Cowper
would have displayed.

'The fear of God can never be taught by constables'
Sydney Smith, *Essays – Proceedings of the Society for the Suppression of Vice* (1809)

Sydney Smith was a clergyman, both sensible and witty,
and by no means a supporter of vice. But nor was he a
supporter of vice suppressors, whose aim was to make
people good by laying charges against anyone they
decided was not as religious as they desired. Sydney
Smith disliked informers, and thought they did at least
as much harm as good. He particularly objected to the
fact that they operated only against the poorer classes
and the smaller kind of tradesman. The rich and fashionable were left alone. In any case, he insisted, religious
devotion must be taught by example and education, and
could not be enforced by law.

'A few more whacks of the ice-axe in the firm snow and we stood on the summit'
Edmund Hillary, in *Life* (13 July 1953)

Hillary and his companion, Sherpa Tenzing, had been
struggling up the last thousand or so feet of Mount
Everest since 6.30 a.m. They reached the summit, aided
by oxygen, at 11.30 a.m. Their first feeling was one of
relief that there were no more steps to be cut in the steep
snow slope. They shook hands, then thumped each
other on the back. Thirty-one years after the first
tentative attempt to scale it, the highest mountain in the
world had been climbed. Hillary took the now very
familiar picture of Tenzing holding a string of flags, and
then attempted photos of every ridge of Everest. Meanwhile Tenzing made a hole in the snow in which to bury
token gifts for the mountain gods. Then, after fifteen
minutes at the earth's highest point, they began the
descent.

'Fifteen men on the dead man's chest –
Yo-ho-ho, and a bottle of rum'
R. L. Stevenson, *Treasure Island*, ch.1 (1883)

The chorus of a song bellowed by a mysterious seaman who had quartered himself at the *Admiral Benbow*, the inn run by the parents of young Jim Hawkins. Captain Billy Bones, as he called himself, was fond of the song, and when he had had more rum and water than he could really carry he would not only sing it himself but compel the company at the inn to join in. They were too afraid of him not to, but too fascinated to stay away. A stroke at length killed him – and left Jim with a treasure chart.

'The first and main error of Masters is want of discretion'
Henry Peacham, *The Compleat Gentleman* (1622)

The author, a graduate of Trinity College, Cambridge, was not a bigoted opponent of teachers. Indeed, he was himself a schoolmaster for a time, though he also lived by his pen and by acting as a private tutor. His theme is that too many schoolmasters were both undiscriminating in their methods and brutal in their attitude. They tried to teach all pupils in the same way instead of adjusting the method to the capacity of each individual, and their methods were too often those of the bully. 'These fellows believe that there is no other way of making a scholar than by beating him.'

'Firste he wroghte, and afterward he taughte'
Geoffrey Chaucer, *The Canterbury Tales – Prologue* (c 1387)

In other words, he practised first and then preached. Unlike almost all the other pilgrims on the Chaucerian journey to Canterbury, this idealized Parson is entirely admirable. There is no trace of satire tinging the eulogy. The Parson sets his parishioners an example of upright behaviour instead of merely telling them how to behave. He is reluctant to press any villager to pay the legal tithes, and, indeed, is readier to give money than to grasp it. Nor is he guilty of the absenteeism not uncommon among the clergy in Chaucer's time. 'A bettrë preest I trowe that nowher noon is.'

'Fleet the time carelessly, as they did in the golden world'
William Shakespeare, *As You Like It*, I, i (c 1599)

Charles must have been a very superior sort of professional wrestler, unlike the inarticulate mountains of flesh so often associated with the sport. Asked to give the news from the Court, where he is the usurping Duke's official wrestler, he does so with the confidence and fluency of a television reporter. Describing the activities of the banished Duke in the Forest of Arden, he throws in a classical allusion as nonchalantly as if he were tossing an inexperienced wrestler to the ground. The golden world, according to the imaginations of classical poets, was the first and best age, when men lived in an ideal state of peace and happiness.

'The flowers of the forest are a' wede away'
Jane Elliot, *Lament for Flodden* (1776)

At the battle of Flodden (1513) the Scots were heavily defeated by the English, commanded by Henry VIII's general, the Earl of Surrey. With 10,000 of them slaughtered, the defeat rankled in Scottish minds for years. More than 250 years after the event the poetess puts herself in the place of those who suffered the misery of that disaster. The lassies are moaning and sighing, for there are no young men to take part in harvesting and shearing, or to frolic with the girls in the gloaming. The flowers (young men) of the forest are all withered away. The poem was written as the result of a bet, and published anonymously as an old ballad.

'Fly our paths, our feverish contact fly!'
Matthew Arnold, *The Scholar Gipsy* (1853)

The poet is addressing in imagination a scholar who two hundred years earlier, it was said, had been forced by poverty to leave his studies and join a band of gipsies. He learnt much of their lore, and discovered that 'they could do wonders by the power of imagination'. Arnold was greatly attracted by this old tale and by the legend that the scholar's shade was sometimes seen wandering through the Oxfordshire countryside. He urges the ghostly figure, 'born in days when wits were fresh and clear', to avoid contact with 'this strange disease of modern life, / With its sick hurry, its divided aims'.

'A fool at forty is a fool indeed'
Edward Young, *Love of Fame*, Satire II (1725–8)

Young is indulging in some slashing satire at the expense of various types of people who seek for fame. There are many such, 'so weak are human kind by Nature made'. Asked if he too does not write for fame, Young admits the impeachment, and says to himself:

Thou, too, art wounded with the common dart,
And Love of Fame lies throbbing at thy heart.

To chase after Fame is foolish, and he is mature enough to abandon such folly. 'A fool at forty is a fool indeed.' So he temporarily gave up writing, and married the Earl of Lichfield's daughter instead.

'"Fool," said my Muse to me, "look in thy heart, and write"'
Philip Sidney, *Astrophel and Stella*, I (1591)

According to this opening sonnet of a series, Sidney (1554–86) was racking his brains to think of the best way of addressing his 'dear She' in verse, and finding that 'words came halting forth', until his Muse advised him what to do. The advice was excellent, but it is doubtful whether it is really meant to be taken literally in the case of these love sonnets, written to be circulated in manuscript. The Stella to whom they were addressed was seemingly Penelope Devereux, married unhappily to Lord Rich. Sidney's love for her was probably courtly rather than intense, true to literature rather than to life.

'Fools rush in where angels fear to tread'
Alexander Pope, *Essay on Criticism*, Pt III (1711)

The poet is writing of 'bookful blockheads' who have read everything but are totally deficient in judgment, and who are ever ready with ignorant and destructive criticism. Nothing is safe from their conceited outpourings. There would be no sanctuary from them (he suggests metaphorically) even at the altar of St Paul's Cathedral, for 'Fools rush ... fear to tread'.

'Footprints on the sands of time'
H. W. Longfellow, *A Psalm of Life* (1839)

The lives of great men, Longfellow tells us encouragingly, should inspire us to put forward our best efforts and thus 'leave behind us / Footprints on the sands of time'. Future generations, seeing the result of our good work, will follow our example. But perhaps the poet's metaphor is not altogether well chosen, for nothing is more ephemeral than a footprint on the sand.

'For all sad words of tongue or pen
The saddest are these: "It might have been!"'
J. G. Whittier, *Maud Muller* (1854)

Maud is a farm girl who offers a passing traveller, a judge, a drink and a pleasant chat. He moves on, and each daydreams about the other. Maud thinks of the security she could bring herself and her family, and the good she could do, if such a man were her husband. The judge thinks of the rural happiness suggested by the fair and simple country girl. But the marriage that might have been does not take place. The judge marries a social climber; Maud marries a farmhand and becomes mother of a large family. Bret Harte (1836–1902) wrote a cynically amusing 'sequel', *Mrs Judge Jenkins*, in which the judge did return to marry Maud – but both were disillusioned by the marriage.

'For a man who sticks to it there's a lot to be done in a shop'
H. G. Wells, *The History of Mr Polly*, ch.4 (1910)

Alfred Polly, a young shop assistant, has just come into a small inheritance. At the time he is staying with his cousin, Harold Johnson, a serious-minded clerk. He takes a thoughtful and kindly interest in Polly's affairs, advising him that there is a lot to be said for opening a shop of your own, and working out figures to help him. Eventually Polly does open a shop, but only after saddling himself with an incompetent and disagreeable wife. The venuure is a sad failure. Mr Polly, alas, does *not* stick to it.

'Foreigners always spell better than they pronounce'
Mark Twain, *The Innocents Abroad*, ch.19 (1869)

This wisecrack of the famous American humorist was provoked by a European tour which brought his party to Milan. Here they were shown some sketches by Leonardo da Vinci. Twain had no trouble with 'Leonardo', but was surprised to find 'Vinci' pronounced 'Vinchy'. The party also visited da Vinci's painting *The Last Supper*. He poked fun at the insincere (as he thought) tributes paid by visitors to the painting, which was so dark as to be almost invisible. 'After reading so much about it, I am satisfied that *The Last Supper* was a miracle of art once. But that was three hundred years ago.'

'Forever most divinely in the wrong'
Edward Young, *Love of Fame*, Satire VI (1725–8)

This satire attempts to put women in their place by offering a whole portrait gallery of (fictitious) ladies, each of whom has some specific weakness. Lavinia is proud, especially in church; Flavia lives in sin; Amasia is too eager not to be thought prudish; Lucia is so eager for riches that she marries a wealthy fool. However, she is more sensible than Tullia, who is intelligent enough to talk cleverly but likes to shine by arguing against accepted views. 'She thinks it vulgar to defend the right.' So her tongue wags a great deal, but always 'most divinely in the wrong'.

'For every time she shouted "Fire!" They only answered "Little Liar!"'
Hilaire Belloc, *Matilda* (1907)

This was the experience of Matilda, in Belloc's amusing *Cautionary Tales*. Her dreadful vice was telling lies, and a fearful fate was the result. One evening she tried to kill boredom by telephoning the Fire Brigade. The firemen came galloping in from every direction (these were the days of horses), only to find that it was a false alarm. A few weeks later, when Matilda was again on her own, a fire really did break out. Nobody now took any notice of her calls for help, and when her Aunt returned from the theatre she found that 'Matilda, and the House, were burned'.

'For God's sake look after our people'
Captain R. F. Scott, *Last Journal* (29 March 1912)

This was the last entry in the journal kept by Scott recording the day-to-day events of his famous and tragic journey to the South Pole. The journal and the bodies of Scott and two companions were found eight months after an unexpectedly long-lasting blizzard prevented them from leaving their tent to reach a depot of food and fuel only eleven miles away, and little more than a hundred miles from the base. The 'people' referred to were, of course, the relatives of the men who had died on the return from the Pole.

> *'For he on honey-dew hath fed,*
> *And drunk the milk of Paradise'*
> S. T. Coleridge, *Kubla Khan* (1797)

Coleridge tells that he once saw in a vision a girl playing a dulcimer, and singing so magically that if only he could recall the words and music he would be filled with inspiration. So rapturous would he be that people would fear his 'flashing eyes, his floating hair', and would hastily seek to protect themselves by drawing magic circles around him. Moreover they would cry that he had drunk the nectar of the gods. Not long before writing *Kubla Khan* Coleridge had begun to take a less desirable nectar – opium.

> *'For her own person, it beggared all description'*
> William Shakespeare, *Antony and Cleopatra*, II, ii (c 1607)

Cleopatra was sailing down the river in her golden barge to her first meeting with Antony. Shakespeare subtly gives the poetic description of her to the plain blunt soldier, Enobarbus, and it strikes the ear all the more effectively coming from a normally rough tongue. The details come largely from North's translation of Plutarch's *Life of Marcus Antonius* (2nd edition 1595). Cleopatra lay under a cloth of gold canopy, fanned by little boys dressed as Cupids. 'Royal wench!' declared Enobarbus's listener, half in admiration, half in reference to Cleopatra's previous seduction of Caesar. ('Wench' used to mean 'whore'.)

> *'The formal bullfight is a tragedy, not a sport, and the bull is certain to be killed'*
> Ernest Hemingway, *Death in the Afternoon* (1932)

Though fascinated by a practice that to most civilized people is revolting, Hemingway admitted in his study of the psychology of cruelty that bullfighting, however exciting, was not a sport. If the bull failed to be killed by the matador it was, by law, taken out of the ring and killed outside. Bulls were not allowed to be fought more than once, for an experienced bull would be likely to kill most of the bullfighters. Although many people outside Spain might say 'a good job too', the Spanish government sees things differently.

> *'For nature then*
> *To me was all in all'*
> William Wordsworth, *Lines Composed a Few Miles above Tintern Abbey* (1798)

When he was an unthinking boy Wordsworth was enraptured by waterfalls, mountains, and woods. That time is past, 'and all its aching joys are now no more'. But in recompense he has learned to find a deeper meaning in Nature, one that helps him to understand man through his mystical vision. He appears to believe that Nature is conscious of doing good. 'Nature never did betray / The heart that loved her.' The subtitle *On Revisiting the Banks of the Wye during a Tour* is more appropriate than the title; the poem was composed during several days' walking.

*'For nearly a century after his death Shakespeare remained
more a theme for criticism by the few than a subject of
adulation by the many'*
Ivor Brown, *Shakespeare*, ch.1 (1949)

Shakespeare's reputation was by no means extravagantly
high during the greater part of the seventeenth century.
'Dryden acclaimed him, but also criticized and rewrote
him.' During the Restoration period and the first half of
the eighteenth century his plays were usually garbled on
the stage and not greatly revered in the study. Not until
Garrick began a Stratford Festival in 1769 did bardolatry
make its appearance. Since then Shakespeare worship
has become almost an industry. Ivor Brown, one of the
outstanding dramatic critics of this century, offers an
admiring but level-headed portrait of the bard.

*'For old, unhappy, far-off things,
And battles long ago'*
William Wordsworth, *The Solitary Reaper* (1807)

In 1803 Wordsworth visited Scotland, where he was
deeply moved by hearing a girl singing a melody in Erse
as she wielded her sickle. Unable to understand what
she is singing, he lets his imagination offer suggestions.
Scottish history was full of melancholy incidents, and
perhaps the poet's guesses were not too wide of the
mark.

'For the Snark was a Boojum, you see'
Lewis Carroll, *The Hunting of the Snark* (1876)

The Snark, a creature of Lewis Carroll's lively imagination, is being pursued by a group whose main common
characteristic is the letter B. The Bellman is captain, and
those with him include a Boots, a Barrister, a Banker, and
a Baker. The last-named is anxious that the Snark, when
captured, shall not prove to be a Boojum Snark. Alas, the
creature, he at length discovers, *is* a Boojum, the result
being that in the midst of his cry of triumph the Baker
'softly and suddenly vanished away'. That was the effect
Boojums had on Bakers.

'For this relief much thanks'
William Shakespeare, *Hamlet*, I, i (c 1601)

The first scene of the play shows us a sentry (Francisco)
on midnight duty at Elsinore Castle, the home of King
Claudius, his wife Gertrude, and his nephew Hamlet.
Francisco is extremely thankful to be relieved by another
sentry, for it is a bitterly cold night, and he was also
afraid that the ghost of Hamlet's murdered father, seen
on two previous occasions, might appear once more. The
night had in fact passed quietly, but the ghost did show
itself again after Francisco had left.

'For we were nurst upon the self-same hill'
John Milton, *Lycidas* (1638)

On the early death of his college friend, Edward King, Milton wrote a memorial poem which was first published in a volume containing verses (some Latin and Greek) by various hands. Milton borrowed the pastoral style from Virgil, in whose *Eclogue III* Lycidas is a shepherd. The allusions in the poem follow the same line, with Christ's College, Cambridge being referred to as the hill where young shepherds would learn their skills.

'Four legs good, two legs bad'
George Orwell, *Animal Farm*, ch.3 (1945)

After the animals on Manor Farm had revolted and driven out the farmer, the pig leaders of the rebellion found that most of the creatures were unable to learn the seven rules of Animalism drawn up for them. The rules were therefore reduced to a single maxim, as quoted. The birds at first objected, but it was pointed out to them that a wing was an organ of propulsion, not manipulation, and could therefore be regarded as a leg. The maxim was learnt by heart, and the sheep would bleat it for hours – a satirical dig at political slogans.

'The freelance is a tramp touting for odd jobs'
Arnold Bennett, *The Truth about an Author* (1903)

Fairly early in his literary career Bennett spent a period freelancing, as most authors do. He did not like it. After two or three years he was lucky enough to obtain a post as an assistant editor, and from then on he trod a successful path. He looked back on his freelancing days with disgust and wrote of them with asperity. Though not dependent on writing (he had a job in a lawyer's office), he found the return of rejected manuscripts humiliating. 'And the shame of the freelance is none the less real because he alone witnesses it – he and the postman.'

'From bias free of every kind
This trial must be tried'
W. S. Gilbert, *Trial by Jury* (1875)

The Usher of the Court was instructing the jurymen in their duties, stressing that all prejudices must be set aside in the breach of promise case about to be dealt with. Being a Gilbertian Usher he mixed his insistence on impartiality with the most flagrant bias, almost sobbing over the distress of the plaintiff and advising the jury to take no notice of what the ruffianly defendant might say. The judge and jury displayed equal partiality, and the defendant's chances would have been slim if the judge had not decided to marry the plaintiff himself.

'Funny peculiar or funny ha-ha?'
Ian Hay, *Housemaster*, Act III (1936)

Users of English have long noted the ambiguity of the word 'funny', but the first character in literature to give clear and neat expression to the problem was a fourteen-year-old girl with the unlikely name (or nickname) of Button. Moreover she was to be found in what in 1936 was a very unlikely place indeed – a boys' public boarding school. Three girls, aged fourteen to twenty, are dumped – for inadequate reasons – on a public school housemaster. They almost wreck his career, in a light-hearted way, but not before their dialogue has introduced a classic and popular phrase to the English language.

'Gals is nat'lly made contrary; and so, if you thinks they've gone one road, it is sartin you'd better go t'other'
Harriet Beecher Stowe, *Uncle Tom's Cabin* (1851)

Eliza, the coloured maid of a kindly slave-owning family in nineteenth-century America, discovers that her employers have had to sell some of their slaves to a trader, and her own little son is among them. She takes flight with her child towards the northern States where slaves are free. The slave trader, Haley, prepares to give chase, assisted by two negro slaves, Sam and Andy. But while pretending to be assiduous in helping him they secretly do their best to hinder. Before the chase even begins Sam confuses Haley as to which road Eliza might have taken.

'Gather ye Rose-buds while ye may'
Robert Herrick, *To Virgins, to Make Much of Time* (1648)

The rapid passing of time was a theme that often occupied Herrick's mind, though he himself managed to survive, in a very troubled century, to the age of eighty-three. Here he is advising maidens to make the most of their youth, and seize the opportunity of marrying before advancing years made them miserably ineligible:

> While ye may, go marry:
> For having lost but once your prime,
> You may for ever tarry.

'Get her a flannel waistcoat and flannel drawers, ma'am'
E. C. Gaskell, *Cranford*, ch.1 (1853)

This suggestion was not a fashion hint for a lady susceptible to the cold, but a piece of advice concerning an Alderney cow. The animal was greatly prized by an elderly lady of Cranford, that quiet and delightful Cheshire village of the early nineteenth century. Unfortunately, one day the cow tumbled into a lime-pit and although it was rescued it lost most of its hair, and came out looking cold and miserable. Its owner was terribly distressed, but the blunt Army officer, Captain Brown, came forward with a remedy. He was possibly joking, but Miss Barker took him at his word, and the cow flourished in its unusual costume.

'Gentlemen of fortune ... usually trust little among themselves, and right they are'
R. L. Stevenson, *Treasure Island*, ch.11 (1883)

Long John Silver was himself a gentleman of fortune – in other words a villainous pirate. At present he is acting the part of an affable sea cook aboard the treasure-seeking *Hispaniola*. He is here convincing a young member of the crew that the lad can safely throw in his lot with the rogues who are preparing, under Silver's leadership, to seize the ship and the treasure. Although pirates rarely trust one another, Long John points out, there is not a man who would dare to try and cheat Silver himself.

'The gentry would have accepted a starving poet, living for his art, if only he had washed'
A. Calder-Marshall, *The Magic of My Youth*, ch.I (1951)

The gentry were the professional middle-class inhabitants of the little Sussex town of Steyning. The poet was Victor Neuberg who, though a genuine poet, was more notable for his one-time association with the notorious occult magician, Aleister Crowley, than for his poetry. But his muse had dried up when young Calder-Marshall knew him, and his activities were taking the dog for a walk and doing the shopping. He was indifferent to his appearance, washing and shaving only occasionally and wearing frayed and unpatched clothes.

'Get up and bar the door'
Anon, Old Ballad

A Scotsman and his wife are both reluctant to make the effort to bar their door. At last they agree that whoever is the next to speak shall do it. They remain resolutely silent – even when a couple of gentlemen arrive seeking hospitality. Getting no response to their questions, the men set to and finish up the puddings that the wife has been boiling. Then for fun they decide that one of them shall make love to the wife while the other shaves off the husband's beard, using the water the puddings have been boiled in. This at last stirs the man to utter a protest, whereupon his wife leaps up in delight and cries, rather belatedly:

Goodman, you've spoken the foremost word –
Get up and bar the door!

'Great wits are sure to madness near allied'
John Dryden, *Absalom and Achitophel*, Pt 1 (1681)

Achitophel (or Ahitophel) was a traitorous counsellor who conspired with Absalom, King David's son, against the King (2 Samuel, xv). The reference in the quotation is to 'Achitophel', who represents Anthony Ashley Cooper, First Earl of Shaftesbury, a man of great intelligence ('wit'), who pursued a furious anti-Royalist policy in the later years of his life. Dryden, a Royalist supporter, suggests in his satire that Shaftesbury shows his madness by intense political activity at a time of life when he should more properly be relaxing and resting his 'pigmy body'. 'Absalom' was the Duke of Monmouth, the natural son of Charles II ('David').

'Girls now at sixteen are as knowing as Matrons were formerly at sixty'
Edward Ravenscroft, *The London Cuckolds*, I, i (1681)

This situation seems to have been as prevalent in the seventeenth century as it no doubt is today. But Wiseacre, a London alderman, thinks he has successfully solved the problem. He has brought up an ignorant girl to be free from all contact with the outside world, thus (he believes) providing himself with a young wife too simple to have a will of her own or to cuckold him. His precautions, of course, are futile, and he is as badly let down by his silly young wife as is his friend, Alderman Doodle, by a witty one. For almost a century this rumbustious farce was acted every year in London on Lord Mayor's Day, perhaps to cock a snook at London's mayor and aldermen.

'Give me liberty, or give me death'
Patrick Henry, *Speech in the Convention of Virginia* (23 March 1775)

Henry, lawyer and politician, was a fiery opponent of British rule in America. In 1775 he strongly supported the arming of the Virginia militia against Britain, and indicated his attitude, already well-known, with a dramatic speech. Although not immediately recorded, the speech was later put together by some who had heard it. In it he denied that the Americans were too weak to fight. 'Three millions of people, armed in the holy cause of liberty . . . are invincible by any force which our enemy can send against us.' The war, he declared, had already begun, and peace was not to be gained at the price of liberty.

'Glory be to God for dappled things'
Gerard Manley Hopkins, *Pied Beauty* (1877)

The poems of Hopkins (1844–89) were not published until thirty years after his death. A Roman Catholic priest, teacher, and professor, he wrote mainly religious poetry in his own strange style. *Pied Beauty* praises objects that are particoloured – 'skies of couple-colour', fish with stippled scales, the wings of finches, the patchwork pattern of differently cultivated fields. The poet goes on to praise things that are not merely variegated but are in sharp contrast: 'swift, slow; sweet, sour; adazzle, dim'.

'Go and catch a falling star'
John Donne, *Song* (1633)

The song is a youthful exercise in cynical anti-love poetry. The reader is invited to perform all manner of fantastic feats – e.g. to grasp a star, to make a mandrake root pregnant, or to prove that mermaids can be heard singing – which are no more impossible (the poet says) than to find a woman who is fair and true. Carrying cynicism to its extreme, he asserts that even if he received a letter telling him that the girl next door was honest and innocent he would not bother to seek her out, for her virtue would have been lost by the time the letter arrived.

'God bless us every one!'
Charles Dickens, *A Christmas Carol* (1843)

The Ghost of Christmas Present takes miserly Scrooge (in a vision) to the home of his underpaid clerk, Bob Cratchit. In spite of their poverty the family are making the most of their modest fare in a cheerful spirit. Cratchit's youngest son Tiny Tim, a poor little cripple, is as cheerful as anyone, and (in the quotation) echoes his father's 'A Merry Christmas to us all . . . God bless us all.' Scrooge is duly impressed by the vision, and his complete conversion is not far off.

'God give thee strength, O gentle trout, To pull the rascal in'
John Wolcot, *To a Fish of the Brook* (1801)

An unusual attitude towards angling, especially in the days when animal welfare was scarcely thought of. The poet was better known by his pseudonym, Peter Pindar, under which he satirized the Royal Academy and the Royal Family with merciless and sometimes unrefined wit. In this much gentler little poem, the doctor-clergyman-poet encourages a fish not to fear him, for he has no intention of catching it. On the contrary, he invites the fish to retaliate on the angler by pulling him in!

'God is always for the big battalions'
Voltaire, *Letter to François Leriche* (1770)

The French philosopher, at the age of seventy-six, was writing to a Besançon official warning that the number of blockheads was always greater than the number of intelligent men, and that the former were more likely to prosper than the latter. Hence a frontal attack of the minority against the majority was futile: attack had to be more surreptitious. Voltaire's own attacks on Christian ideas and priestly behaviour in France had made it necessary for him to seek safety in Geneva, from where he wrote. The theme of the quotation was borrowed from a letter written by a French noble a hundred years earlier (Comte de Bussy, 1618–93).

'God made the country, and man made the town'
William Cowper, *The Task*, Bk I (1785)

The theme is put forward here by Cowper, a quiet and gentle country-lover. Though he champions the country, he admits that the arts flourish best in towns, and that London is 'this queen of cities', though imperfect. His main objection to the town is that the Sabbath is neglected: 'Knees and hassocks are well-nigh divorced'. It was doubtless very different in Cowper's church at Olney, Bucks. But what Cowper (and others) have tended to overlook is that the fields and woods of the 'natural' countryside are largely as man-made as a city street. God's country is primitive jungle or barren desert.

'Go down to Kew in lilac-time, in lilac-time, in lilac-time
Go down to Kew in lilac-time (it isn't far from London)'
Alfred Noyes, *The Barrel Organ* (1907)

The title of the poem reveals the kind of rhythm the poet
had in mind – the lively *tum-ti-tum* characteristic of the
old-fashioned barrel organ. Noyes himself used to recite
the poem while turning the handle of an imaginary
organ. Kew Gardens, in the south-west of London, is an
extensive botanical garden noted (among other things)
for its bluebells and its lilacs.

'God's in His heaven –
All's right with the world'
Robert Browning, *Pippa Passes* (1841)

Pippa, a young Italian girl working in the silk mills, is
given a single day's holiday, which she is anxious to
make the most of. She goes cheerfully through the town,
sometimes bursting into song. Each song that she sings
has a powerful effect on those who hear her. In this, her
first song, she unwittingly wrecks the life of her employer, Ottima, who has just encouraged her lover, Sebald, to
murder Ottima's elderly husband. Pippa's song causes
Sebald to feel remorse and to turn against his mistress.
Browning, like Pippa, was something of an optimist, but
it must not be forgotten that it is Pippa, not the poet
himself, whose feelings are expressed in the quoted
lines.

'God tempers the wind to the shorn lamb'
Laurence Sterne, *A Sentimental Journey* (1768)

Maria is a poor half-witted girl met by Yorick (Sterne) on
his journey through Italy. She tells him of her wander-
ings – to Rome and back, across the Apennines, all over
Lombardy, 'through the flinty roads of Savoy without
shoes'. How she had managed all this she could not say,
but 'God tempers the wind to the shorn lamb'. She
obtained this pleasant (though quite untrue) metaphor
from a French proverb, but with Sterne's help she has
contributed a popular saying to the English language.

'The good are always the merry'
W. B. Yeats, *The Fiddler of Dooney* (1892)

The fiddler, himself the speaker, claims that people love
to hear him playing, and when they do they always
dance 'like a wave of the sea'. His brother and cousin are
religious-minded, but he himself is fonder of secular
tunes. Yet when they all three get to Heaven, St Peter
will invite him in first, for good people are nearly always
merry.

> And the merry love the fiddle
> And the merry love to dance.

'Good fences make good neighbours'
Robert Frost, *Mending Wall* (1914)

There is a New England practice of 'walking the line' each Spring, when the owner of a field goes along the dry-wall boundary to replace the stones that always seem to fall during the winter. Frost follows this custom with his stolid neighbour, each on his own side of the wall. Having a livelier and more mischievous mind than his companion, the poet is sometimes tempted to ask *why* fences make good neighbours, and what exactly the fence is keeping in, or keeping out. But the neighbour is not really mending the wall for any specific purpose. He is doing it because he, and his father before him, have always done the same.

'Good wine needs no bush'
William Shakespeare, *As You Like It*, Epilogue (*c* 1600)

In Elizabethan times it was the custom to hang an ivy bush (sacred to Bacchus, god of wine) outside taverns and other wine houses to advertise that wine was sold therein. The actor playing Rosalind suggests that although good wine does not really need to be thus advertised, for its quality will make it known, none the less bushes are always used to draw attention to good wine. Similarly, although a good play should not need an epilogue to draw attention to its merits, yet 'good plays prove the better by the help of a good epilogue'.

'Good without evil is not given to man'
T. L. Peacock, *Gryll Grange*, ch.28 (1861)

A specially written play is being performed by Mr Gryll and friends at Gryll Grange. Mr Gryll, as an ancient Greek, is awakened from a sleep of three thousand years to be shown how civilization has progressed. He finds it full of innovations which are very mixed blessings. Steamships collide or blow up, and trains crash. Brilliantly gas-lit theatres burst into flames. (Covent Garden Theatre was burnt down in 1856 during a ball.) Three optimists assert that the ills brought by social progress are far less than the benefits, but the ancient Greek is not convinced.

'Go on with the story about the wedding-cake'
T. S. Eliot, *The Cocktail Party*, Act I (1949)

One of the not very many amusing items in this rather serious comedy is the attempt by forgetful Mrs Shuttleworth to tell a funny story about Lady Klootz and the wedding cake. There are so many interruptions that the story never gets told. And in the end Mrs Shuttleworth disclaims all knowledge of Lady Klootz and has no recollection of either wedding or wedding-cake. In the main this clever but super-subtle play consists of characters talking at some length about their states of mind, in fluent conversational blank verse, and mostly in irresolute despair.

'Go out and govern New South Wales!'
Hilaire Belloc, *Cautionary Tales – Lord Lundy* (1907)

Belloc's tongue-in-cheek tale is a warning against excessive tearfulness. Lord Lundy was intended by his family to enjoy a distinguished political career, but unfortunately from his earliest years he 'was far too freely moved to tears'. A question addressed to him in the House would cause him to shake with sobs, a distinct handicap to a Cabinet Minister. Thus he sank lower and lower in political rank. Finally his aged grandsire, the Duke, banished him to the lowest position he could think of – the governorship of New South Wales. 'And gracious! how Lord Lundy cried!'

'Government of the people, by the people, for the people shall not perish from the earth'
Abraham Lincoln, Speech delivered at Gettysburg (19 November 1863)

This fine-sounding sentiment was uttered by the American President during the Civil War in a brief but pungent speech which attracted little notice at the time but has since become historic. The occasion was the dedication of a national cemetery on the spot where a desperate battle had been fought a few months earlier. Cynics may doubt whether the type of government described has yet been achieved.

'Great God! this is an awful place'
Captain R. F. Scott, *Last Journal* (17 January 1912)

These words were written at the South Pole. Scott's party arrived after tremendous efforts only to discover that the Norwegian, Amundsen, had reached it a month earlier. Scott added that the area around the Pole was 'terrible enough for us to have laboured to it without the reward of priority'. It is a mistake, however, to suppose that disappointment gravely affected him or his party. Scott, unlike Amundsen, was engaged in a serious scientific expedition of which a journey to the hitherto undiscovered South Pole was only a part (though an important part). Amundsen was engaged primarily in a race to reach the Pole before Scott.

'The great roads march on boldly, with scarce a curve or bend, From some huge smoky Nothing, to Nothing at their end'
F. W. Harvey, *Gloucestershire Friends – The Little Road* (1917)

The poem is intended as a tribute to the little roads or lanes of England, and in particular those of Harvey's home county. He eschews the great Roman road, full of all kinds of traffic, and turns to the byroad, where the only noise to be heard is the sound of 'little tongues of water' and the rustling of leaves. Unfortunately Harvey allows his simple muse to become rather commonplace as he descends to

The secret winding misty road
That leads to Fairyland.

'Grieve not, my child, chase all thy fears away'
William Cowper, *On the Receipt of My Mother's Picture* (1790)

Cowper was six when his mother died. He was almost sixty when he was presented with a portrait of her, but this had a powerful effect on him. He blessed the artist who could paint her face so vividly that she seemed to be soothing his worries away just as she did in his childhood. He recalls her death and funeral, though he was too young to understand fully what was happening. At first he had expected her to return, but 'learnt at last submission to my lot'.

'Grow old along with me!
The best is yet to be'
Robert Browning, *Rabbi Ben Ezra* (1864)

The opening lines of a typical Browning poem, in which the poet's optimistic philosophy of life is expressed through the mouth of an ancient Jewish scholar. This learned man lived in the twelfth century, and was noted for his *Commentaries on the New Testament*. Though nothing very tangible emerges from the 32-stanza poem, it does stress the comforting idea that everything is for the best. Even old age has its blessings; life is but the fashioning of the pitcher by the master potter.

'The gulf between us and the brutes
Though deep, seems not too wide'
Louis Macneice, *Jigsaw III* (1957)

The poet suggests that we have a great deal in common with animals. Though they do not indulge in games with rules, like cricket and football, their play seems to have the same motivation as ours. Their instincts and desires are like ours, and so are their movements, if we substitute hands for paws, fins, or wings. Our distinctive qualities are only the tip of the iceberg; the submerged nine-tenths we share with the rest of creation.

'Had she come all the way for this,
To part at last without a kiss?'
William Morris, *The Haystack at the Floods* (1858)

A grim, powerful poem, fictional but dealing with historical characters. An English knight in France, Robert de Marney, after the fourteenth-century Battle of Poitiers (where the Black Prince defeated the French), was riding through the rain with his mistress, Jehane, and a small band of men. Suddenly they were ambushed by a large force of Frenchmen. Robert's men treacherously betrayed him. He was bound and gagged, and even Jehane's attempt to snatch a parting kiss was foiled. Robert was then brutally murdered.

This was the parting that they had
Beside the haystack in the floods.

'Hail to thee, blithe Spirit!
Bird thou never wert'
P. B. Shelley, *To a Skylark* (1821)

To Wordsworth the skylark was first of all a bird with a nest on the ground and a mate to whom the singing was addressed. Shelley, however, tends to soar away into ethereal realms. He is more concerned with the effect of the lark's song on his own mind than with the bird itself. Significantly he first thinks of it as 'like a poet hidden in the light of thought'. Then he passes to other similes: 'like a high-born maiden'; 'like a glow-worm golden'; 'like a rose embower'd'. He is fascinated by the lark's 'profuse strains', which make him envious. If he himself could be taught the same gladness (he thinks) the world would listen to him as intently as he now listens to the lark.

'Handsome is that handsome does'
Oliver Goldsmith, *The Vicar of Wakefield*, ch. 1 (1766)

When the Vicar's two daughters were praised by neighbours for their looks his wife would conceal her gratification by replying deprecatingly that they were handsome enough provided that they were good 'for handsome is that handsome does'. Common usage has altered 'that' to 'as' to suggest that behaviour is more important than appearance.

'A harmless, necessary cat'
William Shakespeare, *The Merchant of Venice*, IV, i (1600)

The cat (as any mouse or bird knows) is neither harmless nor necessary, though delightful to most right-thinking humans. Shylock, the Jewish money-lender, is asked to explain his malice towards the merchant Antonio. He replies that some people dislike pigs, others are disturbed by bagpipes, and yet others by 'a harmless, necessary cat'. Yet they cannot give reasons for having an aversion to these things. Similarly he cannot and will not give reasons for his feelings towards Antonio.

'Have you ever seen gingerbread with gilt on it?'
Noel Coward, *Cavalcade* (1931)

A honeymoon couple, Edith and Edward, are talking fondly on the deck of a big ocean liner. Edith is wondering if their love for each other will fade one day, 'when the gilt wears off the gingerbread'. Edward insists that it will not, and counters her metaphor by implying that gingerbread does not have gilt on it. His riposte is neat but inaccurate, for up to the middle of the nineteenth century gingerbread cakes were often made in the form of people or animals, and decorated with material that looked like gold leaf. Their talk about the future is, in fact, charged with dramatic irony, for when Edith removes her cloak from the deck-rail, the name of the ship is seen on a life-belt – S.S. *Titanic*.

'Have you heard of the wonderful one-hoss shay
That was built in such a logical way?'
Oliver Wendell Holmes, *The Deacon's Masterpiece*

According to this humorous poem, 'The Deacon' was an eighteenth-century carriage-builder who decided to construct a shay (chaise) on a new principle. Normally there is always a weakest spot in a carriage, and this leads it to break down. The Deacon was determined to have no weak spot; every part of his new chaise was built of the very strongest material. The vehicle was finished in 1755, and it remained as strong as ever year after year. But in 1855, one hundred years to the day since it had been completed, it suddenly disintegrated into a heap of timber. All the parts, being equally strong, had given way together!

'Have you not Maggots in your brains?'
Beaumont and Fletcher, *Women Pleased*, III, iv (1647)

In other words, 'Aren't you suffering from bats in the belfry?' The question was addressed to Lopez, a sordid old miser with a handsome young wife. He had called in his neighbours to be witnesses of his wife's infidelity, as he (not unfairly) supposed. But as his only evidence was that he had scratched her face – and even that so-called evidence was mistaken – the neighbours not unnaturally doubted his sanity. The authors were taking their task rather too lightly in this minor and rather scatter-brained comedy, and tossing together any kind of nonsense without much regard to its credibility.

'Heads I win, and tails you lose'
Duke of Rutland, Letter to J. W. Croker (1846)

The remark was occasioned by the Protection duties imposed on corn by France at a time when Sir Robert Peel wished to remove them in England in order to reduce the cost of living. France, Rutland says, is in a position where she cannot lose. English farmers would be unable to sell their corn to her, while she would still be in a position to dump her corn in England. Both the Duke and Croker (a prominent literary journalist) opposed the repeal of the Corn Laws.

'Heard melodies are sweet, but those unheard
Are sweeter'
John Keats, *Ode on a Grecian Urn* (1819)

The unheard melodies are those of the youth playing his pipes to a nymph in the pastoral scene depicted on the side of the urn. Imagination, Keats implies, can produce even more delightful sounds than those of a real instrument.

'The heathen Chinee is peculiar'
F. Bret Harte, *The Heathen Chinee* (1870)

In a tale in verse of the American West in mid-nine-teenth-century days, a simple Chinaman, Ah Sin, agreed to play at cards with a couple of Californians, though he did not understand card games. One of the Americans, Bill Nye, was a thorough card-sharper. Strangely enough, however, the child-like Chinaman kept winning. But at length he put down a hand of cards so suspicious that there was an angry scuffle. In the course of it cards by the dozen poured from the Chinaman's capacious sleeves. The innocent-seeming Chinee was not only peculiar but a much better trickster than the Americans.

'Heaven has no rage like love to hatred turned, Nor hell a fury like a woman scorned'
William Congreve, *The Mourning Bride*, III, viii (1697)

Zara, a captive African queen, has just discovered that Osmyn (also known as Alphonso), the man she loves, is closely attached to another woman. Her fury is under-standable; but her rage is short-lived, for in due course she kills herself for love when she believes Osmyn to have been murdered. The passionate Zara, a role created by Mrs Barry, was a favourite part of many great tragediennes, especially Mrs Siddons.

'Heaven lies about us in our infancy'
William Wordsworth, *Ode on the Intimations of Immortality* (1807)

The poem is based on the curious Platonic doctrine that the soul has had a life before entering the human body. From this former life it brings recollections which are clear in infancy but fade as we grow older. By the time we reach schooldays the soul's vision is already begin-ning to fade: 'Shades of the prison-house begin to close / Upon the growing boy'. The vision has disappeared altogether in manhood.

At length the Man perceives it die away,
And fade into the light of common day.

'He called for his candle, his bell, and his book'
R. H. Barham, *The Ingoldsby Legends – The Jackdaw of Rheims* (1840)

The Cardinal Lord Archbishop of Rheims removes a costly ring from his finger before washing his hands at the table. The ring is placed beside his plate, but when he goes to put it on again he finds it is missing. Indignantly he calls for candle, bell, and book, and proceeds to lay a solemn and comprehensive curse upon the rascally thief. To everyone's surprise nobody at first appears 'one penny the worse'. The reason soon becomes clear. The thief is discovered to be the Cardinal's pet jackdaw, which the curse has reduced to a pitiful state.

Then the great Lord Cardinal called for his book,
And off that terrible curse he took.

'He could raise scruples, dark and nice,
And after solve 'em in a trice'
Samuel Butler, *Hudibras*, Pt I, c. 3 (1663)

For a time Butler was secretary to Sir Samuel Luke, a
rigid Cromwellian army officer. This gave Butler a
splendid opportunity for studying the weaknesses of the
Puritans, and the result was *Hudibras*, a pungent satire
on their activities, with Sir Samuel presented (perhaps
unfairly) as Sir Hudibras, an absurd Puritan knight.
Butler is here mocking the Puritan tendency to indulge in
religious quibbles, raising artificial difficulties which
could be immediately answered:

As if Divinity had catch'd
The itch, on purpose to be scratch'd.

'He died with his face to you all'
Elizabeth Barrett Browning, *The Forced Recruit* (1862)

Mrs Browning's poem was written shortly after the
bloody battle of Solferino, fought between the Austrians
and the combined French and Sardinian forces. She
imagines a young Italian living in Austria and forced into
the Austrian army, but refusing to load his rifle or shoot
his countrymen or allies, preferring to meet his death by
their bullets. The battle of Solferino, one of the bloodiest
of the nineteenth century, at least had one beneficial
consequence. A Swiss banker, Henri Dunant, was so
shocked at the appalling state of the numerous wounded
that he founded the Red Cross organization.

'Heedless of grammar, they all cried, "That's Him!"'
R. H. Barham, *The Ingoldsby Legends – The Jackdaw of Rheims*
(1840)

After the Cardinal Archbishop of Rheims had solemnly
cursed the thief who stole his ring, the sacristan suddenly noticed that the jackdaw which was usually to be
seen hopping perkily around the Cardinal was in a sorry
state.

His pinions drooped – he could hardly stand –
His head was as bald as the palm of your hand.

The identity of the thief was obvious. The monks and
friars all cried excitedly: 'That's the scamp that has done
this scandalous thing!' The ring was duly found in the
jackdaw's nest, the terrible curse was removed, and the
bird at once recovered his health.

'He had never tried to carry a woman, but on the cinema it
always looked an easy piece of heroism'
Aldous Huxley, *Crome Yellow*, ch. 17 (1921)

Anne had injured her ankle in the garden at night.
Denis, young, inexperienced, and very much in love
with her, for once feels master of the situation. A little
older than himself in years, and a lot in poise, Anne
usually makes him seem gauche. Now, he thinks, the
position is reversed. He confidently starts to lift her but
he is not very muscular. He takes a few staggering steps
and then has to drop her with a bump. Anne shakes with
laughter. Denis's moment of assurance is gone, and his
painful humiliation is complete. The episode is youthful
mortification typified.

'He had used the word in its Pickwickian sense'
Charles Dickens, *The Pickwick Papers*, ch. 1 (1836–7)

Mr Pickwick, President of the Pickwick Club, had been called a humbug by one of the members, Mr Blotton, after a learned lecture had been delivered by the President. There was a good deal of disturbance, but at length the chairman drew from Mr Blotton the statement that he had used the word 'humbug' not in the usual sense but in its Pickwickian sense. How this differed from the ordinary sense was not made clear, but the controversy has provided the English language with a useful term that we can employ when we would like to be rude to someone without (we hope) giving offence.

'He has outsoared the shadow of our night'
P. B. Shelley, *Adonais*, xl (1821)

Shelley modelled his lament for the death of John Keats on the laments for Adonis written by the pastoral poet Bion (c 100 B.C.). In stanza xl he at last finds some consolation by reflecting that death has brought Keats freedom from the earthly ills experienced by those still living. Shelley believed mistakenly that Keats's death had been partly caused by a savage criticism in the *Quarterly Review* (1818), and in the Preface to *Adonais* he indignantly attacked those responsible.

'Heigh ho, would she were mine'
Thomas Lodge, *Rosalynde* (1590)

Readers familiar with *As You Like It* (c 1599) will know the story of Lodge's novel, *Rosalynde*, for Shakespeare dipped into it with both hands. Like Orlando, Rosader is a disinherited young man in love with charming and lively Rosalynde, who (like Shakespeare's heroine) is pretending to be a youth under the name of Ganymede. Invited to describe Rosalynde, Rosader recites a love poem, each verse of which ends with the quoted line. Her eyes are sapphires, her lips like budded roses, her neck a stately tower. As Ganymede rather sceptically observes, she seems to be 'far above wonder'.

'He is the wisest, the happiest, and the best, inasmuch as he is a poet'
P. B. Shelley, *A Defence of Poetry* (1821)

Shelley is trying to convince himself and us that as a poet inspires others with 'the highest wisdom, pleasure, virtue and glory' (so he believes) he must necessarily be the best and happiest of men. The fact that all too often poets are not a bit like this did not disconcert Shelley, whose ability to shut his eyes to reality was infinite. His eloquent but rather rambling *Defence* was nominally a reply to T. L. Peacock's *The Four Ages of Poetry*, but it is really, as Peacock said, 'a defence without an attack'. Peacock's essay was a witty *jeu d'esprit*, and serious-minded Shelley was not the man to answer it.

> *'He left the name, at which the world grew pale,*
> *To point a moral, or adorn a tale'*
Samuel Johnson, *The Vanity of Human Wishes* (1749)

The world grew pale at the name of Charles XII, King of Sweden (1697–1718), for he had a passion for warfare. 'Peace courts his hand, but spreads her charms in vain.' He rejected all peace offers, and both the Danes and the Russians felt the might of his mailed fist. In the end he was killed by a stray bullet while besieging a petty Norwegian fortress. The terrible figure who made the world tremble left behind him only a name. And the moral? Why, the vanity of human wishes.

> *'Hell is paved with good intentions'*
Samuel Johnson, in Boswell's *Life of Johnson* (1791)

Johnson was inclined to regard himself as a lazy man, and kept making resolutions to improve himself. For example, he once drew up resolutions for his Sunday behaviour. They included decisions to read the Scriptures, to go to church twice, and 'to rise early, and in order to it, to go to sleep early on Saturday'. But no one was more conscious than Johnson of failure to keep to pious plans, and he often scolded himself for his inadequacy. The well-known quoted saying was typical of his attitude.

> *'He nothing common did nor mean*
> *Upon that memorable scene'*
Andrew Marvell, *Horatian Ode Upon Cromwell's Return from Ireland* (1650)

Interrupting the praise of his hero, the poet (though an ardent Cromwellian) inserts a few lines to commend the calm and dignified bearing of Charles I at his execution by Cromwell's army. After being condemned to death by an illegal tribunal which he refused to recognize, Charles was beheaded on a scaffold erected outside Whitehall Palace on 30 January 1649. Cromwell's return from Ireland in 1650 left its inhabitants 'ashamed/To see themselves in one year tamed'. It also left many of them with a lasting feeling of bitterness.

> *'Here she comes i'faith full sail, with her fan spread and*
> *streamers out, and a shoal of fools for tenders'*
William Congreve, *The Way of the World*, II, v (1700)

Mirabell, the hero, describes the entrance of his delightful but maddening mistress, Millamant, likening her to a galleon sweeping through the water. The description is perhaps witty rather than apt, for Millamant is too lively to bear comparison with a great sailing ship. She sweeps through life with laughing disdain rather than with dignity. She and Mirabell are the supreme representatives of those typical seventeenth-century characters, the witty couple, forever sparring with each other.

'Here tulips bloom as they are told'
Rupert Brooke, *Grantchester* (1912)

The young poet, normally resident in the Cambridge-shire village of Grantchester, was staying temporarily in the regimented Germany of the period shortly before the First World War (1914–18). There he found himself longing for the more informal English way of life. Seated in a Berlin café he gives expression to his feelings in lively verse. He includes a humorous suggestion that even the flowers adopt their respective national characteristics. In contrast to the rigid rows of German tulips he mentally pictures 'an English unofficial rose' growing in happy disorder in an English hedge.

'He ruleth all the roste
With bragging and with bost'
John Skelton, *Why Come Ye nat to Court?* (c 1522)

Skelton, at one time tutor to Henry VIII, is having a good hard smack at Cardinal Wolsey, accusing him of ruling the Star Chamber Court so domineeringly that no other member of it dare oppose his views. Skelton, not surprisingly, became rather unpopular with Wolsey, from whom he sought sanctuary at Westminster. There is some uncertainty about the rhyme. Did Skelton's 'roste' mean 'roost'? Then Wolsey is seen as the bragging cock perched on his roost, and the modern phrase 'ruling the roost' seems to accept this. But 'roste' has also been interpreted as 'roast', and 'to rule the roast' is to be lord of the kitchen. Brewer favours the latter version.

'Her women fair; her men robust for toil'
Thomas Campbell, *Theodric* (1824)

Believe it or not, the quotation refers to England, 'Where Nature, Freedom, Art, smile hand in hand.' Theodric is a gallant Austrian officer who in an interval between wars comes on a sightseeing visit to England, where he finds 'vigorous souls, high-cultured as her soil'. London in festive mood delighted him. Above all he was fascinated by the lovely ladies, 'fairest of the land', who rode in open carriages through the streets and parks. One of them attracted him so much that he prolonged his visit in order to get to know her, and in due course he married her.

'He sees his bride as if he saw her not'
David Mallet, *Elvira*, I, i (1763)

Almeyda is not really a bride but is the girl to whom King Alonzo has promised his son, Don Pedro. The reason why the Prince hardly looks at Almeyda is that he is married already to Elvira. This married couple spend a good deal of the play lamenting their unhappy situation. Not without cause, for the King is annoyed at having his plans upset, and condemns both his son and Elvira to death. However, when Elvira produces the two offspring of her marriage there are tears all round, and Alonzo relents. But there has to be at least one death in order to make the play a tragedy, so Elvira obliges, poisoned by Almeyda's angry mother.

'He sighed for the love of a ladye'
W. S. Gilbert, *The Yeomen of the Guard*, Act I (1888)

Jack Point and Elsie Maynard are strolling players who entertain a crowd outside the Tower of London with a song entitled *The Merryman and his Maid*. It tells the story of a jester who sighed for the love of a lady, the Merrymaid. She was in love with a lord, and scorned the Merryman. The lord, however, 'turned up his noble nose with scorn' at the girl. In the end the Merrymaid begged forgiveness from the jester, and all ended happily. The song in some ways paralleled the case of Jack Point and Elsie – but there was no happy ending for Jack Point.

'He smote them hip and thigh'
Bible, Judges, xv, 15 (*c* 600 B.C.)

Hip and thigh is a wrestling action in which the opponent is thrown head first over the leg. Here it denotes complete slaughter. The action is hardly to Samson's credit. He had grossly neglected his wife, but was incensed when her Philistine father gave her to someone else. His idea of retaliation was to set fire to the Philistines' crops. They responded by burning the wife and her father. Samson now carried on the senseless vendetta by killing as many Philistines as he could (smiting them hip and thigh), and then taking up a defensive position 'in the top of the rock Etam' (an unidentified place) – a Biblical thug gone to roost.

'He that is down can fall no lower'
Samuel Butler, *Hudibras*, Pt I, c. 3 (1663)

Hudibras is a mock-heroic poem which jeers at the Puritans by making Sir Hudibras a ridiculous figure – a Don Quixote of a very inferior kind. He usually gets the worst of any contest. He and his argumentative squire, Ralpho, had won a temporary victory over a crowd of revellers, Hudibras being against any kind of enjoyment. But when hostilities are renewed Hudibras is knocked flying by a sturdy Amazon named Trulla, who proceeds to sit on him. He begs her not to scoff at him, for 'he that is down can fall no lower'.

'He that outlives this day, and comes safe home,
Will stand a tip-toe when this day is named'
William Shakespeare, *Henry V*, IV, iii (1599)

In days when war was regarded as glorious, Henry was answering a nobleman who had wished for more troops before the battle of Agincourt. Henry boastfully asserts that if there were more English soldiers available it would lessen the honour of defeating the French. (There were about nine thousand English troops to about thirty thousand French.) He prophesies that the battle will become so renowned that those Englishmen who have taken part in it will hold themselves high whenever the day on which it was fought (St Crispin's day, 25 October) is mentioned.

*'He told me, as a matter of pride, that he had sometimes
wrung a dirty dishcloth into a customer's soup before taking
it in'*
George Orwell, *Down and Out in Paris and London* (1933)

The offender was Jules, a Magyar waiter in a Paris
restaurant where Orwell was working as a dish-washer.
He was both proud and lazy, shirking his work as far as
possible and stealing as a matter of principle. His
treatment of customers' soup was not due to any
personal quarrel. Jules was an ardent and voluble Com-
munist; on principle he sometimes decided to revenge
himself on a customer for being a member of the
bourgeoisie. The moral seems to be that it is advisable to
find out a waiter's politics before dining in Paris.

'He was a man who used to notice such things'
Thomas Hardy, *Afterwards* (1917)

The poet wonders whether, when he dies, his neighbours will recall the interest he took in the details of
nature – the delicacy of a moth's wings, the flight of a
hawk, his care for the humble hedgehog, his patient
watching of the stars in the night sky. Though he
nowhere says so explicitly, it is clear that he hopes this
aspect of his nature will be long remembered.

'He was a rake among scholars, and a scholar among rakes'
T. B. Macaulay, *Review of Aikin's Life of Addison* (1843)

Macaulay's bon mot relates not to Addison but to
Richard Steele (1672–1729). It has at least a tinge of truth,
but is characteristically oversimplified to make an epigram. Though a bit of a rake in certain respects, Steele
was a good deal more than that. He virtually originated
sentimental comedy, and he founded the social essay,
offering good sense and humour to the man in the coffee
house – the average intelligent person of the day. In both
The Tatler (1709) and *The Spectator* (1711) Steele was
closely allied with Joseph Addison, which is how he
came to be drawn into Lucy Aikin's *Life* of the latter.

'He was as fresh as is the month of May'
Geoffrey Chaucer, *The Canterbury Tales – Prologue* (c 1387)

Every medieval knight had his squire, and the knight
who rode with other pilgrims to Canterbury was squired
by his son. He was a fine young fellow, about twenty
years old. In spite of his youth he had seen service on the
continent and carried himself well. He wore clothes that
were beautifully embroidered with flowers, and was as
accomplished in peaceful pursuits as he was in war. He
could sing, dance, draw, and write poetry, as well as
joust.

'He was not for an age, but for all time'
Ben Jonson, *To the Memory of my Beloved, the author Mr William Shakespeare* (1623)

This tribute to Shakespeare, paid by an admiring contemporary, is from a poem in the preface to the First Folio, the first collected edition of Shakespeare's plays. The Folio was arranged by two fellow actors, Heminge and Condell, seven years after Shakespeare's death. In this poem, Jonson claims that although Shakespeare was no learned scholar ('thou hadst small Latine, and lesse Greeke'), he equalled or excelled the greatest writers of Greece and Rome.

'He who'd make his fellow-creatures wise
Should always gild the philosophic pill'
W. S. Gilbert, *The Yeomen of the Guard*, Act I (1888)

The Lieutenant of the Tower of London has a vacancy for a jester, and Jack Point is offering his own qualifications. Jack can rhyme, quip, be merry, tell stories and jests, and pose riddles. He adds a song explaining what a jester can do in the way of blending philosophy with humour:
When they're offered to the world in merry guise,
Unpleasant truths are swallowed with a will.

'His heart runs away with his head'
George Colman (the younger), *Who Wants a Guinea?* I, i (1805)

John Torrent, squire of the manor in a Yorkshire village, wishes to help his tenants after a disastrous fire. But his impetuous generosity is undiscriminating, so Heartly (a useful level-headed friend) proposes to take a hand in the distribution of charity, for Torrent 'often produces most harm when he shows most benevolence'.

'His honour rooted in dishonour stood,
And faith unfaithful kept him falsely true'
Alfred Tennyson, *Idylls of the King – Lancelot and Elaine* (1859)

Sir Lancelot, chief of King Arthur's knights, was also the secret lover of the Queen, Guinevere. When he is tended in sickness by the lovely Elaine, who has fallen in love with him, he is tempted to return her feelings. But he is held back by his desire to honour his love for the Queen, though that in itself was dishonourable to King Arthur. So 'his honour rooted in dishonour stood'. The second line of the quotation is a favourite example of *oxymoron*, that figure of speech in which contradictory terms are combined.

'His little nameless, unremembered acts
Of kindness and of love'
William Wordsworth, *Lines Composed a Few Miles above Tintern Abbey* (1798)

Wordsworth had returned after five years to the River Wye district. During that time he had often experienced in retrospect the peace of mind brought by the beauty and serenity of the scene. Feelings thus inspired were often unconscious, just like the kind and affectionate actions of a good man, performed so naturally that he does not even think of them. This reflective poem, one of Wordsworth's best contributions to the *Lyrical Ballads*, was composed during four or five days of a walking tour which began near Tintern, the 160 lines being kept entirely in his mind until the end of the journey.

'His time has come, he ran his race;
We hope he's in a better place'
Jonathan Swift, *Verses on the Death of Dr Swift* (1731)

Dean Swift is humorously portraying the scene which he thinks will take place when his death is announced. He imagines his 'female friends' receiving the news while engaged in a game of cards. They will hear it, he suggests, quite calmly, scarcely taking their minds off the game.

The Dean is dead (*and what is trumps?*)
Then Lord have mercy on his soul.
(*Ladies, I'll venture for the Vole.*[1])
Six deans, they say, must bear the pall.
(*I wish I knew what king to call.*)

'Hitch your wagon to a star'
R. W. Emerson, *Civilization* (1870)

Emerson is stressing the importance of morality to civilization. 'Everything good in man leans on what is higher.' Readers are counselled to abjure paltry and evil acts. Thinking of the gods as stars, he warns that no god will help those who act wrongly. If we do wrong 'we shall find all their teams going the other way – Charles's Wain, Great Bear, Orion, Leo, Hercules: every god will leave us.' Whether his high opinion of the gods was justified the reader must decide for himself.

'Hold on, never mind about the cargo, hold on'
Thor Heyerdahl, *The Kon-Tiki Expedition*, ch. 7 (1950)

These were Heyerdahl's words as the famous balsa-wood raft, *Kon-tiki*, reached the end of its 4,000-mile voyage across the South Seas from Peru to Polynesia. As the raft was being driven towards a great coral reef the leader gave the friendly but urgent instruction to his five colleagues to hold on. Each man held grimly to one or other of the ropes. The sea presently seized the raft, flung it on to a section of the reef, and completely submerged it. It was considerably damaged, but all the adventurers survived. And Heyerdahl not only proved his point that such a voyage was practicable and could have been carried out in early times. He also wrote a world best-seller about the expedition.

[1] The winning of all the tricks

'Home is the sailor, home from sea'
R. L. Stevenson, *Requiem* (1884)

Stevenson wrote his own epitaph, which is duly inscribed on his tomb in Samoa, where he died. Though not, of course, a professional sailor, he chose his metaphor aptly, for he was a man with a zest for travel and adventure. The two-stanza *Requiem* begins:

Under the wide and starry sky,
Dig the grave and let me lie.

It ends:

Here he lies where he longed to be;
Home is the sailor, home from sea,
And the hunter home from the hill.

'An honest man's the noblest work of God'
Alexander Pope, *Essay on Man*, Epistle IV (1733)

Pope is pointing out the folly of a desire for fame. Those supposedly clever or great, he says, are less important than those who are honest and straightforward. But whether Pope genuinely believed that simple honesty was more significant than genius may be doubted.

'Honeymooning is a very overrated amusement'
Noel Coward, *Private Lives*, Act I (1930)

Honeymooning is very much the main theme of this Act, arguably one of the best first Acts of any twentieth-century comedy. The speaker, Amanda, is on honeymoon with her second husband, having divorced her first, Elyot, because of their frequent quarrels. By a remarkable coincidence, permissible only in comedy, Elyot has unknowingly come to the same Deauville hotel for *his* second honeymoon. Amanda and Elyot presently meet by chance alone on their respective balconies. They remember vividly their first honeymoon and intimacy, and realize that they are still in love with each other. By the end of the Act they have decided to leave together for another, though illicit, honeymoon, leaving their respective spouses behind.

'Honour and life to Willow the King'
Edward E. Bowen, *Willow the King* (1886)

Bowen, a master at Harrow School, wrote a number of verses to be sung by his pupils. Next to *Forty Years On*, this is perhaps the best-known. Willow the King is, of course, the cricket bat, with his courtiers (the stumps) standing three in a row. His reign is disturbed by the coming of the Leathery Duke, who knocks the courtiers flying. There is a hidden pun here, for Duke was the name of a leading cricket-ball maker of the period. In the last verse the Leathery Duke becomes filled with air, changing to a football, and Willow the King is put to bed for the winter.

'Hope springs eternal in the human breast: Man never Is, but always To be blest'
Alexander Pope, *Essay on Man*, Epistle I (1733)

In his Essay the poet examines human nature in verse, holding that he can express his views more concisely thus than in prose. Here he reflects that ignorance of the future is a blessing in disguise. Just as the lamb would not gambol so happily in the fields if it were aware of the butcher's knife, so man, not knowing his precise destiny, is able to enjoy the blessing of hope.

'A horse! A horse! My Kingdom for a horse!'
William Shakespeare, *King Richard III* (1597)

The last words of the villainous King Richard, providing the actor with a splendid line for his final exit. Though his horse has been slain under him (off stage) in the battle against the future Henry VII, Richard goes off fighting like a tiger. It is something of an anticlimax when the victor enters a few moments later to announce that 'the bloody dog is dead'. The quoted line appears in a slightly earlier play about Richard III, *The True Tragedie* (1594). But no matter who wrote it, this bold cry of a desperate King is splendid theatre.

'The house is still but a sort of porch at the entrance of a burrow'
H. D. Thoreau, *Walden* (1854)

A cellar, which was to be found in almost all nineteenth-century houses in England and America, is likened to the burrow made by many animals. The cellar was the place where essential supplies were stored. It often remained long after the house was gone. Thoreau was an educated American dedicated to the simple life. In 1845 he withdrew for two-and-a-half years to a solitary place near Walden Pond, where he built himself a hut (with cellar) and lived alone. *Walden or Life in the Woods* is a descriptive account of the time he spent there.

'How are the mighty fallen!'
Bible, 2 Samuel, i, 19

The mighty are Saul, King of Israel, and his son Jonathan, slain by the Philistines at the battle of Mount Gilboa. David, Saul's successor, though estranged from Saul, utters a sincere lament over the death of 'the Lord's anointed'. 'The beauty of Israel is slain upon thy high places: how are the mighty fallen!'

'How happy could I be with either
Were t'other dear charmer away'
John Gay, *The Beggar's Opera*, Act II, ii (1728)

The handsome highwayman, Captain Macheath, has been arrested through the treachery of Mr Peacham, his employer. While he is in prison he is visited by his jailer's daughter, Lucy Locket, to whom he has promised marriage, and Polly Peacham, whom he has secretly married. Each girl accuses him of infidelity, and he bursts into song to indicate his inability to satisfy either of them. Ultimately he temporarily disowns Polly and encourages Lucy in order to get her to steal her father's keys and enable him to escape.

'How I wonder what you are!'
Jane Taylor, *The Star* (1806)

This early-nineteenth-century children's writer started planning books at the age of eight, though she had to wait until she was twenty-one before having a book published – *Original Poems for Infant Minds* (1804), written in collaboration with her sister. 'Twinkle, twinkle, little star' is an invitation to the heavenly body to continue shining all night, followed by the somewhat improbable assertion that the night traveller 'Could not tell which way to go' without the light of the star to guide him. The poem invited parody, and Lewis Carroll duly had the Mad Hatter singing 'Twinkle, twinkle, little bat! / How I wonder what you're at!' (*Alice's Adventures in Wonderland*, ch. 7).

'How many good and clean wits of children be nowadays
perished by ignorant schoolmasters'
Thomas Elyot, *The Boke Named the Governour* (1531)

Elyot's *Boke*, the first book on education written in English, is concerned particularly with the training of those destined to govern. In Henry VIII's day all such instruction dealt mainly with Greek and Latin, and Sir Thomas Elyot (classical scholar and diplomat) was indignant at the bad teaching which too often prevailed. Anyone, he complains, is able to set up as a schoolmaster, even if he has only 'a spoonful of Latin'. Such men will teach so incompetently that what is learnt 'will be washed away with one shower of rain'.

'How now, Sir Hugh! No school today?'
William Shakespeare, *The Merry Wives of Windsor*, IV, i
(*c* 1600)

Mistress Page is expressing the usual concern of a parent at finding there is an unexpected school holiday. The episode was doubtless introduced so that Shakespeare could enjoy having a good-humoured knock at a schoolmaster who had taught him (in Jonson's phrase) small Latin and less Greek. A Welsh master named Thomas Jenkins taught at the Stratford Grammar School when Shakespeare was about twelve, and was most probably the model for Sir Hugh Evans. The Latin catechism through which Evans puts one of his pupils in this scene was typical of the Elizabethan style of teaching, and so, too, was the casual threat of a flogging.

'The hungry sheep look up, and are not fed'
John Milton, *Lycidas* (1638)

Milton passes from lamenting the death of his friend
Edward King to lamenting the state of religion. King
would have taken holy orders if he had lived, and such a
man, Milton felt, could ill be spared. Milton sees the
clergy of the day neglecting their parishioners ('the
hungry sheep') and concerned only with material interests. Moreover, firm Protestant that he was, he was
worried by the grim wolf which 'daily devours apace,
and nothing said'. The wolf was the Catholic Church,
which he saw making constant surreptitious attempts to
seek converts, while the Church of England remained
indifferent to the danger.

'I always feel with Norman that I have him on loan from somewhere, like one of his library books'
Alan Ayckbourn, *Table Manners*, II, i (1973)

This is the second play in Ayckbourn's brilliant trilogy,
The Norman Conquests. Norman, an amusing but
emotionally unstable librarian, is married to Ruth, a
clever, brisk, emotionally cold businesswoman. Norman
has tried to arrange an illicit weekend with Ruth's sister,
Annie. The attempt is frustrated, and Annie apologetically assures her sister that she was not trying to take
Norman away from her. Ruth unemotionally replies that
she does not own Norman any more than she owns a
library book. 'I'll get a card one day,' she adds with
caustic exaggeration, 'informing me that he's overdue
and there's a fine to pay on him.'

'I am a lone lorn creetur', and everythink goes contrairy with me'
Charles Dickens, *David Copperfield*, ch. 3 (1849–50)

Dan Peggotty lived in a house made out of an upturned
boat, where he gave a home also to the widow of a
former partner in the fishing business, Mrs Gummidge.
She suffered from an obsesssion that she was neglected
and uncared for, all alone in the world, with fate against
her. She constantly complained that she felt mishaps and
discomforts more than other people did. To Dan Peggotty, always good-natured, her widowhood excused everything. 'She's been thinking of the old 'un,' was his
invariable comment.

'I am alone the villain of the earth'
William Shakespeare, *Antony and Cleopatra*, IV, vi (c 1607)

Antony's most reliable and capable soldier, Enobarbus,
has become increasingly dismayed by his master's in-
fatuation with Cleopatra and his deterioration as a
soldier. At length in despair he forsakes Antony and
reluctantly joins the enemy, leaving his possessions
behind. As soon as Antony learns that his valued friend
has left him he magnanimously sends the deserter's
possessions after him, with additional bounty. It is a
shattering experience for Enobarbus. Overcome with
remorse at having forsaken such a leader, he dies of
grief, cursing himself.

'I am a very 'umble person'
Charles Dickens *David Copperfield*, ch. 16 (1849–50)

Uriah Heep, the fawning clerk of Mr Wickfield, a lawyer
with whom David lodges, is constantly stressing his
humility. To indicate his lowliness he frequently rubs his
hands together 'as if to squeeze them warm and dry',
and he often engages in 'snaky twistings of his throat
and body'. In reality he is a cunning schemer, aiming at
getting control of his employer's practice. This he succeeds in doing in due course, but his misdeeds are
exposed at last.

'I am done with apple-picking now'
Robert Frost, *After Apple-Picking* (1914)

On the surface this is a poem about the end of autumn,
the apple-picking season. The ladder remains against the
trees, there is an unfilled barrel nearby, and there are still
a few unpicked fruits. The frosts have already begun,
and the poet is even able to look at the fruit through a
slab of ice skimmed off the drinking-trough. Now he is
tired out with the labour of carefully plucking fruit
without allowing it to fall. Besides this simple interpreta-
tion of the poem an allegorical one may also be found,
with apple-picking representing life itself, and the pick-
er's drowsiness a peaceful readiness for death.

'I am just going outside, and may be some time'
Captain L. E. G. Oates, Recorded in Captain Scott's *Last Journal* (16–17 March 1912)

These are the last words of one of the four men who
accompanied Scott on his sledge journey to the South
Pole. On the ill-fated return from the Pole, Oates
suffered so badly from frost-bitten feet that he was
unable to continue walking. Knowing that his disability
might hinder his companions from reaching safety if he
remained with them, he deliberately went out into the
blizzard to die. Although his heroism failed to save his
friends, it remains a notable example of self-sacrifice.

'I am never less alone than when alone'
William Hazlitt, *Table Talk – On Going a Journey* (1821)

Hazlitt prefers to be alone when walking in the country.
'I cannot see the wit of walking and talking at the same
time.' He does not want the bother of trying to explain
why he finds this or that flower attractive, or of indulging in the kind of witty conversation that can be
delightful indoors. By himself he can look at what he
pleases, think what he pleases, and do what he pleases.
'I laugh, I run, I leap, I sing for joy.' If he did have a
companion the only subject he would want to talk about
on a journey would be food – 'what one shall have for
supper when we get to our inn tonight'.

'I am not going to be shot in a wheelbarrow, for the sake of appearances, to please anybody'
Charles Dickens, *The Pickwick Papers*, ch. 19 (1837)

Mr Pickwick, being lame with rheumatism, is being trundled in a wheelbarrow to accompany a shoot organized by his friend, Mr Wardle. He demands that Mr Winkle, walking behind him, shall carry his gun with the muzzle pointing to the ground, despite Winkle's objection that this is not the correct sportsman's way. Mr Pickwick's wisdom is shown soon afterwards when the gun goes off, seemingly of its own accord, fortunately with no damage to anyone. The fact is that Mr Winkle's skill with a gun is as illusory as his other supposed accomplishments.

'I am poor Brother Lippo, by your leave'
Robert Browning, *Fra Lippo Lippi* (1855)

Poor Brother Lippo was a real person, Filippo di Tommaso Lippi (1412–69), who was placed in a Carmelite monastery as a child and stayed there till he was twenty. But he was essentially an artist; released from his religious vows he cheerfuly pursued his real vocation. Browning's dramatic monologue begins with an attempt by the local watchmen to arrest him as a suspicious character when they find him wandering the streets after midnight. He is able to shake off their suspicions, which are finally drowned in a round of drinks. Browning obtained his factual details from Vasari's *Lives of the Illustrious Painters* (1550).

'I am rich beyond the dreams of avarice'
Edward Moore, *The Gamester*, III, 2 (1753)

This exciting affluence lay not in cash but in contentment. Mrs Beverley, the doting wife of a reckless gambler who is on the road to ruin, assures him that she will regard herself as a wealthy woman provided he loves her contentedly. Her unwise fondness is unavailing, and he ends by taking his own life in this grim but powerful domestic melodrama. Garrick first produced it, and a little later Mrs Siddons as the distressed wife reduced Drury Lane audiences to tears.

'I am screaming out loud all the time I write and so is my brother which takes off my attention rather'
Charles Dickens, *Nicholas Nickleby*, ch. 15 (1838–9)

The author of this would-be pathetic letter is Fanny, daughter of Mr Squeers, a brutal schoolmaster, who himself has recently been thrashed by his greatly provoked assistant, Nicholas. Fanny Squeers is writing revengefully to the young man's uncle, who had obtained Nicholas the post. She asserts that her father is too badly hurt to write, while she and her brother have suffered internal injuries. Her highly inaccurate account is readily accepted by Ralph Nickleby, who is no friend to his nephew. But Miss Squeers's hope that Nicholas 'is sure to be hung before long' was fated to be unfulfilled. In the end it is Ralph who hangs himself, while Nicholas prospers.

'I am the last and highest court of appeal in detection'
A. Conan Doyle, *The Sign of Four*, ch. 1 (1890)

The supreme detective in fiction is, of course, Sherlock Holmes of Baker Street. He points out to the invaluable Dr Watson that even official police inspectors are sometimes driven to come to him for assistance when they are baffled. They were the readier to ask his help inasmuch as he claimed no public credit. The analytical work itself was sufficient reward for him. In *The Sign of Four* the portly Athelney Jones is the police inspector, rather patronizing at first, but in time driven to acknowledge that 'Mr Sherlock Holmes is a wonderful man'.

'I am the master of my fate:
I am the captain of my soul'
W. E. Henley, *Invictus* (1875)

Henley is noted for the vigour and robustness of his verse. This is the more remarkable in that he was a cripple from boyhood, and *Invictus* was written from a hospital bed. There was nothing feeble, however, about Henley's mind, which is bravely reflected in the four stanzas of the poem. He thinks of his resistance to misfortune as a battle.

Under the bludgeonings of chance

My head is bloody, but unbowed.

These were not merely bold words. He refused to allow crippling tuberculosis of the hip to destroy his active life, and he became an industrious literary critic and editor (of the *Magazine of Art, National Observer,* etc.) and a poet.

'I am told there are people who do not care for maps, and find
it hard to believe'
R. L. Stevenson, *My First Book* (1894)

Stevenson's enthusiasm for maps was fortunate, for it gave the world one of the finest adventure stories ever written. His young stepson, Lloyd Osbourne, had drawn the map of an imaginary island. Stevenson began elaborating it and giving exciting names to the various localities, such as Skeleton Island and Spyglass Hill. He was soon writing the first pages of a story called *The Sea Cook.* A magazine publisher looking for new writers for *Young Folks* became interested. The serial was published in 1881, and the book appeared two years later as *Treasure Island.* Sadly, the original map was lost.

'I awoke one morning and found myself famous'
Lord Byron, quoted in T. Moore's *Life of Byron* (1830)

By commenting pungently in accomplished verse on contemporary writers and critics, Byron, in his *English Bards and Scotch Reviewers* (1809), launched himself on the literary world as a young poet of talent and wit. When the first two cantos of his *Childe Harold's Pilgrimage* were published three years later they created a sensation that had scarcely been known before. The first edition was sold out in three days, and Byron at once became the leading literary figure of the day. '*Childe Harold* and "Lord Byron" became the theme of every tongue,' his friend Thomas Moore observed, and he quotes the statement made by Byron himself.

'I beheld great heaps of coin and quadrilaterals built of bars of gold'
R. L. Stevenson, *Treasure Island*, ch. 33 (1883)

At last young Jim Hawkins sees the treasure which had been buried on a desert island by the notorious pirate, Captain Flint. Ex-pirate mutineers from the private treasure-ship *Hispaniola* had found the treasure-spot, with the aid of a chart, but the treasure had gone! In fact it had already been discovered by Ben Gunn, an unfortunate seaman who had been left marooned alone on the island three years earlier. He had removed the treasure bit by bit to a distant cave. Here it was held by the rightful treasure-seekers, Squire Trelawney, Dr Livesey, and Jim, ready to be shipped aboard the *Hispaniola* for the homeward voyage.

'I came to myself in darkness, in great pain, bound hand and foot'
R. L. Stevenson, *Kidnapped*, ch. 7 (1886)

This is the key situation in Stevenson's famous novel. David Balfour, true heir to the estate held by his villainous uncle, has been enticed on board the brig *Covenant* at his uncle's instigation. Here he has been suddenly knocked down by a blow on the head from behind. When he gradually regains his senses he realizes that he has been kidnapped. His uncle's intention was that he should be shipped out to the Carolinas and sold, virtually as a slave, in the plantations. But fortunately for David the brig is wrecked, and his uncle's plan goes awry.

'I cannot go as fast as I would, by reason of this burden that is upon my back'
John Bunyan, *The Pilgrim's Progress*, Pt 1 (1678)

Christian, the hero of Bunyan's allegory, has left his home in the City of Destruction to seek refuge in the Celestial City, on the advice of Evangelist (the personification of the wise preacher). Christian has persuaded his neighbour, Pliable, to go along with him, but in response to his companion's request to 'mend our pace', Christian points out that he is carrying a heavy load (the burden of Sin). Why Pliable does not have a similar burden is not explained; but in any case they shortly afterwards fall into the Slough of Despond. Pliable has had enough and returns home.

'I can read anything which I call a book'
Charles Lamb, *Detached Thoughts on Books* (1822)

Lamb loved reading, and had widely ranging tastes. But he could not stomach 'books which are no books': court calendars, directories, scientific treatises, almanacks, statutes at large. Less offensive are books such as the *History* of Josephus or Paley's *Moral Philosophy*, though they would tempt few people to remove them from the shelf. Most frustrating of all are deceptive books. Most of us, perhaps, have sometimes shared Lamb's disgust at taking down what looks like a nicely bound book of old plays, only to find that it is (say) an *Essay on Population*.

'I can't get out, I can't get out'
Laurence Sterne, *A Sentimental Journey – The Passport* (1768)

Sterne heard these pitiful words when he was passing through a hotel corridor. They came from a starling shut up in a little cage. 'I'll let thee out, cost what it will!' cried Sterne as he tried to open the cage door. But he failed to undo it, and in due course found that the bird belonged to an English lad who had caught it before it could fly, fed it, and taught it the four simple words that enabled it to impersonate an English prisoner. Sterne later bought the bird, but instead of releasing it he gave it away to an English nobleman, presumably preferring kudos to kindness.

'I care for nobody, no, not I,
If no one cares for me'
Isaac Bickerstaffe, *Love in a Village*, I, v (1762)

This sturdy sentiment is a fiction within a fiction. It is expressed by the Jolly Miller of Dee, a fictitious person who appears in a song sung by Squire Hawthorn, himself a fictitious character in Bickerstaffe's lively comic opera. This was partly based on Wycherley's *The Gentleman Dancing Master* (1672). Squire Hawthorn is a hearty man who shares the miller's attitude to life, maintaining that 'the cheerful man's a king'.

'I care not two-pence'
Beaumont and Fletcher, *The Coxcomb*, V, i (1647)

It is easy to understand this contempt today, when 2p is virtually the smallest coin in common use. (Inflation has almost eliminated the 1p and ½p.) But in the seventeenth century, the penny was a silver coin by no means insignificant in value. There must be something in the word 'twopence' which invites scorn. In *The Coxcomb* the words are spoken by a Justice who is plainly a satirical portrait, probably based on Shakespeare's Justice Shallow (*The Merry Wives of Windsor*). The *Coxcomb* Justice is opinionated, foolish, and quite indifferent to the laws of evidence.

'I could never endure to shake hands with Mr Slope'
Anthony Trollope, *Barchester Towers*, ch. 4 (1857)

For an author to write so personally about one of his characters suggests a strong belief in his own work. Trollope was always prepared to analyse his success in character drawing, and he rightly regarded the Reverend Obadiah Slope as one of his best efforts. This unpleasant, unctuous, hypocritical clergyman, eager to be the power behind the bishop's throne, is a convincing villain, the more convincing because his faults are not overdone. The reference to his handshake is a touch of genius. The cold, clammy perspiration which exudes from his palms seems to fit his oily character perfectly.

'I could not love thee (Dear) so much,
Lov'd I not honour more'
Richard Lovelace, *To Lucasta, Going to the Warres* (1649)

After the surrender of Charles I to the Scots in 1646 Lovelace fought for the French king. But later he probably took up arms for Charles again, and he was imprisoned in London in 1648. While in prison he prepared for the press his book of poems entitled *Lucasta*. The 'Warres' may well have been the Civil War before the King's surrender, when the poem was very likely written. Lucasta was said to be Lucy Sacheverell.

'I count religion but a childish toy,
And hold there is no sin but ignorance'
Christopher Marlowe, *The Jew of Malta – Prologue* (c 1591)

The Prologue of this rather patchy play was spoken by an actor personating Machiavel (Machiavelli, 1469–1527), whose cynical doctrines were well known at Cambridge in Marlowe's time at the University. Marlowe used him to introduce the play, as Machiavelli's scheming approach to life matches that of the crafty Jew. Audiences were no doubt pleasantly shocked to hear this notorious Italian brazenly offering his opinions. There is no evidence that Marlowe shared Machiavel's attitude to religion, but he probably enjoyed putting the daring views into Machiavel's mouth.

'I did delude my noble father with a feigned pilgrimage, and
dressed myself in habit of a boy'
Beaumont and Fletcher, *Philaster*, V, v (1611)

Girl dressed as boy was a very popular device in Elizabethan and Jacobean romantic plays. Beaumont and Fletcher's Euphrasia was treading in the footsteps of Shakespeare's Rosalind and Viola. It was easy for a boy actor to play a girl pretending to be a boy. In this play Euphrasia, daughter of a lord at the King's court, falls hopelessly in love with Philaster, heir to the throne, and disguised as a boy becomes his page. Later on he passes her over to his secret sweetheart, Arethusa. In due course the supposed youth and Arethusa become involved in a series of melodramatic misunderstandings which are something of a strain on plausibility.

'I did in Drury Lane see two or three houses marked with a
red cross upon the doors'
Samuel Pepys, *Diary* (7 June 1665)

This grim sentence marked Pepys's introduction to the signs of the Great Plague, 'the first of the kind that, to my remembrance, I ever saw'. Matters must have been made worse by the heat, for this was the hottest day he had ever experienced. After seeing the plague signs he bought some tobacco to smell and chew, believing that this would protect him. Three days later he learnt that the terrible disease had reached the City, where he lived. He decided to draw up his will, 'in case it should please God to call me away'. Fortunately it did not.

'An idiot race to honour lost'
Robert Burns, *Lines on Viewing Stirling Palace*, (1787)

In 1787 Burns paid a visit to the ruined Stirling Castle, once the home of the Scottish kings. For some reason his Stuart sympathies were excited. With a diamond pen he scratched some lines of a verse on the window of a Stirling inn, abusing the Hanoverians.

A race outlandish fills the throne,

An idiot race to honour lost.

A few weeks later he regretted these rather foolish and mildly treasonable words, so he hurried back and smashed the window. Too late: copies had been made.

'I disapprove of what you say, but I will defend to the death your right to say it'
Often attributed to Voltaire (1694–1778)

This is such an impressive saying that it is a pity Voltaire did not actually say it. The statement is an exposition of Volaire's attitude as expressed in the book *The Friends of Voltaire* (1907) by Evelyn Beatrice Hall. The French philosopher Helvétius had written a work entitled *De l'Esprit* (1758) which the authorities condemned as full of dangerous doctrines. They had it burnt publicly. Voltaire disagreed with the book, regarding most of it as commonplace, dubious, or false, but he also disapproved of its ruthless suppression. Miss Hall expresses his feelings in the form of an imaginary quotation.

'I do not know the method of drawing up an indictment against a whole people'
Edmund Burke, *Speech for Conciliation with the Colonies* (22 March 1775)

Burke was attempting to persuade the House of Commons that it was folly to try to suppress the American colonies by force, as though their objections to the taxation system were a crime. It was absurd to make no distinction between ill-conduct by individuals against the state, and differences of opinion between communities within an Empire. It was unrealistic to condemn the whole American people (with their own parliaments and law courts) as if they were merely common criminals needing to be punished.

'I do not love thee, Doctor Fell, The reason why I cannot tell; But this alone I know full well, I do not love thee, Doctor Fell'
Tom Brown, *Epigram* (c 1683)

Brown (1663–1704) was an Oxford undergraduate who had got into trouble with the dean of his college (Christ Church), Dr John Fell, a worthy man who was considerably responsible for the development of the Oxford University Press. Brown revenged himself by turning his translation of an epigram by Martial (A.D. 40–104) into a satirical jingle about his dean. It is unfortunate that so admirable a man should have come to typify unpopularity; and it is poetic justice that Brown's later writings are now almost forgotten, and only his trivial jingle is remembered.

'I don't care where the water goes if it doesn't get into the wine'
G. K. Chesterton, *Wine and Water* (1914)

The wine-loving poet imagines Noah stocking his ark with immense quantities of wine, and indifferent to the waters of the Great Flood as long as they do not adulterate his cellar. 'The water has drowned the Matterhorn as deep as a Mendip mine / But I don't care where the water goes if it doesn't get into the wine.' Chesterton goes on to suggest that the modern idea of abstinence is really a punishment for man's sins: 'A great big black teetotaller was sent to us for a rod.'

'I don't like this cruise; I don't like the men: and I don't like my officer'
R. L. Stevenson, *Treasure Island*, ch. 9 (1883)

This blunt opinion was the opening comment by Captain Smollett on the voyage he had been asked to lead in the *Hispaniola*. His unfavourable attitude was not unjustified. All the crew appeared to know more about the treasure-seeking purpose of the expedition (supposed to be secret) than he did. Nor did he think it right for the crew to be chosen without his being consulted. As for the officer (mate), he was too free in his manner with the men. Squire Trelawney, who was paying for the expedition, was indignant with the Captain, but his companion, Dr Livesey, was better balanced. Smollett, despite his criticisms, was retained as Captain, which was just as well for the treasure-seekers. All the Captain's fears were justified. Most of the crew were ex-pirate rogues.

'I don't like this pernicious modern jargon about shopkeepers and gentlefolk being much the same. There's far too much truth in it to be agreeable'
St John Hankin, *The Return of the Prodigal*, Act II (1905)

A worthy successor to Oscar Wilde, St John Hankin makes Lady Faringford, the speaker here, almost as delightfully objectionable as Lady Bracknell in *The Importance of Being Earnest* (1895). She is pointing out to her daughter that owing to their position in society such people as the Faringfords, though poor, are greatly sought after. If it became accepted that there was no real difference between gentlefolk and tradesmen, a very comfortable position in the social system would be lost. 'No, no, my dear, rank and birth and the peerage may be all nonsense, but it isn't *our* business to say so.'

'I don't mind if I do'
Ted Kavanagh, *ITMA*, BBC radio comedy series (1939–49)

One of the most popular of the many characters thought up by Ted Kavanagh for the B.B.C. *ITMA* programme was Colonel Chinstrap, a bibulous army officer whose mind was centred on liquid refreshment. Any word in the conversation which remotely suggested the offer of a drink was promptly misheard and seized upon. Should a word such as 'frisky' enter the conversation it would inevitably be followed by the Colonel's 'Whisky, sir? I don't mind if I do!' Chinstrap was played (together with several other characters) by Jack Train.

'I dreamt that I dwelt in marble halls'
Alfred Bunn, *The Bohemian Girl* (1843)

Arline, a gipsy girl, relates (in song) that she has dreamt she was living in luxury, blessed with 'riches too great to count'. Well might she enjoy such a dream, for she was really no gipsy but the abducted daughter of Count Arnheim. She had been stolen in childhood by a gipsy chieftain, lived with gipsies for many years, and fallen in love with one of them, to whom she sings her song. The Irish composer, M. W. Balfe, wrote the music for the opera, the libretto being the work of a theatre manager who controlled both Covent Garden and Drury Lane theatres. The opera was a great success at Drury Lane, and brought Bunn a marble statue in the Rotunda.

'If a horse sweats in the stable, Moll White has been upon his back'
Joseph Addison, *The Spectator*, no. 117 (1711)

Though Moll White was fictitious she was far from imaginary. She typified the traditional village witch, feared and sometimes ill-treated by the local inhabitants because they thought she was responsible for spoiling the butter, maltreating the cattle, sweating the horses, and a variety of other misdeeds. Addison hesitated to commit himself completely, but he was firmly on the side of sanity and humanity. He condemned or gently ridiculed the belief (freely held in the seventeenth and eighteenth centuries) that old women such as Moll White really possessed evil powers or were in any way responsible for village misfortunes.

'I fear the Greeks, even though they bring gifts'
Virgil, *Aeneid*, Bk II (*c* 29–19 B.C.)

When the wily Greeks were attacking Troy they managed to seize the city through the device of the Wooden Horse – a huge structure in the form of a horse left behind on the shore after the Greeks had pretended to sail away. The Trojans were in two minds. Some, encouraged by a phoney Greek deserter, wanted to drag the horse into the city as a prize. Others were in favour of its destruction. Prominent among these was Laocoon, priest of Apollo, a man who (as the quotation indicates) was rightly suspicious of anything Greek. In the end the horse was pulled into Troy, where in the night it disgorged a gang of Greek desperadoes.

'I felt as if we were all sitting at ease somewhere at the bottom of the Pacific'
J. B. Priestley, *Self-Selected Essays* (1932)

Priestley was writing of a visit to a billiards hall where a championship match was in progress. He was struck by the atmosphere of absolute calm, the feeling of utter remoteness from external life. The solemn, impersonal voice of the marker calling the score helped the illusion: 'it did as much as the four walls and the thickly curtained windows to withdraw us from ordinary life'. Billiards has now gone out of fashion, but its multi-coloured replacement, snooker, still provides something of the same peaceful spirit, despite television coverage.

'If he'll only turn out a brave, helpful, truth-telling Englishman, and a gentleman, and a Christian, that's all I want'

Thomas Hughes, *Tom Brown's Schooldays*, ch. 4 (1856)

If this was all that Squire Brown wanted, it seems strange that he did not keep Tom at home and set him a good example. Sending him away to strangers, many of whom were likely to be the very opposite of the Squire's requirements, was hardly a reasonable act. However, it was fortunate that he pursued this illogical course or we would have been deprived of a novel that gives a wonderfully vivid and robust picture of school life in the days of the justly renowned Dr Arnold of Rugby.

'If he were ever animated enough to be in love, [he] must long have outlived every sensation of the kind'

Jane Austen, *Sense and Sensibility*, ch. 8 (1811)

The poor old fellow who has outlived the possibility of love, according to Marianne Dashwood (seventeen years old) is Colonel Brandon (aged thirty-five). Apart from his age and his rather stiff manner, Brandon had complained of a rheumatic twinge in one shoulder and also mentioned a flannel waistcoat. 'A flannel waistcoat is invariably connected with aches, cramps, rheumatisms, and every species of ailment that can afflict the old and feeble,' Marianne asserts, and she dismisses as ridiculous the suggestion that he had fallen in love with her. Naturally Jane Austen slyly brings them together forty chapters later.

'If I had served God as diligently as I have done the King, he would not have given me over in my grey hairs'

Thomas Wolsey, Quoted in George Cavendish, *The Life of Cardinal Wolsey* (c 1556)

Wolsey's reluctance to enable Henry VIII to take Anne Boleyn as his wife, and his failure to secure from the Pope a satisfactory divorce from Katharine of Aragon, turned the self-centred and savage King against his former chief minister. Wolsey was arrested at York. On the journey back to London, where the Tower awaited him, he fell sick. At Leicester he uttered the well-known words of the quotation, and died soon afterwards. Cavendish was a gentleman of Wolsey's household.

'I find a general opinion prevailing that your policemen are not paid sufficiently'

J. W. Croker, *Letter to Sir Robert Peel* (28 September 1829)

This statement, repeated many times during the following 150 years, was made immediately after Peel first organized the Metropolitan Police force. Croker, a prominent politician and man of letters, maintained that three shillings a day, without adequate opportunities for increase and promotion, was not enough for a man required to be on duty at night, in all weathers, 'in a state of perpetual trouble, labour, and disquiet, that other folks may enjoy their rest'. Peel replied defending his rate of pay, but rather uneasily. The debate continues, and doubtless will continue to do so as long as policemen are required to keep a check on public behaviour.

> *'If I should die, think only this of me:*
> *That there's some corner of a foreign field*
> *That is for ever England'*
> Rupert Brooke, *The Soldier* (1915)

This sonnet presents an idealized conception of soldierly sacrifice. Brooke bids his friends think of his heart as a pulse in the Eternal Mind, transmitting English scenes and values to the world. He was the most popular poet of the early part of the Great War; his war sonnets seemed to catch the patriotic, dedicated mood better than the work of any other verse writer. Whether this mood would have survived the long and bitter trench warfare of later years can only be guessed. He died unglamorously of septicaemia in the Dardanelles early in 1915.

> *'If it be necessary for you to live by your work, do not begin*
> *by trusting to literature'*
> Anthony Trollope, *An Autobiography*, ch. 11 (1883)

Trollope is warning would-be authors against setting out to live by their pens before they have proved that they are likely to succeed. As a member of the Royal Literary Fund committee he had seen a great deal of the sufferings of authors. He himself would have failed dismally if he had not had another job while making his efforts. Some of his work was lucrative when he was well-known, but for ten years 'I did not earn enough to buy me the pens, ink, and paper which I was using'. Take an office job, he advises, and write in your leisure time.

> *'If only we could persuade ourselves to be quiescent when we*
> *are happy!'*
> Richard Jefferies, *The Open Air* (1885)

Before going on the River Thames, Richard Jefferies had mentally pictured its delights. Now, resting quietly near a weir, lazily watching the green cascade of water shooting beneath his skiff and a reed-sparrow pottering about near by, he felt wonderfully content. 'This was really like the beautiful river I had dreamed of.' If only he could have been satisfied to sit still and feast his eyes on the scene! But some instinct prompted him to open a newspaper lying about – and the first item that caught his eye was an account of someone being drowned close to a weir. In a flash the feeling of happiness was gone.

> *'If people only made prudent marriages, what a stop to*
> *population there would be'*
> W. M. Thackeray, *Vanity Fair*, ch. 16 (1848)

This is the novelist's own comment, relative to the marriage of Captain Rawdon Crawley to Becky Sharp. This marriage was imprudent, perhaps, in the sense that Crawley's wealthy aunt was angry at his marrying the daughter of a French dancer instead of an heiress or an aristocrat, and therefore cut him out of her will. In many respects, however, the marriage could not really be called imprudent. Becky was clever, attractive, and easy-going, and she handled their affairs far better than he could have done himself – until her lack of regard for him brought the marriage to an end.

'If the French should conquer, what would become of English liberty?'
Oliver Goldsmith, *The Citizen of the World*, IV (1760)

The quotation, long before the Napoleonic period, relates to the Seven Years' War (1756–63), a conflict resulting largely from a clash of interests between England and France in America and India. Love of liberty, the essay suggests, is a special characteristic of the English, and Goldsmith introduces a nice touch of ironic humour here, for the words of the quotation are uttered not by a political orator but by a prisoner conversing with friends through the bars of his gaol.

'If the prophet Isaiah were to appear in London today he would be at once arrested'
A. P. Herbert, *More Misleading Cases* (1933)

The prophet would in fact be guilty, under the law, of making predictions concerning the future. Herbert's exact knowledge of legal matters (he qualified, without practising, as a barrister) enabled him to present some amusing and pungent sidelights on the law. Here he is dealing with the Vagrancy Act of 1824 – still in force when he wrote – under which people were sometimes convicted for professing to tell fortunes. Herbert humorously but convincingly ridicules the ancient law by showing that this is precisely what the racing tipsters of national newspapers regularly do.

'If there be one vicious mind in the set, 'twill spread like a contagion'
R. B. Sheridan, *The Rivals*, II, i (1775)

The reference is to a country dance, where the ladies are passed from one man to another in the course of the movement. Faulkland, a very jealous fellow, has been told that his sweetheart has been joining in country dances during his absence. He is somewhat upset, his easily-inflamed imagination suggesting to him that in 'the lascivious movement of the jig ... the atmosphere becomes electrical to love'. He is in fact doing his sweetheart an injustice – she is far more devoted than his jealousy deserves – but his unreasonable doubts are cured at last.

'If there must be a lion in the household, then let it be as small as possible'
Joy Adamson, *Born Free*, ch. I (1960)

This seemed to be the point of view of the African servants of George and Joy Adamson. George was Senior Game Warden of a huge area in Kenya. He had occasion to kill a dangerous lioness which had three tiny cubs. He took these back to his home, and they were brought up by hand, feeding from an improvised baby's bottle. When they were about five months old it became clear to the Adamsons that they could not indefinitely keep these fast-growing lion cubs. Two were therefore to be sent to a Dutch zoo. The servants all wished to keep the smallest, which later became famous as Elsa.

'If the world does not please you, you can change it'
H. G. Wells, *The History of Mr Polly* (1910)

This realization suddenly flashed upon Mr Polly after he had set fire to his house, intending to commit suicide, and had accidentally made himself a hero by rescuing the old lady next door. For fifteen years he had endured a wretched life with an incompetent and unsympathetic wife and an unsuccessful shop. It dawned on him that he could just clear out, leaving his wife the fire insurance money. So Mr Polly left his wife and ruined home, to find a different and much more interesting life.

'If ... they tip me the black spot'
R. L. Stevenson, *Treasure Island*, ch. 3 (1883)

'Captain Billy Bones' was one of the leaders of a former pirate gang. He had absconded with a map showing where a substantial treasure had been buried on a remote island, and was always afraid of being tracked down by his old shipmates. One day the worst happened and he was tipped (given) 'the black spot'. This was a small circle of paper blackened on one side and bearing a fearful warning on the other – a message to indicate that vengeance was about to overtake him. The warning had such an effect on Bones that he had a fatal stroke.

'If you attempt management on the single-star system, nothing – not even my genius added to your own – can save you from final defeat'
George Bernard Shaw, *Letter to Mrs Patrick Campbell* (3 July 1912)

Shaw was desperately anxious to prevent Mrs Patrick Campbell from presenting *Pygmalion* herself, without a really strong male co-star in the part of Professor Higgins, and he stressed that such one-star productions were always failures in comparison with two-star shows. She was prepared to accept the argument, but refused to go into partnership with the actor Shaw wanted (Robert Loraine). After many vicissitudes the play was at last produced in London in April 1914, after it had been played in America, with Beerbohm Tree as Higgins and producer, and Mrs Patrick Campbell as Eliza. (She wished she were twenty-five years younger.)

'If you can wade through a few sentences of malice, meanness, falsehood, perjury, treachery, and cant ... you will perhaps be somewhat repaid by a laugh at the style of this ungrammatical twaddler'
Charles Dickens, *The Pickwick Papers*, ch. 51 (1837)

Dickens is making fun of the journalistic rivalry shown in the local newspapers of the day. Eatanswill has two journals, the *Independent* and the *Gazette*, each supporting a different political party, and each offering extravagant criticism of the other. The respective editors of these papers have met by chance at an inn in the presence of Mr Pickwick and some of his friends. Each editor reads the other's paper, making unfavourable comments aloud. Finally, Mr Slurk of the *Independent* offers the quoted comment about the *Gazette*, and precipitates a physical contest.

'If you choose to get drunk and break the law afterwards you must take the consequences'
John Galsworthy, *The Silver Box*, III, i (1906)

Although this persuasive play cannot be said to show that there is one law for the rich and another for the poor, it does show how useful it is to have money. A magistrate is here talking to Jones, an unemployed working-man who, while drunk, has taken a silver cigarette-box from the house of the well-to-do Barthwicks. The Barthwicks' undergraduate son, Jack, has snatched a purse from a prostitute in a drunken tiff. But whereas Jones receives a prison sentence for his drunken theft, Jack escapes scot-free, as his father repays the prostitute to save a fuss, and no one charges him with stealing.

'If you had told Sycorax that her son Caliban was as handsome as Apollo she would have been pleased'
W. M. Thackeray, *Vanity Fair*, ch. 4 (1848)

All mothers like to hear their sons praised for good looks, and the sons like it too. Becky Sharp, though only nineteen, showed great astuteness in whispering loudly 'He's very handsome' to Joseph Sedley's sister, Amelia, when she was first introduced to him. Not only was it likely that Mrs Sedley would be told, but Joseph himself (as Becky had hoped) had overheard the whisper and was duly flattered. Becky's purpose was simple and not entirely reprehensible. Alone in the world, she wanted a husband, and had no parents to find one for her, so she was reduced to finding one for herself. It was sheer bad luck that this attempt just failed.

'If you have it [charm], you don't need to have anything else'
J. M. Barrie, *What Every Woman Knows*, Act I (1908)

Maggie Wylie is defining charm for the benefit of her father and brothers. 'It's a sort of bloom on a woman. The local minister has had the bad taste not to ask Maggie to marry him but has become engaged to someone else, who must obviously have charm. Maggie's brother, James, asserts that she too has charm, but Maggie firmly denies it. However, the rest of the play is devoted to proving that she has, and the most charming actress available is always chosen for the part.

'If you only took time and trouble enough the figures would always work out and balance up, unlike life'
J. B. Priestley, *Angel Pavement* (1930)

Narrow-minded intellectuals too often assume that a man on an office stool is nothing but a grey drudge, laboriously slaving over dreary figures. Priestley gives the lie to this misleading conception in his portrait of Mr Smeeth, chief cashier in a small city firm. He was a man who enjoyed manipulating figures and could handle them with skill. Far from being a servile drudge, he grew in stature when he entered the office. He had joined the firm as office boy thirty-five years earlier, and the office boy still lurking within him looked at his slow but steady rise to the dignity of cashier as something of a romance.

'If you're anxious for to shine in the high aesthetic line'
W. S. Gilbert, *Patience*, Act I (1881)

It is well known that Gilbert's comic opera was a satire on the aesthetic poseurs of the day, notably Oscar Wilde. It is a mistake, however, to think that Gilbert was satirizing the author of *The Importance of Being Earnest* or any other play. The aesthete mocked by Gilbert – a composite of Wilde and one or two others – was based on the young man who paraded Bond Street in exquisite garments, a tulip or a lily in his hand, and who had as yet written nothing of note. He offered a perfect subject for parody, and Gilbert was an expert marksman. Wilde's first play appeared eleven years later.

'If your friend has made the pilgrimage once, distrust him; if he has made the pilgrimage twice, cut him dead'
A. W. Kinglake, *Eothen*, ch. 16 (1844)

The pilgrimage concerned is the Moslem one to Mecca, and the saying is a cynical Turkish one. The theory is that as pilgrimages are commonly made to counterbalance bad conduct, those who make them are likely to be bad characters. Kinglake introduces the topic in connection with his stay in Jerusalem. He suggests that the Turkish maxim should not be taken too seriously. The pilgrims he saw in Jerusalem were 'a well-disposed, orderly body of people', not at all criminally inclined.

'I gave the Arabs to understand that I regretted their perishing by hunger, but that I should bear this calmly, like any other misfortune not my own'
A. W. Kinglake, *Eothen*, ch. 17 (1844)

Kinglake is not quite so unfeeling as the quotation may suggest. The Arabs were the owners of the four camels that he had engaged to carry himself, servants, and baggage across the Arabian desert. His interpreter assured him that the Arabs had agreed to provide their own food. On the second evening they announced that they had brought no food with them. Kinglake gave them the quoted reply. This was clearly the right approach. As soon as they realized that he meant what he said, they regarded him with great respect and produced a hidden bag of meal to make their own bread.

'I had not a friend or a toy, But I had Aladdin's lamp'
J. R. Lowell, *Aladdin* (1869)

According to the distinguished American author Aladdin's lamp is the gift of lively youthful imagination and hope. When you are young, he tells us, however poor and friendless you may be, you can none the less enjoy life by imagining the wonderful things that are to come. You build 'beautiful castles in Spain'. As you get older, though you may gain in material possessions, you lose the imaginative fire of youth. 'I own no more castles in Spain.'

'*I have a little shadow that goes in and out with me*'
R. L. Stevenson, *A Child's Garden of Verses – My Shadow* (1885)

The child finds the shadow curious, for though it is very like him from the head to the heels, it has a way of altering rapidly in size, sometimes getting so little 'that there's none of him at all'. The shadow seems to be rather cowardly, for it always stays close to the child. It is also lazy, for one morning when the child got up early, before sunrise,

My lazy little shadow, like an arrant sleepy-head,
Had stayed at home behind me and was fast
asleep in bed.

'*I have been here before,
But when or how I cannot tell*'
D. G. Rossetti, *The House of Light – Sudden Light* (1881)

The familiar lines come from a short 'Song' (IV) in a series inspired by Rossetti's love for his wife, who married him in 1860 and died in 1862. The poems were written over a period of years. *Sudden Light* consists of three brief stanzas, based on the idea of pre-existence, suggesting that he and his wife met in an earlier age and are now repeating a love that had taken place years before. 'You have been mine before ... I knew it all of yore.'

'*I have been in the scholastic profession long enough to know
that nobody enters it unless he has some very good reason
that he is anxious to conceal*'
Evelyn Waugh, *Decline and Fall* (1928)

Paul Pennyfeather has been sent down from his university (quite unjustly) for indecent behaviour. In despair he seeks a teaching post. When asked by his prospective employer, Dr Fagan, why he left college so suddenly he honestly admits the reason. Fortunately the headmaster is not put off, having his own cynical belief as to why young men take up schoolmastering. Evelyn Waugh himself was for a short time a master at a private school.

'*I have been led beyond my intention, I hope by the honest
desire of giving useful pleasure*'
Samuel Johnson, *Lives of the Poets – Preface* (1779)

The intention was to write a brief prefatory note to each of the poets whose works were to be issued by a trio of London publishers. The note was to contain a few dates and a general character of the poet. But Johnson got carried away by his own interest, and some of the brief notes developed into long and admirable essays. This was the kind of thing that Johnson could do better than anything else. Few people will agree with all his judgments, but there is a downrightness and a vigour in the *Lives* that keep them very much alive.

'I have come to the borders of sleep'
Edward Thomas, *Lights Out* (1916)

This poem, written when Thomas was soon to be in the thick of one of the worst battles of the First World War, was inspired by a camp bugle call. He uses sleep as a metaphor for the death which he feels he is quite likely to meet, and he accepts the situation almost willingly. Suffering, as he so often did, from moods of deep depression, he was curiously ready for 'the unfathomable deep forest where all must lose their way'. He was killed on the morning of 9 April 1917, at the Third Battle of Arras, probably by a stray bullet, though some accounts speak of a direct hit by a shell.

'I have it here in black and white'
Ben Jonson, *Every Man in His Humour*, IV, ii (1598)

Black and white are, of course, ink and paper. But in this early use of the phrase there is a deliberate contrast with 'black and blue', for the document concerned is a legal warrant obtained against the bullying Captain Bobadil by his landlord, Cob, who had been beaten by the Captain for the innocent offence (now accepted by the doctors as a virtue) of condemning the smoking habit. 'I have it here in black and white for his black and blue,' Cob tells his wife as he produces the document.

'I have measured out my life with coffee spoons'
T. S. Eliot, *The Love Song of J. Alfred Prufrock* (1917)

The poem is a confused portrayal of diffidence, self-pity, and futility. Prufrock is indecisive and mediocre. He realizes this but cannot change. The quoted line effectively indicates that his life has been a round of trivial pursuits of little significance. The title is ironic; the poem is not a love song but a lament. It is significant that the poem appeared at a gloomy period of the First World War, when the futility of war, and of life, was thrusting itself increasingly upon intellectuals. Eliot's idiom, casual but precise, conversational but obscure, appealed to many.

'I have nothing to declare except my genius'
Oscar Wilde, quoted in Frank Harris's *Oscar Wilde* (1918)

On his visit to America on a lecture tour in 1881 Wilde was asked by a New York Custom House official whether he had anything to declare. Like Shaw, Wilde constantly adopted a half-serious, half-humorous pose of superiority, and the above well-known quip was a typical example.

'I have nothing to offer but blood, toil, tears, and sweat'
Winston Churchill, *speech to the House of Commons* (13 May 1940)

Early in May 1940 deep feelings were expressed in the House of Commons that a stronger Government was needed to conduct the war successfully. Neville Chamberlain resigned as Prime Minister. On 10 May his place was taken by Winston Churchill, who formed a new Government drawn from members of all political parties. Three days later he spoke to the House, asking for unity of effort and warning members of the grave difficulties ahead. His now famous words were no doubt based on Garibaldi's cry to the legion besieged in Rome in 1849: 'I offer only hunger, thirst, forced marches, battles, and death'.

'I have not slept one wink'
William Shakespeare, *Cymbeline*, III, iv (*c* 1610)

The insanely jealous Posthumus, wrongly believing his wife, Imogen, to be unfaithful to him, has ordered his servant Pisanio to kill her. Pisanio is sensibly unwilling to carry out such an order. He tells Imogen about it, adding that the business has worried him so much that he has had no sleep. A 'wink' in Elizabethan English was not a deliberate twitch of one eye but a closing of both eyes.

'I have often noticed that almost everyone has his own individual economies'
E. C. Gaskell, *Cranford*, ch. 5 (1853)

The narrator of the novel is thinking particularly of Miss Matty Jenkyns, with whom she is staying. Miss Jenkyns is charming and refined, but she will allow only one candle at a time to be burned in the livingroom. If a second is lit she will put out the first. The narrator also recalls an old gentleman who bore a serious financial loss quite calmly, but made a great fuss about a trivial waste of writing-paper. She herself admits to the collecting of odds and ends of string, and acknowledges that she gets quite cross if someone cuts the string of a parcel instead of untying it.

'I have something to expiate
A pettiness'
D. H. Lawrence, *Snake* (1923)

In Sicily, Lawrence sees a dangerous snake come to drink at his water trough. He is in two minds what to do. On the one hand his civilized instinct, egged on by his knowledge that this type of snake is venomous, tells him that he ought to kill the reptile. On the other hand he is fascinated by its appearance, 'earth-golden from the burning bowels of the earth'. In the end, just as the creature is disappearing, he flings a piece of wood towards it, making it vanish in a flash. Immediately he despises himself for a paltry act towards a kingly creature that had sought his hospitality.

'I have today hoisted the national ensign of the United States of America at this place'
Robert E. Peary, *The North Pole* (1910)

These were the opening words of the brief record left at the North Pole by its discoverer on 6 April 1909. For over twenty years the attainment of the North Pole had occupied almost all Peary's waking thoughts. This was his eighth journey into the Arctic wilderness. Yet, ironically, as soon as his observations had made it certain that he had truly reached the Pole he was too exhausted to feel any elation. 'There was not a thing in the world I wanted but sleep.' Mental exaltation came later.

'I hope I shall never be deterred from detecting what I think a cheat, by the menaces of a ruffian'
Samuel Johnson, *Letter to Macpherson*, quoted in Boswell's *Life of Johnson* (1791)

Johnson is referring to James Macpherson, a Scottish scholar who had published *Fingal* (1762) and *Temora* (1763), purporting to be by an ancient Gaelic poet named Ossian. Though not entire fabrications they were considerably Macpherson's own work, boosting the exploits of a mythical Gaelic hero. Some critics, including Johnson, were sceptical concerning the authenticity of the poems, and said so. Macpherson in due course wrote threateningly to Johnson, in terms never precisely disclosed. Johnson's reply was open, and was reinforced by the purchase of a stout stick. This kept Macpherson at bay; but cheat or not, he managed to get himself buried in Westminster Abbey.

'I am monarch of all I survey'
William Cowper, *Verses supposed to be written by Alexander Selkirk* (1782)

Selkirk was a Scottish sailor who quarrelled with the captain of his ship in 1704. At his own request he was put ashore on Juan Fernandez, an uninhabited island in the Pacific Ocean about 400 miles from Chile. Here he lived alone for over four years. His experience probably inspired Defoe to write *Robinson Crusoe*, and it certainly led Cowper to compose one of his best-known poems. Himself often subject to melancholia, he found it easy to imagine the despair of a castaway who, though 'lord of the fowl and the brute', was also 'out of humanity's reach'.

'If the murderer is wise he will let well alone, but murderers are seldom wise'
Agatha Christie, *After the Funeral*, ch. 13 (1953)

It is because fictional murderers will not let well alone that fictional detectives are so universally successful. This famous detective, M. Hercule Poirot, was deliberately made as different as possible from Sherlock Holmes. Thus he was equipped with an egg-shaped head and magnificent moustaches. His nationality was suggested by the presence at Torquay (Agatha's home town) of some Belgian refugees during the Great War. She wanted him to be proud of his brains, and so 'the little grey cells' became familiar to all detective story readers.

'I loved you, Evelyn, all the while'
Robert Browning, *Evelyn Hope* (1855)

The verse is spoken by a middle-aged man to the corpse of the girl of sixteen that he loved, and who he hoped would have loved him if she had lived. Although she scarcely knew him, he rather presumptuously sets out to claim her in the next world ('I claim you still, for my true love's sake'), and then sentimentally puts a leaf in her dead hand as a symbol of their future life and love together. The poem seems to suggest some mysterious episode in Browning's life, but in fact there is no reason to think that it is anything more than a vividly imagined fiction. It was one of his most popular poems, according to a ballot conducted by the *Pall Mall Gazette*.

'I love not Man the less but Nature more'
Lord Byron, *Childe Harold's Pilgrimage*, IV, clxxviii (1818)

As Childe Harold (who closely resembles Byron) reaches the end of his pilgrimage the poet drops the disguise. In his own person he expresses his love of nature and solitude – his 'pleasure in the pathless woods' and his 'rapture on the lonely shore'. He goes on to invite the 'deep and dark blue ocean' to 'roll on' – advice which the ocean appears to have taken, for it has continued rolling on ever since.

'It is easier to take away a good name than to restore it'
Sir Walter Scott, *Old Mortality – Introduction* (1816)

The aphorism follows a true story which Scott relates of Old Mortality (Robert Paterson) who used to visit grave-yards to clean and repair tombstones. One day some children pestered a nearby sexton to know what he did with the bits of old coffins that he sometimes dug up. Three of the boys were grandchildren of a cooper who made and sold wooden bowls and spoons. For a joke Paterson told the boys that the coffin pieces were sold to their grandfather for making his bowls. The information was spread around in the village, to the indignation of the cooper, who in fact used old wine casks. But although Paterson admitted the joke, the cooper's business was ruined.

'It is in the nature of a Forsyte to be ignorant that he is a Forsyte'
John Galsworthy, *The Man of Property*, ch. 10 (1906)

Galsworthy's Forsytes (typically Victorian/Edwardian of their class) were a varied crowd, but they shared an attitude to life. They tended to be cautious, solid, property-conscious, possessive, often stubborn and de-termined, sometimes softhearted and susceptible, seiz-ing the substance but often losing the soul. In their hansom cabs, exclusive clubs, lawyers', stockbrokers', or business offices, and their elaborate drawingrooms, they were all Forsytes in the broad sense. And because they were Forsytes, they never thought of themselves as possessing special characteristics. To themselves they were the norm; all other types were oddities.

'It is possible to be below flattery, as well as above it'
T. B. Macaulay, *History of England*, ch. 2 (1848)

Macaulay was alluding specifically to Charles II, averring that his contempt for flattery was not really a virtue. Macaulay had many qualities of a great historian, but his judgments are often unreliable. On Charles II he is hopelessly at sea. Far from being (as Macaulay thought) ignorant of politics and administration, he was – as modern historians now understand – a man whose casual manner usually concealed a quick grasp of affairs, and sometimes a firm determination to direct them.

'I know a bank whereon the wild thyme blows'
William Shakespeare, *A Midsummer Night's Dream*, II, i (1600)

Oberon, the fairy King, knows that the bank is one where Titania, his Queen, is wont to sleep. Having fallen out with her, he spitefully decides to pay her back by making her ridiculous. He streaks her eyes with a love potion while she sleeps, thus making her fall in love with a yokel who has been given an ass's head by magic. Titania duly dotes on him, until Oberon decides to remove the charm and heal the breach. There is a certain charm in the fairy speeches, but their portrayal by all-too-solid actors and actresses usually presents the producer with a problem that he never quite solves.

'I know he is a Devil, but he has something of the angel yet undefac'd'
George Etherege, *The Man of Mode* (1676)

The description is of Dorimant, the play's hero (if that is the word), given by one of his discarded mistresses. The character is indeed a curious one. He is shown as coarse, callous, and even malicious towards his various mistresses. However, the play ends with the heroine eager to marry him. Dorimant was most probably based on the dissolute but talented Earl of Rochester, whose friend Etherege was. Perhaps in life something of the angel was visible, but it is not evident on the printed page. The title of the play applies to Sir Fopling Flutter – one of the first of a long line of coxcombs in the 'Comedy of Manners'.

'I know I have the body of a weak and feeble woman, but I have the heart and stomach of a King'
Elizabeth I, *Speech to troops at Tilbury* (1588)

When the mighty Spanish Armada had set sail to crush England once and for all, the Queen's safety was of paramount importance. She herself was inclined to meet her enemies with her troops on the coast. The Earl of Leicester persuaded her to stay at Havering, Essex, a few miles inland, and from there pay a visit to the fort at Tilbury on the Essex coast, where a large body of troops was drawn up to repel invasion. Here she made a famous encouraging speech to them. In fact their courage was never tested, for the Armada was already virtually defeated by the English fleet, with convenient assistance from storms.

> *'I know that I shall meet my fate*
> *Somewhere among the clouds above'*
> W. B. Yeats, *An Irish Airman Foresees his Death* (1918)

The airman was Robert Gregory, an Irishman who joined the Flying Corps in the First World War. He feels driven to take part in the air battles by 'a lonely impulse of delight' which convinced him that his present activity was the only reality. He was killed over Italy in 1918, fighting for 'those . . . I do not love' against 'those . . . I do not hate'.

> *'I'll come to thee by moonlight, though hell should bar the*
> *way'*
> Alfred Noyes, *The Highwayman* (1906)

The speaker is the gaily-dressed highwayman, planning to visit his sweetheart Bess, the landlord's daughter, after a hold-up. His words are overheard, and a troop of soldiers wait for him in the inn, binding his sweetheart, with a musket pointing at her heart to prevent her from giving any signal. When she hears her lover approaching she warns him in the only way she can – by getting a finger to the trigger and pressing it. Her sacrifice is in fact useless, for when next day he hears how Bess died he gallops furiously back to the inn and is shot like a dog on the highway. On a winter's night, the poem concludes, 'when the road is a ribbon of moonlight over the purple moor', a ghostly highwayman can be heard riding up to the old inn door.

> *'The ill consequences of exercise are precarious (doubtful),*
> *but those of sitting still are certain'*
> Catherine Hutton, *Life of William Hutton* (1816)

Miss Hutton is writing of her father, a well-known Birmingham bookseller and author whose autobiography, edited by his daughter, attracted a great deal of attention after his death in 1815. He was a man of resolution, who educated himself under considerable difficulties. As he grew old he refused to allow physical handicaps to force him to his bed, but insisted on carrying on with his accustomed activities to the last possible moment. His daughter attributed his long life (he died at ninety-two) to these determined exertions. She herself, a popular novelist of the day, lived till she was ninety.

> *'I'll drink it if you like. I'm used to it, and use is everything'*
> Charles Dickens, *David Copperfield*, ch.5 (1849–50)

When young David is being sent to London, a stop is made at a Yarmouth inn where a meal has been ordered for him. But the rascally waiter takes advantage of the child's innocence. Pretending to give friendly help, he eats most of the boy's dinner, and also lies that the beer is so strong as to be dangerous. He kindly offers to drink it himself. 'I don't think it'll hurt me if I throw me head back and take it off quick.' Which he does, and gullible David is quite pleased to find that the obliging waiter remains very much alive.

'An ill-favoured thing, sir, but mine own'
William Shakespeare, *As You Like It*, V, iv (c 1599)

During his sojourn in the Forest of Arden the clown, Touchstone, has agreed to marry a country wench, the goat-girl Audrey. Feeling that anyone connected with the court, even a jester, is not expected to mate with a rural maid, he offers the Duke, whom he has just met, an apologetic explanation of the match. His fiancée is not bright enough to resent the apology. Provincial though he was himself, Shakespeare had no hesitation in ridiculing country folk for the amusement of Londoners.

'I'll have no favourites on my ship'
R. L. Stevenson, *Treasure Island*, ch. 9 (1883)

Jim Hawkins is officially cabin boy aboard the treasure-seeking ship *Hispaniola*. He is not too pleased when Captain Smollett, the blunt, outspoken commander of the vessel, sees him looking round the ship and orders him below to his duties. There was something to be said on both sides. The Captain's attitude to discipline was right and proper, but perhaps Jim had a slight grievance. Although Squire Trelawney was responsible for fitting out the expedition, no one but Jim could really claim ownership of the treasure chart.

'I'll keep his picture while I've a room to put it in'
R. B. Sheridan, *The School for Scandal*, IV, i (1777)

Charles Surface, the extravagant but generous young nephew of Sir Oliver Surface, decides to sell off the family portraits in order to get some ready money. His uncle (whom he has never seen), though horrified at the proposed sale, poses as a prospective purchaser. There is just one portrait that Charles refuses to sell – that of Sir Oliver himself. 'I'll not part with poor Noll. The old fellow has been very good to me.' Sir Oliver is so ridiculously delighted that he forgives everything, and startles Charles by paying even more than agreed for the portraits.

'I'll meet the raging of the skies, But not an angry father'
Thomas Campbell, *Lord Ullin's Daughter* (1803)

She therefore persuaded the boatman at the ferry to row herself and her lover, a Highland chief, across Lochgyle despite the violent storm. Meanwhile Lord Ullin with a band of armed men came chasing after them, eager, most unreasonably, to slay the lover. But as they reached the shore and the father saw his daughter about to be overwhelmed by the waves 'his wrath was changed to wailing'. He called out his forgiveness. It was a bit late in the day, however, for a change of heart, and the daughter and her lover were drowned.

The waters wild went o'er his child,
And he was left lamenting.

'I'll put a spoke among your wheels'
John Fletcher, *The Mad Lover*, III, vi (1647)

A cheerful old soldier overhears a crafty love plot being hatched against his commanding officer, and resolves to counter it. The spoke in his figure of speech was not the spoke of a wheel in the present-day sense but a wooden stave used for braking purposes. It was thrust through a hole in the carriage wheel to act as a drag. Hence to put a spoke in someone's wheel was to hold him back or hinder him.

'I'll see you again
Whenever Spring breaks through again'
Noel Coward, *Bittersweet*, I, ii (1929)

The theme song of what the author himself called a play of semi-nostalgic sentiment. It is sung by Carl, a music teacher, and his pupil Sarah, who is about to be married to another man. Carl and Sarah suddenly elope to his native Vienna, where, after their marriage, he is tragically killed by an officer who has been forcing his attentions on Sarah. The cleverly constructed lyrics, persuasive melodies, and restrained sentiment combined to make *Bittersweet* one of the playwright's most effective and popular plays. He himself said that it gave him more complete satisfaction than any other of his plays.

'I'll sell her for five guineas to any man that will pay me the money'
Thomas Hardy, *The Mayor of Casterbridge*, ch. 1 (1886)

A significant episode in the first chapter of Hardy's novel is the sale of his wife by Michael Henchard, a hay trusser looking for work. He is not fully sober, and his fuddled mind sees his simple wife and their child as an encumbrance. So in a tent at the Weydon-Priors Fair he sells her to a sailor passing by. Afterwards he regrets his act, and it has a harmful effect on him later in his life. Although there was no legality in such sales, some uneducated people believed them to be authentic. The novel was probably suggested to Hardy by an actual wife-sale that took place some years earlier at Portland, Dorset.

'I'll squeeze thee, like a Bladder, there;
And make thee groan thyself away to Air'
John Dryden, *The Conquest of Granada*, Pt 2, IV, iii (1672)

Unlike Hamlet, whose first attitude to his father's ghost is thoroughly respectful, Almanazor begins by treating his mother's ghost with scant consideration, threatening either to grab her and drag her into the light, or else squeeze her into nothingness. Not surprisingly 'The Ghost retires'. Later she reappears, and a more suitable conversation ensues. 'Speak, Holy Shade, thou Parent-form, speak on,' Almanazor begs. The quoted lines have often been offered as an example of dramatic banality. They are certainly not Dryden at his best, nor heroic tragedy at its most impressive.

'I may by degrees dwindle into a wife'
William Congreve, *The Way of the World*, IV, v (1700)

The lively heroine, Millamant, is at last being brought by her lover, Mirabell, to give a straight and definite answer to his proposal of marriage. In one of the most famous of all comic scenes she lays down the numerous terms on which she will agree to marry. They include the right to lie in bed as long as she pleases; to be free from nauseous terms of endearment ('wife, spouse, my dear, joy, jewel' etc.); to write and receive letters at will; to have her closet inviolate; and to be empress of her own tea table. 'These articles subscribed ... I may by degrees dwindle into a wife.' Mirabell proceeds to lay down *his* terms, adding that if these are accepted, 'I may prove a tractable and complying husband'.

'I'm going to do nothing for ever and ever'
Anon, in J. M. Cohen's *Penguin Book of Comic and Curious Verse* (1952)

This anonymous verse voices the thoughts of a tired housewife, killed by overwork. She rejoices that in the place to which she is going (she seems to assume it is Heaven) there will be no cooking, laundry, or sewing, and no dishes to wash. She won't even be concerned in the regular performances of anthems, 'for having no voice I'll be quit of the singing'. Her idea of paradise is just to do nothing at all. No doubt the thought seems attractive to a wife who has been a kitchen drudge, but one suspects that after a while she will become bored and be looking round for a few haloes to polish.

'I'm no angel'
W. M. Thackeray, *Vanity Fair*, ch. 1 (1848)

Most people would suppose the famous film actress, Mae West, to be the originator of this well-known confession, but in fact she took the words (consciously or not) from Becky Sharp. That keen-witted young woman had been insultingly treated in the young ladies' seminary where, a poor orphan, she had been placed as an apprentice teacher. Accordingly she hated the haughty headmistress. Her charming friend, Amelia, gently reproved her for uttering revengeful thoughts. 'Revenge may be wicked, but it's natural,' Becky replied truthfully enough, and cheerfully disclaimed angelic status.

'I must down to the seas again, to the lonely sea and the sky'
John Masefield, *Sea Fever* (1902)

Masefield was partly educated on the ship *Conway*, which trains boys for the merchant service. At the age of fifteen he went to sea as an apprentice on a windjammer, in which he voyaged round Cape Horn. Though he soon gave up life on the ocean, he remained fascinated by the sea, as many of his writings show. The present poem comes from his first publication, *Salt-Water Ballads* (1902). 'All I ask is a tall ship, and a star to steer her by.' Then the wheel's kick, the song of the wind, and 'a grey dawn breaking' will satisfy his fever.

'In a few weeks I had settled down happily to a life of deception'
A. A. Milne, *It's Too Late Now*, ch.6 (1939)

Looking back to his days at Westminster School, Milne is dealing revealingly with the common practice of getting pupils to exchange papers at correction time, with the supposed intention of preventing cheating. He points out that far from achieving its object, exchanging papers may very well make cheating more certain. A boy who would hesitate to cheat for his own advantage will do so with a perfectly clear conscience to benefit a schoolmate, especially if the mate is a popular one, good at sport.

'In a full-hearted evensong Of joy unlimited'
Thomas Hardy, *The Darkling Thrush* (1900)

On a grim winter evening in a gloomy landscape that made the earth seem like a corpse, the poet was suddenly uplifted by the 'full-hearted evensong' of an old thrush perched on a barren twig. It made him feel that as there was so little to sing about in the bleak surroundings, the bird must have been inspired by some secret Hope unknown to man.

'In all our little quarrels, my dear, if you recollect, my love, you always began first'
R. B. Sheridan, *The School for Scandal*, III, i (1777)

Sir Peter and his young, headstrong wife are trying to make up their differences, and have just agreed that they will never quarrel again. Unfortunately Sir Peter chooses this blissful moment to advise Lady Teazle that she must watch her temper, for it is she who is always responsible for starting their arguments. Though he endeavours to soften the accusation with endearments, his wife bristles indignantly at this tactless attitude, and soon they are quarrelling again more fiercely than ever.

'In did come the strangest figure'
Robert Browning, *The Pied Piper of Hamelin* (1845)

The figure was that of a piper, dressed half in yellow, half in red. He offered to rid the little town of Hamelin of the swarm of rats which plagued it, and the Corporation readily agreed to pay far more than the modest one thousand guilders that he asked. He was as good as his word, piping a tune that drew all the rats away, and drowning them in the River Weser. But when he came to collect his money the Mayor tried to treat the agreement as a joke, and refused to pay. The piper thereupon played another tune, with disastrous effect on the Hamelin children. The story is a very old Westphalian legend.

'I never can forget 'ee, for you was a good man and did good things'
Thomas Hardy, *The Woodlanders*, ch.48 (1885)

The closing words of what, in effect, is an epilogue to Hardy's fine novel. Giles Winterbourne has died through his over-chivalrous care for the woman he loves, who is married to another man. Giles handed over his humble dwelling to her, thereby worsening an illness that proved fatal. Marty South, a country girl who has always loved him without hope of response, faithfully tends his grave; and her simple eulogy is worthy of a poet. 'Whenever I get up I'll think of 'ee, and whenever I lie down I'll think of 'ee again. Whenever I plant the young larches I'll think that none can plant as you planted.'

'I never heard the old song of Percy and Douglas, that I found not my heart moved more than with a trumpet'
Philip Sidney, *An Apologie for Poetrie* (c 1580)

The old song that Sidney refers to is the ballad *The Battle of Otterbourne*, telling of a desperate fight between the forces of the Scottish Earl Douglas (slain) and the Northumbrian Lord Percy (captured). Sidney is writing of the power of poetry to move men's hearts, claiming that even if the ballad is crudely sung by a rough minstrel it still affects the emotions. He adds that in Hungary, a warlike country, it was the custom for songs of their ancestors to be sung at feasts to kindle the courage of their fighting men.

'I never lived in any cathedral city, except London, never knew anything of any Close: and had enjoyed no peculiar intimacy with any clergyman'
Anthony Trollope, *An Autobiography*, ch.5 (1883)

Many readers of Trollope's Barchester novels have imagined that his detailed picture of life among cathedral dignitaries must have been inspired by a long connection with a well-known cathedral; Salisbury was sometimes named. This was not so. Trollope had no personal familiarity with cathedral life. One evening, while in Salisbury in the course of his postal duties, he wandered round the lovely Close and was struck by the thought that such a setting would be excellent for a novel. He then conceived the stories of *The Warden* and *Barchester Towers*. The characters were all imaginary.

'I never saw daffodils so beautiful'
Dorothy Wordsworth, *Journal* (15 April 1802)

Although for poetic purposes Wordsworth professed to have 'wandered lonely as a cloud' when he came upon the host of golden daffodils that inspired his famous poem, in fact his sister Dorothy was with him. Afterwards she herself recorded her encounter with the daffodils, and her description forms a delightful companion piece to her brother's lyric. 'They grew among the mossy stones about and above them; some rested their heads upon these stones, as on a pillow, for weariness; and the rest tossed and reeled and danced, and seemed as if they verily laughed with the wind that blew upon them over the lake.'

'I never will desert Mr Micawber'
Charles Dickens, *David Copperfield*, ch.12 (1849–50)

Mrs Micawber, emotional and easily upset, is asked by the youthful David whether she will accompany Mr Micawber if he goes to Plymouth in the hope of finding work. He had just been discharged from a debtor's prison, and she had often been reduced to selling or pawning the few family treasures. But the mere idea of parting from her improvident but good-natured husband reduces her to tearful hysterics. 'He is the parent of my children! He is the father of my twins! He is the husband of my affections; and I ne—ver—will—desert Mr Micawber!'

'The inexorable law of caste ... that commands like to mate with like, and forbids a giraffe to fall in love with a squirrel'
T. W. Robertson, *Caste*, Act I (1867)

This was probably the first significant play on the theme of marriage with a partner from a lower social class. Captain Hawtree is warning his friend, Hon. George D'Alroy, not to think of marrying a common actress who has a drunken father. But George insists that Esther is a natural lady, and he marries her in spite of his aristocratic mother's disapproval. He is proved right in the end, and the haughty Marquise comes round to admiring her baby grandson. The giraffe has successfully mated with the squirrel. Robertson's attempt at realism in story and characters was a genuine innovation, and despite its limitations *Caste* remains a landmark in dramatic history.

'An infant crying in the night'
Alfred Tennyson, *In Memoriam*, liv (1850)

The poet fears that the memorial he is writing to his dead friend, Arthur Hallam, is not worthy of him. Then he reflects that men must do the best they can. Good and bad are always found together, and ultimately everything will be for the best. This optimistic philosophy buoys him up, but a more realistic feeling reminds him that it is only a dream, and that we really know nothing of what is ahead.

> So runs my dream: but what am I?
> An infant crying in the night ...
> And with no language but a cry.

'Infinite riches in a little room'
Christopher Marlowe, *The Jew of Malta*, I, i (c 1591)

The play opens with Barabas, a wealthy Jew, counting his treasure, piled up in front of him. He pushes aside the silver coins: 'What a trouble 'tis to count this trash.' Gold is better, but it becomes wearisome to count it as the years go by. Best of all are jewels:

> Bags of fiery opals, sapphires, amethysts,
> Jacinths, hard topaz, grass-green emeralds,
> Beauteous rubies, sparkling diamonds.

Just one of these would be enough to ransom a king. Here indeed 'infinite riches in a little room' (i.e. small space) may be found.

'*In his owne grees I made him frie*'
Geoffrey Chaucer, *The Canterbury Tales – Wife of Bath's Prologue*
(*c* 1387)

The Wife of Bath, one of the pilgrims to Canterbury, is telling of her fourth husband, a lecher who annoyed her by having a mistress. She repaid him in his own coin by making him bitterly jealous. 'I was his purgatory,' she says, cheerfully recalling the situation. She is clearly a forceful personality, by no means a typical wife at a period when women were very much the underdogs. It is highly probable, therefore, that Chaucer was drawing a portrait from life – though not necessarily from personal experience.

'*In poetry enough is not only not so good as a feast, but is a beggarly parsimony*'
J. R. Lowell, *The English Poets* (1888)

The poetry specifically referred to here is that of Spenser. Lowell is repudiating the criticism that the Spenserian stanza led the poet into tedious circumlocutions. He insists that although the gist of a verse may be tersely expressed in prose, it is precisely in the richness and careless abundance of such poetry as Spenser's that its quality lies. His verse rolls forward with generous fluency and splendour. Spenser's 'dilation', Lowell suggests, 'is not mere distension, but the expansion of natural growth in the rich soil of his own mind'.

'*In spite of all temptations
To belong to other nations
He remains an Englishman!*'
W. S. Gilbert, *H.M.S. Pinafore*, Act II (1878)

Ralph Rackstraw, a fine upstanding seaman of low rank, ventures to fall in love with the daughter of his captain. Their attempt to elope is intercepted by the captain. Ralph defends his temerity in loving his social superior by asserting proudly that he is an Englishman. The Boatswain supports Ralph's claim in a delightful send-up of conventional patriotic songs. It needed only a wave of Gilbert's wand-like pen to make fun of the Senior Service by causing Ralph and the captain to change places, thus removing all obstacles to the marriage.

'*In the bottom of our hearts envy and discontent still lurked, like coiled serpents*'
Aldous Huxley, *Along the Road* (1925)

The cause of the envy was a powerful sports car. Huxley and a companion were travelling through the Italian Alps in a small Citroen car, climbing a long winding pass in second gear. Three times they were overtaken by a huge red Alfa Romeo racing-car which roared past them at three times their speed, and then descended. The red car was merely engaged in hill climbing tests, but although Huxley and his friend tried to persuade themselves that they were quite happy with their little Citroen, envy and discontent were not easily banished.

'In the future days, which we seek to make secure, we look forward to a world founded upon the four essential freedoms'
Franklin D. Roosevelt, *Inaugural Address* (6 January 1941)

The American President was speaking some months before the U.S.A. entered the war, but he was already looking ahead to peacetime. The four freedoms he had in mind were:

Freedom of speech
Freedom of worship
Freedom from want
Freedom from fear

Few people, alas, would feel that the world today has achieved what Roosevelt envisaged.

'In the Spring a young man's fancy lightly turns to thoughts of love'
Alfred Tennyson, *Locksley Hall* (1832)

This very quotable line is not entirely appropriate to the story. The narrator is revisiting in his maturity the home (Locksley Hall) where he had spent his youth. In those days he had fallen in love with his cousin, Amy, but her parents had persuaded her to throw him over and marry a wealthier man, far inferior (the narrator considers) to himself. He had loved her not lightly but so deeply that in his bitterness against Amy and against society he almost decides to leave Europe and find 'some savage woman' to mate with and rear his children.

'In this country (England) it is a good thing to kill an admiral from time to time to encourage the others'
Voltaire, *Candide*, ch.23 (1759)

Candide is on board a ship which calls at Portsmouth, where he sees a crowd watching an execution. It proves to be that of a naval officer, Admiral Byng, in whose unfortunate case Voltaire, though a Frenchman, had taken a great interest, which is why the incident is dragged into the novel. Byng's offence was that he had shown less than wholehearted zeal in attempting to relieve a fort in Minorca, the task for which he had been sent out. His execution disturbed some Englishmen as well as the French satirist, but others maintained that a high-ranking officer was as much entitled to the privilege of being shot as a low-ranking one.

'I only wanted to make you happy'
Alan Ayckbourn, *Round and Round the Garden*, II, ii (1973)

The closing line of *The Norman Conquests*, doubtless the most quotable comic trilogy ever written. There are three separate plays, all telling exactly the same story of a planned weekend that fails to come off. Yet although they cover the same ground, with the same characters and virtually the same incidents, there is a slight shift of angle. Each play deals with episodes that occur off-stage in the other two. The result is not only technically brilliant but also enormously funny. Norman's blundering attempt to take his sister-in-law for a secret weekend is misunderstood by everyone, and his last despairing cry is worthy of Chekhov.

'I paint the Cot
As Truth will paint it, and as Bards will not'
George Crabbe, *The Village*, Bk I (1783)

Crabbe is scornful of the artificial way in which poets have too often portrayed rural life, drawing on outworn classical similes. Happy swains and piping shepherds disguise the harsh realities endured by villagers and country dwellers. These people labour incessantly, often in the heat, and live in a countryside where rank weeds eat up the land. The true shepherd may be an elderly man, with little to look forward to except the poorhouse and death.

'I really don't think that I could consent to go to heaven if I thought that there were to be no animals there'
George Bernard Shaw, *Androcles and the Lion*, Act I (1912)

Shaw himself, in a letter, called this play 'a bawling, shouting, roaring, bustling, brutal affair'. He was doing it an injustice, for it is in fact a penetrating study of religious experience – and at the same time an immensely funny pantomime, based on the familiar tale (from a Latin author of the second century A.D.) of an animal lover who pulled a thorn from the foot of a forest lion, was later captured and thrown to a lion in the sacrificial arena, to be recognized by the animal as its benefactor. Androcles is here begging a fellow Christian not to suggest that animals have no souls.

'I remember, I remember
The house where I was born'
Thomas Hood, *I Remember, I Remember* (1827)

In this melancholy little poem by a professional humorist the poet reflects that the happiness he had known in childhood has now departed. He remembers how the sun 'never came a wink too soon' at his window.

> Now 'tis little joy
> To know I'm farther off from heaven
> Than when I was a boy.

In spite of his humour, Hood's life was not a cheerful one. He suffered a good deal both in health and from economic difficulties. He finally received a Civil List pension, but died at the early age of forty-six.

'I resolved to begin as I meant to end'
Samuel Johnson, in Boswell's *Life of Johnson* (1791)

This was how Johnson's weddingday started, as described by him to Topham Beauclerk, and through him to Boswell. The pair rode to the church together, each on horseback. The wife-to-be, following the example of fine ladies in the old romances, began acting capriciously, first complaining that Johnson rode too fast, then objecting that he was lagging behind. She would have done better to have studied *The Taming of the Shrew* than the romances, for Johnson was no more disposed to be the slave of a woman's caprice than Petruchio. He pushed on briskly till he was out of sight, leaving her to follow. The policy evidently worked, for the marriage proved to be a happy one, though the wife was nearly double the age of the husband.

'I saw an aged aged man
A-sitting on a gate'
Lewis Carroll, *Through the Looking-Glass*, ch.8 (1871)

This comes from a song which the White Knight sings to Alice. It is, he tells her, 'very, *very* beautiful' and will probably bring tears to her eyes. It does not do this, for it is really a rather cheeky parody of Wordsworth's *Resolution and Independence* in which the old leech-gatherer is asked 'What is it you do?' The White Knight's aged man is asked precisely the same question. His answers, however, are a good deal less practical than the leech-gatherer's – for example, looking for butterflies to make into mutton pies, or hunting for haddocks' eyes to use as waistcoat buttons.

'I saw the Iron enter into his soul'
Laurence Sterne, *A Sentimental Journey; Paris – the Captive* (1768)

Sterne was so sentimentally inclined that the sight of a starling in a cage very much upset him. He began thinking of the miseries of imprisonment. Picturing in his mind a wretched captive, he seemed to see the unhappy man chained by the legs, able to do little in the dim light but mark the slowly passing days by cutting notches on bits of stick. The iron of the chain had almost become a part of his nature. Although the picture was an imaginary one, Sterne was so affected that he burst into tears – not for the first time (or the last) on his sentimental continental journey.

'I see no reason why the author of a play should not regard a first night's audience as a candid and judicious friend'
R. B. Sheridan, *The Rivals – Preface* (1775)

This is precisely how young Sheridan (he was twenty-three) *did* regard the first-night audience of *The Rivals*. The play was unfavourably received and strongly criticized, especially because of its length, and was withdrawn after the first night. With some extensive cutting and an acting change it was staged again eleven days later and was a great success. None the less, it may be doubted whether a dramatist is wise to leave the work of revision until the play is actually before the public. One suspects that Sheridan's *Preface* was excusing a slackness rather than presenting a plan.

'I shall sleep like a top'
William D'Avenant, *The Rivals*, III (1664)

A top at the height of its spinning appears almost motionless. To sleep like a top, therefore, is literally to sleep standing up. This quite rational simile first appears, oddly enough, in a mad song. Celania has gone mad through love. She intends to dress like a man and go searching the forest for her lover. In her song she longs for a hawthorn bush to lean against to keep herself awake, 'or else I shall sleep like a top'. D'Avenant's play (not to be confused with Sheridan's a century later) was based on Fletcher's *The Two Noble Kinsmen* (1634).

'I should not dare to call my soul my own'
Elizabeth Barrett Browning, *Aurora Leigh*, Bk II (1857)

Aurora, narrating the story in verse, tells how a rich and arrogant cousin offered to marry her when she was almost twenty. She refused him, for she felt that the proposal was not inspired by love but by his desire for a helpmate, 'a wife to help your ends'. Later she reflects that if she had married him he would have regarded her as something bought and paid for, and she would have been left without a soul of her own. When his circumstances change and his life is dogged by misfortune, her own attitude changes, and they come together.

'I sing of brooks, of blossoms, birds, and bowers'
Robert Herrick, *Hesperides* (1648)

The opening lines of Herrick's introductory poem to his remarkable collection of lyrics. The verse neatly summarizes the contents. They include 'Maypoles, hock-carts, wassails, wakes', not to mention youth, love, cleanly wantonness, and the Court of Mab. He even writes of hell, and finally of heaven, and hopes 'to have it after all'. The word *Hesperides* relates to the 'Daughters of Evening' who helped to guard the golden apples of the Fortunate Isles.

'I sink a few more ships, it's true,
Than a well-bred monarch ought to do'
W. S. Gilbert, *The Pirates of Penzance*, Act I (1880)

The speaker, or rather singer, is perhaps justified in sinking ships, for it is his trade. He is King not of a country but of the Pirates. He justifies himself also with the reflection that more-orthodox kings often carry out secret activities that are worse than piracy. He is not, in fact, a very successful pirate, owing to the sentimental regard which his gang have for orphans. Any prospective victim who pleads the loss of his parents is allowed to escape.

'Is it really true that Johnson had better have gone on producing Irenes *instead of writing his* Lives of the Poets*?'*
Matthew Arnold, *The Function of Criticism at the Present Time* (1864)

Arnold is answering those writers (Wordsworth in particular) who had put forward the view that critics would be better employed in original composition. He instances Dr Johnson, whose original tragedy *Irene* (1749) had little success and little merit, but whose criticisms in his *Lives of the Poets* (1779–81) were of lasting value. While accepting that 'the critical power is of lower rank than the creative', he maintains that criticism is none the less a valuable art. He points out that Wordsworth's rather tedious *Ecclesiastical Sonnets* (1821), for example, are of less value than the famous Preface to the *Lyrical Ballads* (1800), which is full of interesting critical opinion.

*'Is not a Patron, my Lord, one who looks with unconcern on
a man struggling for life in the water, and, when he has
reached ground, encumbers him with help?'*
Samuel Johnson, *Letter to Earl of Chesterfield* (7 February 1755)

Johnson's letter to Chesterfield, criticizing the noble lord
for not offering more help while the great *Dictionary* was
being compiled, has often been admired; but how far it
was truly justified is another matter. Chesterfield had
taken a polite interest in the plan of the dictionary and
wrote two commendatory papers when it finally appeared. What else he should have done remains uncertain. It seems likely that at one stage Johnson visited
Chesterfield's fine home (perhaps hoping for financial
help), but failed to see the Earl – possibly through a
servant's fault.

*'Isn't it funny
How a bear likes honey?
Buzz! Buzz! Buzz!
I wonder why he does?'*
A. A. Milne, *Winnie the Pooh* (1926)

This was the little song sung by Winnie the Pooh,
perhaps the most famous bear in literary history (whose
name has never been satisfactorily explained). Hearing
the sound of buzzing near an oak tree, Pooh (though a
bear of very little brain) deduced that there were bees
about. Bees mean honey, so he started to climb towards
the buzzing. However he never succeeded in obtaining
any honey. First a branch broke; and then, when he
attempted to float up with a balloon, disguised as a
cloud, it only aroused the bees' suspicions, and he had to
be shot down.

*'Isn't ... life extremely flat
With nothing whatever to grumble at!'*
W. S. Gilbert, *Princess Ida*, Act III (1884)

King Gama is objecting to the vile treatment to which he
is being subjected by his neighbour, King Hildebrand,
who is holding him prisoner. He is suffering terrible
agonies of frustration. His greatest pleasure in life is to
upset people by making unkind, sneering remarks, and
by uttering complaints about everything. Yet he is now
being treated with such kindness and consideration that
it is quite impossible for him to find any fault with
anybody. His sarcasm and ill-nature are met with friendly smiles, and he cannot even *bribe* anyone to contradict
him. He is so upset that he bursts into tears.

'I sought the simple life that Nature yields'
George Crabbe, *The Village*, Bk I (1783)

Crabbe sought it in vain in his village, finding instead
that 'Rapine and Wrong and Fear usurped her place'. He
was born at Aldeburgh (Suffolk), a fishing village, in
1754. After a limited training as an apothecary's apprentice, he returned to Aldeburgh as a surgeon-apothecary
in 1775 but later exchanged medicine for religion. As
curate in 1782 he found himself preaching to 'unfriendly
faces'. The village had deteriorated. Farm workers who
used to engage in healthy sports now spent their leisure
helping smugglers, and worthy fishermen had turned
wreckers.

'I spent the night in ecstasy almost'
Samuel Pepys, *Diary* (6 December 1665)

The ecstasy was mainly musical. During the afternoon Pepys had put himself in a musical mood by working on his setting for the song *Beauty Retire*. Later he and his wife went to the house of a Mrs Pierce where there was a gathering of music lovers, including the delightful actress and singer, Mrs Knipp. 'The best company for music I ever was in, in my life,' Pepys declared. 'I wish I could live and die in it.' Not only was the music splendid but there were the faces of Mrs Pierce, Mrs Pepys, and Mrs Knipp to gaze on, the last-named being 'pretty enough, but the most excellent, mad-humoured thing, and sings the noblest that ever I heard in my life'.

'I sprang to the stirrup, and Joris, and he; I galloped, Dirck galloped, we galloped all three'
Robert Browning, *How They Brought the Good News from Ghent to Aix* (1845)

This well-known dramatic ride was not, as is sometimes thought, based on an historical incident. Browning made the whole thing up while on a sea voyage, inspired by a longing for a gallop on one of his own horses. The lines were scribbled on the blank pages of a book he happened to have with him. But non-historical though the gallop is, it is geographically correct, as we can see if we consult a map of Belgium. The route follows the valleys of the river Scheldt and one of its tributaries. As for the news which the three riders set out so desperately to take to Aix-la-Chappelle, we must invent that for ourselves. Browning omitted to tell us.

'I still had hopes, my long vexations past, Here to return – and die at home at last'
Oliver Goldsmith, *The Deserted Village* (1770)

'Here' was 'sweet Auburn', Goldsmith's probably imaginary village, built up of all the pleasing times he had experienced in rural places. Attempts by some critics to situate the village in Ireland (Lissoy was the chosen one) were misguided, though doubtless youthful Irish recollections contributed to the total picture. The narrator is imagining himself retiring to spend his last days in the quiet village, eventually sinking into the grave with resignation. Sir Joshua Reynolds, to whom the poem was dedicated, returned the compliment by dedicating his picture 'Resignation' to Goldsmith.

'I stood tiptoe upon a little hill'
John Keats, *I Stood Tiptoe* (1816)

When he was just under twenty-one Keats became friendly with the distinguished essayist, journalist, and poet, Leigh Hunt, who lived at Hampstead. Keats spent a good deal of time here, finding pleasure in what were then the rural surroundings of the village. Resting on a gate leading from the Heath into a field, he composed the lines of this poem. It was early morning, with the dew still on the ground and branches; there was perfect stillness in the air, disturbed only by 'a little noiseless noise among the leaves'.

'It all depends what you mean by ...'
C. E. M. Joad, *The Brains Trust*, BBC radio series

The Brains Trust was a radio series (begun in 1941 and in some ways resembling the later *Any Questions* programme) in which listeners sent in miscellaneous questions which were answered by a panel of four. The panel, however, remained largely the same each week, and there was no audience. For some time the panel usually included Professors Julian Huxley and C. E. M. Joad. The latter often prefaced his answer by sensibly insisting that terms used in the question must be clearly defined before the question could be properly answered. In the course of time the quoted sentence became a catchphrase attached to his name.

'I think ... that it is the best club in London'
Charles Dickens, *Our Mutual Friend*, Bk II, ch.3 (1864–5)

The 'club' is the House of Commons, and the opinion is that of Mr Twemlow, a polite, insignificant old gentleman whose chief qualification for offering an opinion is that he is related to Lord Snigsworth. His friend, Mr Veneering, a newly-rich drug merchant, has decided to purchase a pocket borough, and asks Mr Twemlow: 'What do you think of my entering the House of Commons?' Mr Twemlow, not perhaps without a trace of envy, offers the quoted reply.

'I thought – sir – it would look very well in print'
Fanny Burney, *Diary* (16 December 1785)

Miss Burney's novel *Evelina*, published anonymously when she was twenty-six, created quite a sensation. Two of the book's most notable admirers were Dr Johnson and King George III. The latter came upon the young authoress one day when she was staying with a friend at Windsor, and he started to ask her about the novel. Fanny was so overwhelmed by his interest that she could only stammer that she had written it for her own amusement 'in some odd, idle hours'. 'But your publishing – your printing – how was that?' Confused, Fanny could think of no other answer than the quoted one. Afterwards she declared that it was the silliest speech she had ever made. None the less, it is not at all a bad reason for trying to get published.

'It is a beauteous evening, calm and free'
William Wordsworth, *Sonnet* (1807)

The scene was the beach near Calais, and the peace surrounding the poet – disturbed only by the sound of the waves – moved him to compose one of his most famous sonnets. With him was his natural daughter by Annette Vallon, conceived on an earlier visit to France. 'Dear Child! Dear Girl! that walkest with me here.'

'It is a custom
More honour'd in the breach than the observance'
William Shakespeare, *Hamlet*, I, iv (*c* 1601)

Often wrongly quoted to mean simply that a custom or rule is seldom observed. In fact, Hamlet's comment refers to a custom that he condemns – that of holding a wild orgy of drinking and dancing on any festive occasion. It is more honourable, he asserts, to break such a custom than to follow it. Hamlet is talking to his friend Horatio, pointing out how the deplored custom leads the Danish nation to be despised by other countries.

'It is a far, far better thing that I do, than I have ever done'
Charles Dickens, *A Tale of Two Cities*, ch.15 (1860)

Many people believe that these were Sydney Carton's last words as he waited on the scaffold for the blade of the guillotine to fall. They are mistaken: Carton never uttered them. They are in fact part of the last sentence of a long prophetic passage that he *might* have spoken *if* he had given utterance to his thoughts. The rest of the sentence (ending the novel) is: 'it is a far, far better rest that I go to than I have ever known'. Carton is reputed to be a dissolute barrister, but his love for Lucie, wife of his friend Charles Darnay, leads him to sacrifice himself for Charles, whom he resembles closely enough to take his place on the scaffold.

'It is an ancient Mariner,
And he stoppeth one of three'
S. T. Coleridge, *The Rime of the Ancient Mariner* (1798)

The supernatural experiences of the Old Navigator (as Coleridge liked to call him) were so intense that every now and then he felt an irresistible urge to make some passer-by listen to his remarkable story. The famous poem originated in the humble hope of producing £5 to pay for a short walking tour. The Wordsworths, brother and sister, set off with Coleridge to walk from Alfoxden in Somerset to Lynton in Devon. They planned to produce a magazine poem to defray expenses. The project soon became almost entirely Coleridge's. Ultimately it formed his main contribution to the *Lyrical Ballads* (1798), produced by Wordsworth and himself.

'It is a riddle wrapped in a mystery inside an enigma'
Winston Churchill, broadcast talk (1 October 1939)

Early in the Second World War Churchill, then First Lord of the Admiralty, broadcast to the nation a summary of events during the first month of the war. At this period the attitude of Russia remained obscure, and Churchill expressed this fact in his usual vivid style. He added that the key to the riddle was Russian national interest.

'It is a shocking thing, blowing smoke out of our mouths into other people's mouths, eyes, and noses, and having the same thing done to us'
Samuel Johnson, in Boswell's *Journal of a Tour to the Hebrides* (1785)

Johnson, strangely enough, was not uttering a stern condemnation of a repulsive habit. He was primarily expressing surprise that the smoking habit had decreased. After admitting the unpleasant effects of smoking, he went on to wonder why 'a thing which requires so little exertion, and yet preserves the mind from total vacuity' should have gone out of fashion. Some people may think it curious that any mind – especially Johnson's – should be so vacuous that it needed tobacco smoke to fill it.

'It is a tale told by an idiot'
William Shakespeare, *Macbeth*, V, v (1606)

With his castle about to be fiercely attacked by powerful enemies, Macbeth, who has gained the Scottish kingship by murder and tyranny, begins to realize that his ambition has failed him. While in this mood of grim despair he is brought the news of his wife's death. The feeling that existence is both brief and futile sweeps over him, and in the famous soliloquy, 'Tomorrow, and tomorrow, and tomorrow', he gives expression to his feelings about life.

'It is a truth universally acknowledged, that a single man in possession of a good fortune, must be in want of a wife'
Jane Austen, *Pride and Prejudice*, ch.1 (1813)

It is almost universally acknowledged that this is one of the best opening sentences of any great novel. It gives us the basic theme of the story right from the start, and it leads us at once to the delightful discussion between silly Mrs Bennett and drily cynical Mr Bennett. Since the Bennetts have five daughters, the fact that young and wealthy Mr Bingley has taken the neighbouring estate is of obvious consequence. And, of course, Mr Bingley does in the end marry the eldest and loveliest Miss Bennett, and, what is more important, his even wealthier friend Darcy marries the real heroine, Elizabeth Bennett.

'It is a wise father that knows his own child'
William Shakespeare, *The Merchant of Venice*, II, ii (1600)

Old Gobbo, almost blind, has come to visit his son Lancelot, in service with the Jewish moneylender, Shylock. Meeting Lancelot without knowing him, the old man asks for directions. Lancelot at first pretends to be a stranger. When he presently discloses his identity Old Gobbo is reluctant to believe him. The young man remarks humorously that even if Old Gobbo could see clearly he might 'fail of the knowing of me: it is a wise father that knows his own child'.

'It is better to live rich than die rich'
Samuel Johnson, in Boswell's *Life of Johnson* (1791)

One Sunday in 1778 Johnson was walking home from church when he was accosted by a gentleman he had known forty-nine years earlier. He proved to be a Mr Edwards, who had been at Pembroke College with Johnson. Learning that he had been a lawyer for many years, Johnson presumed that he must now be well-off, but Edwards replied that although he had made a good deal of money he had given much of it away to poor relations. 'Sir,' said Johnson, 'you have been rich in the most valuable sense of the word'. Edwards observed that he would not die rich, and promptly received the quoted answer.

'It is Christmas Day in the Workhouse'
George R. Sims, *The Dagonet Ballads* (1881)

Many people imagine that this line introduces a comic poem. The ballad is in fact a grim one, in which a pauper delivers a fierce attack on the authorities who had allowed his wife to die the previous Christmas by refusing to give relief when she was dying and famished. 'What of my murdered wife?' he cries angrily to the well-fed gentlefolk who have come to patronize the poor on Christmas Day. Sims was a well-known author, playwright, and journalist who for many years wrote regularly for a notable Sunday newspaper, *The Referee*, using the pseudonym Dagonet.

'It is extraordinary how cool any party but the principal can be in such cases'
Charles Dickens, *The Pickwick Papers*, ch.2 (1837)

This particular case is a challenge to fight a duel, received by Mr Winkle, one of the leading members of the Pickwick Club. Winkle is afraid to decline it, for he prides himself on his reputation in the Club as an authority on such matters. However, when he invites another member, Mr Snodgrass, to be his second, he imagines Snodgrass will be so concerned that he will hurriedly take steps to prevent the fight from taking place. To his dismay Snodgrass accepts the duel quite calmly. Winkle is saved only by the discovery at the last moment that the challenge was issued to the wrong man.

'It is impossible to win gracefully at chess'
A. A. Milne, *Not That It Matters* (1919)

The author, in a light essay entitled *A Misjudged Game*, points out that in most games there are certain courtesies which one player can pay to an opponent. If you are bowled first ball at cricket, 'the wicket-keeper can comfort you by murmuring that the light is bad'. Mistakes or misfortunes at tennis or golf can be smoothed over by an opponent's 'Sorry' or 'Bad luck'. But at chess everything is deliberate. An opponent cannot apologize for taking a piece that he has been deliberately threatening for several moves. The final move is worst of all. 'No man yet has said "Mate!" in a voice which failed to sound to his opponent bitter, boastful, and malicious.'

'It is in the hour of trial that a man finds his true profession'
George Bernard Shaw, *The Devil's Disciple*, Act III, iii (1897)

Shaw himself described the play as a melodrama, but it is really a satire on irreligious religion – puritanical conventions without a spark of charity. The man who calls himself the disciple of the Devil is really the only character in the play with truly religious feeling. He is instinctively prepared to sacrifice himself for the local minister, Mr Anderson, without knowing why. Mr Anderson, though a good man and a good minister, is at heart a soldier, and when the decisive moment comes he sheds his ministerial duties to lead the local American militia against the British troops (1775). As he himself says, 'It is in the hour of trial.'

'It is not best to swap horses while crossing the river'
Abraham Lincoln, Address to National Union League delegation (9 June 1864)

The League supported Lincoln's Republican candidature for a second term of office as President of the United States, at a time when there was opposition to some of his policies. In his reply Lincoln suggested half humorously that their selection of him was less due to his merits than to their fear that it might be bad tactics to change candidates during a campaign.

'It is the most insipid ridiculous play that ever I saw in my life'
Samuel Pepys, *Diary* (29 September 1662)

The wretched play thus castigated was Shakespeare's *Midsummer Night's Dream*, which, he says, 'I never saw before, nor ever shall again'. It is unlikely that he ever had the opportunity in any case, for the play seems to have been rarely acted during the Restoration period. This is hardly surprising. The strong fairy element is not easy to cope with at any time, and many modern productions have come a cropper over it. It is unlikely that actors and actresses of the early Restoration period, struggling to find the right style for cynical comedies and heroic tragedies, would make much of the antics of lightly tripping fairies.

'It is usual with young ladies to reject the addresses of the man whom they secretly mean to accept'
Jane Austen, *Pride and Prejudice*, ch.19 (1813)

The words are those of Mr Collins, a pompous young clergyman who is proposing marriage to his cousin, Elizabeth Bennett. He is so conscious of his condescension that he cannot be convinced that she is refusing him. Her repeated efforts to turn him down are merely brushed off as conventional replies intended to increase his ardour. It is only when her silly mother angrily reproaches Elizabeth for being foolish and headstrong that Mr Collins begins to believe that the girl means what she says and, further, that a foolish and headstrong wife might not be so desirable after all.

'It is your mental attitude to the jungle which decides whether you go under or not'
F. Spencer Chapman, *Living Dangerously*, ch.21 (1953)

Chapman was a notable traveller and explorer, whose book *The Jungle is Neutral* (1949) about his experiences in the Malayan jungle, is one of the great classics of the Second World War. Several chapters of the present book also deal with his Malayan adventures. He was left behind in Malaya when the Japanese invaded the country. He entered the thick jungle determined to keep alive and (as a British officer) to do all that was possible to hinder the Japanese. But there were many soldiers similarly left to fend for themselves in the jungle who died simply because they felt sure they could not survive. They felt the jungle to be hostile, whereas it is really neutral. What matters is the person's attitude to it.

'It matters not how a man dies, but how he lives'
Samuel Johnson, in Boswell's *Life of Johnson* (1791)

Johnson was always oppressed by the thought of death, and disliked talking about it. Once when the two were alone, Boswell introduced the topic and mentioned the names of two writers (Hume and Foote) who had said they were not afraid to die. Johnson replied truculently, 'Hold a pistol to their breasts and see how they behave!' But he was more eager to talk of living than of dying. When Boswell tried to press the topic, the great man became so angry that it needed a tactful note from the blundering biographer to smooth the matter over.

'It may be for years, and it may be for ever'
Julia Crawford, *Kathleen Mavourneen* (1835)

An Irish lover begs his loved one to wake up and say goodbye to him, for he is going away. 'Arise in thy beauty, thou star of my night,' he cries. But she appears to be more sleepy than sentimental, and remains deaf to his pleading.
> Kathleen Mavourneen! what, slumbering still?
> Oh, hast thou forgotten how soon we must sever?

But apparently she has, for she remains silent to the end of the song.

'It must be done like lightning'
Ben Jonson, *Every Man in His Humour*, LV, v (1598)

Captain Bobadil, a bragging soldier, is explaining to a couple of cronies the fine art of fencing. He lays stress on the need for a flashing blade. 'You do not give spirit enough to your motion, you are too tardy, too heavy! It must be done like lightning!' As his opponent for the demonstration is a wooden post, he has little difficulty in revealing his skill. He is rash enough, however, to proclaim how he will treat Downright, if they meet. Shortly afterwards his enemy, Squire Downright, appears but Bobadil's sword is most reluctant to show itself.

'It's always best on these occasions to do what the mob do'
Charles Dickens, *The Pickwick Papers*, ch.13 (1837)

Mr Pickwick and a few of his companions have come to
Eatanswill (a place not to be found on ordnance survey
maps) in order to witness an election. The respective
candidates are Samuel Slumkey and Horatio Fitzkin.
Finding themselves at once in the midst of a wild crowd
of Slumkey supporters. Mr Pickwick and his friends join
in the shouting, without the slightest idea of who or
what they are shouting for. Pickwick's attitude is that
when you are in the middle of a mob you had better do
as they do. 'Suppose there are two mobs?' asks one of his
friends. 'Shout with the loudest,' Mr Pickwick advises
sagely.

'It seemed a carnival on ice'
John Evelyn, *Diary* (9 January 1684)

This was a famous occasion with a frost so heavy and
continuous that the River Thames became like concrete.
Shops and stalls were set up, arranged in rows resembling buildings in a street, and packed with goods,
forming a sizeable village. Meat was roasted on the ice. A
printer made a small fortune by printing mementoes
giving people's names and addresses, with the date, and
a note stating that the printing had been carried out on
the River Thames. Coaches ran from Westminster to the
Temple, and activities such as sledging, skating, and
puppet-plays turned the Thames into a fairground.

'It's hell fire that's on that man's tongue'
John Galsworthy, *Strife*, Act II, ii (1909)

The theme of the play is the struggle between two
unyielding personalities. Mr Anthony is the grim old
chairman of a company involved in a workers' strike.
Roberts is the fiery Welsh orator who leads the men.
Neither is prepared to give way. The strike has been
going on for months, and the men and their families
(before the days of social security) are suffering badly.
One striker at length speaks out, warning his colleagues
against Roberts – the man with the fiery tongue. Roberts
almost brings them round to his side again, when the
news is brought that his wife has died of cold and
starvation.

'It's more than a game. It's an institution'
Thomas Hughes, *Tom Brown's Schooldays*, ch.8 (1856)

Cricket is a game that has often been praised rather
solemnly. It is perhaps surprising to meet this solemnity
as early as 1856, when cricket was primarily an informal
sport meant to be enjoyed. Tom Brown, now cricket
captain at Rugby School, is talking to a friendly master
while the school plays a side from Lord's, the headquar-
ters of the game. The master agrees with Tom that it is an
unselfish game, teaching discipline and self-reliance. 'An
institution' Tom calls it, but fortunately not the military
institution it has tended to become 130 years later, with
players padded all over and protected by soldiers'
helmets.

'It's the worst writing I ever saw'
Mark Twain, *The Innocents Abroad*, ch.27 (1869)

This was the type of gambit employed by an American party when they wanted to get some amusement out of their guide in Italy. The guide was so used to foreign parties going into ecstasies at everything they were shown that he was completely thrown when Twain's party remained deliberately indifferent. When shown a specimen of the writing of Christopher Columbus they merely criticized it as a poor specimen of penmanship, driving the guide frantic in his efforts to explain the importance of Christopher Columbus.

'It was a famous victory'
Robert Southey, *The Battle of Blenheim* (1798)

It was indeed a famous victory, duly recorded in all the history books. Blenheim (Blindheim) was a Bavarian village where the British army, under the Duke of Marlborough, combined with the Austrians to defeat the French and Bavarians in 1704, to bring the War of Spanish Succession to an end. Nearly a hundred years later Southey presents an ironic view of the affair. He shows old Kaspar, a stolid, uncomprehending peasant, mouthing the conventional viewpoint of a great victory, and glossing over the terrible misery and slaughter involved. It is left to the innocent grandchild to comment on the evil of war.

'It was amusing to look round the filthy little scullery and think that only a double door was between us and the dining-room'
George Orwell, *Down and Out in Paris and London*, ch.12 (1933)

Orwell was working as a dish-washer and general slave in a big Paris hotel, 'a vast, grandiose place with a classical facade'. The contrast which tickled his fancy was that between the spotless diningroom and the filthy little room where the dishes were washed and the food prepared. The floor was a mess of soapy water, lettuce leaves, and trampled food, and there was a foul stink of food and sweat. The waiters would go straight from this muck and beastliness to the customers' diningroom, putting on their artificial servility as they passed through the double doors.

'It was a time of rapture'
William Wordsworth, *The Prelude*, Bk I (1850)

Wordsworth is writing of his childhood in the Lake District, when the winter evenings were often spent skating with his schoolfellows. 'All shod with steel / We hissed along the polished ice in games' their voices echoing across the lake. Sometimes he would leave the throng to skate by himself. Impressed by Nature, he would stop suddenly at the steep dark cliffs which still appeared to be moving past him. 'I stood and watched / Till all was tranquil as a dreamless sleep.' The poem was first completed in 1805 but was not printed until 1850, after his death.

'It was a word not to be mentioned to ears polite'
E. C. Gaskell, *Cranford*, ch.1 (1853)

The forbidden word was 'death'. In the narrow, refined, charming society of Cranford, a fictional Cheshire village (based on Knutsford, now a substantial town), which slumbered in peaceful gentility in the early nineteenth century, unpleasant things were not spoken of in public. Death and – what was almost as bad – poverty were quietly ignored. When a retired Army officer, Captain Brown, joined the almost exclusively feminine society of the village and spoke of being poor, everyone was so shocked that they resolved to ignore him – a decision that they were quite unable to adhere to.

'It was roses, roses, all the way'
Robert Browning, *The Patriot* (1855)

Based on no particular historical incident, the poem illustrates briefly (in six short stanzas) the rapid change which fortune can bring, and the fickleness of mobs. The first two stanzas tell of a popular hero cheered by a crowd who strew roses in his path and are ready to give him anything he wants. A year later fortune has turned, and the roses have changed to stones. The same mob of people now throng the place where a gallows is erected, waiting eagerly to see him hanged. Why his circumstances have altered we are left to guess, though there is a hint of 'misdeeds'.

'It was the best of times, it was the worst of times'
Charles Dickens, *A Tale of Two Cities*, ch.1 (1860)

Dickens is attempting to summarize the period in which his novel begins – the year 1775, some years before the French Revolution erupted. He is indicating that it was a time of unrest and of extremes: 'the age of wisdom, the age of foolishness, the epoch of belief, the epoch of incredulity'. It was a period which had some virtues, but even more vices; and he dwells more on the vices than the virtues. The rulers of both England and France believed that all was well, but much oppression and injustice prevailed, and political upheaval was near.

'It was the schooner Hesperus
That sailed the wintry sea'
H. W. Longfellow, *The Wreck of the Hesperus* (1841)

This is a ballad in traditional style based on the terrible shipwrecks that Longfellow had read about in the newspapers. The ballad tells how the skipper of the *Hesperus* set sail in bad weather with his little daughter. A storm struck the vessel, and although the skipper had boasted that he could weather the roughest gale, he presently died of cold and exposure, leaving his daughter fastened to the mast for safety. 'Then the maiden clasped her hands and prayed, that savéd she might be.' But no miracle was forthcoming, despite her prayers, and her body was found on the shore next morning, still lashed to the mast.

'It would never have occurred to old Jolyon that it was necessary to wear a look of doubt or defiance'
John Galsworthy, *The Man of Property*, ch.1 (1906)

Old Jolyon Forsyte, the senior member of the family, was in certain respects a typical representative of the well-to-do Victorian upper middle-class. Eighty years old, he had a patriarchal look and was very sure of himself. 'He held himself extremely upright, and his shrewd steady eyes had lost none of their clear shining. Thus he gave an impression of superiority to the doubts and dislikes of smaller men.' There was nothing basically haughty, however, about old Jolyon's apparent superiority. He had usually had his own way for so long that he took it for granted, but he was by no means devoid of affection, sympathy, or sensitivity. The character was based on Galsworthy's own father.

'I've a grand memory for forgetting'
R. L. Stevenson, *Kidnapped*, ch.18 (1886)

David Balfour is present when the King's factor (known as the Red Fox), engaged in evicting people of the Highlands from their property, is shot by a hidden Highlander. David is shocked; and when he realizes that his friend, Alan Breck, was close by the murderer when the shot was fired, he tries to question him. But Alan, himself a well-known Highland activist, will never give away a fellow Highlander and evades David's questions with complete sangfroid.

'I've been taking pills of one sort or another ever since I was eight years old'
Alan Ayckbourn, *Absurd Person Singular*, Act I (1972)

A small Christmas party is being held by Sidney and Jane. Sidney finds one of his guests, Eva, swallowing pills, and she explains that she needs them to keep her sane. She is even more distressed in the second Act, a year later, when the party is in her own home. Her husband has just told her casually that he is going to live with another woman, and Eva spends the whole of a hilarious Act attempting to commit suicide in various different ways, each time unsuccessfully. But in the third Act she has quite recovered, and her husband (still with her) has become the underdog. She no longer needs pills.

'I've got a little list'
W. S. Gilbert, *The Mikado*, Act I (1885)

Ko-Ko, the Lord High Executioner, has a list of people he would like to include among his victims if he should be called upon to act professionally, and who, he suggests, 'never would be missed'. People who have irritating laughs or unpleasant handshakes would suffer. So would praisers of all countries and ages but their own. Judicial humorists and people who try to be funny in private life would also come under the axe. Ignorant of modern racial and sexist ideas, Ko-Ko objected both to 'the nigger serenader' and to 'the lady novelist'. We must decide for ourselves what he meant when he condemned 'statesmen of a compromising kind'.

'I've kings enough below, God knows!'
Lord Byron, *The Vision of Judgment*, IXIV (1822)

Byron's satire against George III and his praiser, Robert Southey, tells of the King's right to enter Heaven being argued by Satan and the archangel Michael, who address each other with perfect courtesy. Their difference, Satan observes, is political, not personal. He adds that his desire to capture King George's soul for Hell is purely a matter of principle, for he already has plenty of kings in the lower regions.

'I viewed her with a world of admiration, but not one glance of love'
John Vanbrugh, *The Relapse*, II, i (1696)

Loveless, formerly an inconstant character, is now convinced that he has conquered his former weakness. To prove his point he tells his charming wife, Amanda, about a very handsome woman whom he recently noticed at the theatre without the least flutter of his heart. Amanda is none the less uneasy, and well she might be, for the handsome lady proves to be Berinthia, an old friend of hers, who soon comes to call. Berinthia is no angel, and Loveless's relapse is only a matter of time and opportunity. The play was a continuation of Colley Cibber's *Love's Last Shift* (1696).

'I was coming to that'
Robert Graves, *Welsh Incident* (1938)

The poem appears to be gently poking fun at the Welsh, hinting that they tend to spin out a simple story into a long one. The story-teller attempts to describe some mysterious creatures said to have come from the sea-caves near Criccieth. They were not like anything known, 'very strange, un-Welsh, utterly peculiar'. To various questions he replies, with assurance, 'I was coming to that', and this is also the last line of a poem which (we feel) could continue almost for ever if the storyteller had his way.

'I was exceedingly surprised with the print of a man's naked foot on the shore'
Daniel Defoe, *The Life and Adventures of Robinson Crusoe*, ch.11 (1719)

When Crusoe, wrecked on a desert island, had lived there alone for nearly a dozen years, he was alarmed one day to see a human footprint in the sand on a part of the island that he did not often visit. There was no sign of person or boat. After his initial fear, he persuaded himself that it was his own footprint; but measurement disproved this. In due course he realized that cannibal savages from a distant mainland very occasionally called at the further side of the island to kill and eat their victims.

'I was the last to consent to the separation: but the separation having been made ... the first to meet the friendship of the United States as an independent power'
George III, *Address to John Adams, first American envoy to Britain* (1776)

George III was a strong believer in the principle that the British Parliament had the right to legislate for the colonies. The attitude was in many ways shortsighted, as such men as Chatham and Burke insisted, though it was not against the feeling of the nation. But when the war was over and Britain had been forced to accept America's viewpoint, George showed himself a sensible loser, quite ready to heal the breach.

'I wear the chain I forged in life'
Charles Dickens, *A Christmas Carol*, Stave 1 (1843)

The ghost of Jacob Marley had come to give warning to his miserly old business partner, Ebenezer Scrooge. The ghost showed the heavy chain that he was doomed to carry about because of his greed and selfishness while he was alive. Scrooge was informed that, to help him to escape Marley's fate, he would be visited by three spirits: Christmas Past, Christmas Present, and Christmas Future. They duly appeared, and Scrooge was converted to benevolence with a speed and exuberance that belong essentially to a Christmas story, when critical faculties are taking a rest.

*'"I weep for you," the Walrus said:
"I deeply sympathize"'*
Lewis Carroll, *Through the Looking-Glass*, ch.4 (1871)

The Walrus and the Carpenter (in the story told to Alice by Tweedledee) invited some oysters to go for a walk, and then callously proceeded to eat them. Alice felt that she preferred the Walrus to the Carpenter because he was at least a *little* sorry for the poor oysters. But Tweedledee points out that in fact he ate more than the Carpenter. And when Alice changes her mind and decides that she likes the Carpenter best, Tweedledee insists that *he* ate as many as he could get. Alice is driven to the conclusion that there is not much to be said for either of them.

'I will arise and go now, and go to Innisfree'
W. B. Yeats, *The Lake Isle of Innisfree* (1890)

Innisfree, an island in Lough Gill, County Sligo, is taken by the poet as a symbol of escape from the complexities of modern life. He uses specific details of simple rural life to represent the peace of mind that he seeks – a simple hut of clay and wattles, nine bean rows, a hive for the honey bee. There he will find peace, which in imagination he sees as 'dropping from the veils of the morning'. Such calm, with the sound of the lake water gently lapping the shore, is continuously in his heart when he dwells in the harshness of the town.

'I will follow thee to the last gasp'
William Shakespeare, *As You Like It*, II, iii (c 1599)

The faithful old retainer, Adam, is offering to accompany his young master, Orlando, in his search for fortune. The old man, though approaching eighty, claims to be 'strong and lusty', but by the time the two have tramped to the middle of Arden Forest he has to be carried. There is a strong tradition that Shakespeare himself played the part. One of the dramatist's younger brothers, when an old man, vaguely recalled seeing his brother act in a play in which he was an old man too weak to stagger to a meal table. On this somewhat slender evidence Coleridge opined that Shakespeare was 'a very great actor'.

'I will give thy flesh unto the fowls of the air'
Bible, I Samuel, xvii, 44 (date uncertain)

This was the boast of the Philistine giant, Goliath, when he came forward to meet the youthful Israelite champion, David, in single combat. The result of the contest (a stone from David's sling lodging in Goliath's forehead) is usually regarded as the triumph of the weak over the strong. This is understandable but misleading. A small man armed with a revolver is not weaker than a big man armed with a stick. Catapults or slings were equivalent to revolvers in the days before gunpowder. Assuming that David was a practised sling-thrower, Goliath, unprotected by a visor, stood little chance against him so long as they remained separated by distance.

'I will have all my beds blown up, not stuffed'
Ben Jonson, *The Alchemist*, II, i (1610)

This is not a deliberate pre-vision of the twentieth-century inflated mattress but an extravagant dream of super luxury by Sir Epicure Mammon, one of Jonson's most effective characters. He has been promised untold wealth by two rogues posing as alchemists. The mere thought inspires Mammon to carry his ecstatic fantasies to wild extremes. His beds will be unbelievably soft, his food served in gold dishes studded with precious stones, his shirts made of silk as light as cobwebs. Even his mistresses will be virtuous wives bought from city merchants. Such pleasures are, of course, illusory, and they cost him all his money.

'I wish the good old times would come again ... when we were not quite so rich'
Charles Lamb, *Old China* (1823)

This is a rather startling comment to come from Charles Lamb, who was certainly never a plutocrat. But wealth is, of course, comparative. He puts the sentence into the mouth of his fictitious cousin Bridget (based on his sister, Mary). She is maintaining that they actually enjoyed pleasures more when it was something of a struggle to gain them. When, for instance, they had to stint themselves to buy an old copy of Beaumont and Fletcher's plays, or to squeeze into the cheap gallery seats at the theatre. But the keener enjoyment, as Lamb realized, was not due merely to poverty. It was also connected with youthful enthusiasm.

'I would advise every young man beginning to compose (i.e. write) to do it as fast as he can'
Samuel Johnson, in Boswell's *Journal of a Tour to the Hebrides* (1784)

Johnson was disputing with Dr Watson, an amiable Scottish Professor of Logic who was in favour of composing slowly for fear of adopting slovenly habits. Johnson's point was that if a writer gets into the habit of getting his ideas down on paper quickly, he can always revise them later to improve their accuracy. 'If a man is accustomed to compose slowly, and with difficulty, there is a danger that he may not compose at all, as we do not like to do that which is not done easily.' Johnson wrote (often at speed) a great deal that is worth reading, while Dr Watson wrote very little. The fact may help us to assess who gave the sounder advice.

'I would have History familiar rather than heroic'
W. M. Thackeray, *The History of Henry Esmond, Esquire*, Bk I (1852)

The story is supposed to be narrated by Henry Esmond, living in the eighteenth century. Esmond opens his narrative by asserting that royal personages are no different from anyone else. 'I think,' he says, 'that Mr Hogarth and Mr Fielding will give our children a much better idea of the manners of the present age in England, than the *Court Gazette*.' This is no doubt true, but in fact the novel has very little to do with the kind of low life dealt with by Hogarth and Fielding. Esmond himself is the son (supposedly illegitimate) of Viscount Castlewood, and the story, admirable though it is, concerns the aristocracy.

'Jam tomorrow and jam yesterday – but never jam today'
Lewis Carroll, *Through the Looking-Glass*, ch. 5 (1871)

Alice has been offered employment by the White Queen at the rate of twopence a week and jam every other day. Alice declines the offer, partly because (unlike most children) she does not like jam. It appears, however, that she would never receive jam anyway, for the rule did not allow for jam *today*. 'Today' was 'tomorrow' yesterday, of course, and will be 'yesterday' tomorrow. Alice found this rather confusing, but the White Queen explained that it was the result of living backwards – a typical Looking-Glass explanation, which left Alice as confused as before.

'John Brown's body lies a-mouldering in the grave But his soul goes marching on'
C. S. Hall, *John Brown's Body* (1860)

John Brown (1800–59) was a passionate opponent of slavery. In 1859 he launched an attack on Harper's Ferry, the site of an arsenal, as part of a plan of violence to free negro slaves. His small band was overpowered by a military force two days later. He was tried, found guilty of treason and murder, and hanged. Though his fanaticism may have been of little help to his cause, he was regarded in the North as a martyr, and *John Brown's Body* became a very popular marching song.

'Jokes came in with candles'
Charles Lamb, *Popular Fallacies*, XV (1833)

Lamb is opposing the proverb that invites us to rise with
the lark and lie down with the lamb. In particular he
questions the wisdom of going to bed at the same time as
sheep, which have nothing better to do. He suggests that
the seriousness of early literature may be due to the fact
that the ancients had to spend so much time in the dark.
Humour needs the light. A smile is meaningless in
darkness. Moreover, neither food, drink, nor even smoking can be properly appreciated without light. As for
reading, the candle is the only satisfactory form of light
for the purpose. Daylight offers too many distractions.

'Just for a handful of silver he left us,
Just for a riband to put in his coat'
Robert Browning, *The Lost Leader* (1845)

The youthful Browning is complaining rather bitterly
that the poet Wordsworth, now over seventy, does not
display the same republican feelings that he had held
earlier in life. Such naivety on Browning's part equals the
naivety with which the young Wordsworth had believed
that the French Revolution was heralding a blissful
dawn. The 'handful of silver' was probably the civil list
pension received by Wordsworth in 1842. The 'riband'
was doubtless the dignity of Poet Laureate. Browning's
implication that Wordsworth's views had been influenced by these awards had no basis in fact. Experience
of life usually tones down the idealistic exaggerations of
youth, and thus it was with Wordsworth. In later years
Browning admitted that the poem was written in his
'hasty youth'.

'Katerfelto, with his hair on end
At his own wonders, wondering for his bread'
William Cowper, *The Task*, Bk IV (1785)

Cowper was discussing the pleasure of reading about life
in the newspaper, seeing the busy world at a comfortable
distance in the 'folio of four pages'. Among the many
newspaper items were accounts of prominent figures of
the day. A notable one in London (1781–5) was Gustavus
Katterfelto, a German quack doctor who combined
empiric medicines with pseudo-scientific lectures and
conjuring tricks. He was a great showman and was very
popular in London when Cowper was engaged on *The
Task*, particularly when an influenza epidemic in 1782
gave him a good chance to peddle his nostrums.

'Kind hearts are more than coronets,
And simple faith than Norman blood'
Alfred Tennyson, *Lady Clara Vere de Vere* (1832)

About 150 years ago the nobility were often regarded
with a kind of awe, and Tennyson's youthful sentiment
was perhaps less trite than it may appear today. The poet
was just over twenty when he wrote this nine-stanza
poem, which reproaches the aristocratic but fickle Lady
Clara for trifling with the affections of a humble admirer,
who has been driven to commit suicide.

'King and Queen of the Pelicans we –
No other birds so grand we see'
Edward Lear, *The Pelican Chorus* (1871)

There is a simple story behind the nonsense of this poem. The daughter of the Pelican King and Queen agrees to marry the King of the Cranes, a very smart bird, who had easily won her heart with the help of a Crocodile's egg and a large fish-tart. The father and mother watch the pair fly off 'to the great Gromboolian plain', aware that they will probably not see their daughter again. None the less they repeat the chorus line 'We think no birds as happy as we', adding the characteristic Lear comment 'We think so then, and we thought so still!'

'The lady doth protest too much'
William Shakespeare, *Hamlet*, III, ii (*c* 1601)

The lady is the player queen in the playlet being performed before the King and Queen of Denmark, Claudius and Gertrude. The playlet has been arranged by Hamlet to imitate the suspected murder of his father by Claudius, who subsequently married the widow, Gertrude. The player queen is protesting (as Hamlet believes Gertrude did) that she will never marry again if her husband dies. Gertrude, herself guilty of marrying Claudius only two months after her husband's death, fails to see the implication, and merely criticizes the actress queen for excessive protestation.

'A lady with a lamp I see
Pass through the glimmering gloom'
H. W. Longfellow, *Santa Filomena* (1857)

The lady with a lamp was, of course, Florence Nightingale, whose nursing activities at Scutari during the Crimean War had ceased the year before. Such a splendid effort as hers was bound to arouse Longfellow's enthusiasm, for it fitted his philosophy to perfection. Picturing her carrying succour to the stricken soldiers, with the men kissing her shadow as she passed through the wards, he called her 'Saint Filomena'. Filomela (Philomela) is the classical and poetic name for a Nightingale.

'The last leaf upon the tree'
Oliver Wendell Holmes, *The Last Leaf* (1831)

This poem was suggested by the regular appearance in the streets of Boston, U.S.A., of an old man (reputed to have been a distinguished patriot in his time) who still dressed in eighteenth-century style, with cocked hat, knee breeches, and buckled shoes – the last leaf upon the tree of a former age. Younger people could not help smiling at his appearance as he wandered the streets, looking rather lost. But Oliver Wendell Holmes, in his early twenties, reflected that he himself might one day be in the same position as this elderly eccentric.

And if I should live to be
The last leaf upon the tree
In the Spring,
Let them smile, as I do now.

'Laugh and the world laughs with you;
Weep, and you weep alone'
Ella Wheeler Wilcox, *Solitude* (1883)

The theme of the poem is the loneliness which misery brings. People are happy to share your joys, but they have too many troubles of their own to want to be bothered with yours. And the final worry, death, is one that must inevitably be experienced by yourself. 'No man can help you die.' The poetess wrote a novel before she was ten, and was soon turning out a couple of poems a day. She regarded her work more seriously than most literary critics have done, but she did sometimes produce some effective lines – such as the above familiar quotation.

'The law is a ass'
Charles Dickens, *Oliver Twist*, ch. 51 (1838)

Often incorrectly quoted as 'the law's an ass'. Mr Bumble, first the bumptious and bullying parish beadle, afterwards master of the workhouse, ill-advisedly marries the matron of this establishment, who turns out to be more than a match for him. When he is told that in the eye of the law he is responsible for his wife's action he indignantly repudiates the law's assumption. 'If that's the eye of the law, the law is a bachelor!'

'The Law of Triviality ... means that the time spent on any item on the agenda will be in inverse proportion to the sum involved'
C. Northcote Parkinson, *Parkinson's Law* (1958)

This, Parkinson's second Law, suggests that any public finance committee will accept large expenditure items with little comment, largely through ignorance of the matter, but will quibble for hours over trifles. He instances a committee considering (for example) the introduction of an atomic reactor at a cost of ten million pounds. This, he suggests, would be accepted at once, as most members of the committee would not really know what a reactor is. But the erection of a bicycle shed at a cost of £350 would be discussed ad infinitum, as all the members would be familiar with bicycles and they all would think they knew how to save a few pounds.

'Learn to be wise, and practise how to thrive'
Ben Jonson, *Every Man in His Humour*, I, i (1598)

Knowell, an old gentleman whose 'humour', or special characteristic, is exaggerated concern for his son's welfare, has some similarity to Polonius, and may even have offered a hint or two to Shakespeare when he came to write or refurbish *Hamlet* a year or two later. Unlike Polonius, however, who gave his best advice to an intelligent son, Knowell tends to scatter his wisdom more indiscriminately. Here he is about to utter some very wise words on moderation in expenditure and dress. Unfortunately his admirable precepts are offered to his nephew, a fool who is unlikely to pay the least heed to them.

'Let Austin have his swynk to him reserved'
Geoffrey Chaucer, *The Canterbury Tales – Prologue* (c 1387)

Let St Augustine of Hippo work if he wants to (but leave other monks alone!). The point of view is that of the very worldly Monk, one of the pilgrims on the road to Canterbury. St Augustine (A.D. 345–430) had advocated that monks should engage in manual work. The Pilgrim Monk disliked work but was a great lover of hunting. He also dressed well and fed well. Chaucer's satirical portrait was probably drawn from life.

'Let it be a caution to myself not to love drink'
Samuel Pepys, *Diary* (17 September 1661)

The occasion was the unfortunate fall from grace of Pepys's former teacher at St Paul's school, Dr Crumlum (or Cromleholme). Ten years or so after leaving, Pepys and another ex-pupil paid a visit to their old school. The master was pleased to see them – so pleased that he drank their health rather too often. He then insisted on taking them to a tavern to while away the evening with a bottle of wine. Here the master met another acquaintance, and after sharing drinks with all three of his friends he became less sober than a schoolmaster should be, which 'did occasion impertinent discourse'. Pepys concludes regretfully, 'I confess my opinion is much lessened of him.'

'Letters of thanks, letters from banks, Letters of joy from girl and boy'
W. H. Auden, *Night Mail* (1936)

Written by a leading poet for a Post Office film about the night mail, the verse has the irregular rattling rhythm of the hurrying steam train 'shovelling white steam over her shoulder'. The journey takes the mail up to Scotland, with every possible kind of letter in the mail bags – bills, gossip, letters of condolence, official, chatty, clever, stupid, and the 'spelt all wrong'. People who are asleep in their homes while the train rattles on will soon awake.

    And none will hear the postman's knock
    Without a quickening of the heart.

This was the first poetic sound track written for a film, the director being John Grierson.

'Let the punishment fit the crime'
W. S. Gilbert, *The Mikado*, Act II (1885)

The 'object all sublime' of the Mikado, Emperor of Japan, is to make the punishments he metes out appropriate to the offence. Thus bores will be compelled to listen to tedious sermons, amateur vocalists obliged to sing to dumb waxworks, writers of graffiti in railway trains forced to ride on the buffers, and billiard players who cheat made to play 'with a twisted cue and elliptical billiard balls'. Gilbert's interest in Japan was aroused by a Japanese sword in his library falling to the floor while he was searching for an idea for his next play. It reminded him of a Japanese Exhibition then open in Knightsbridge.

'Let the young people mind what the old people say'
Jeffreys Taylor, *The Young Mouse*

The 'people' in this nineteenth-century children's poem are in fact four-legged ones with long tails. A young mouse, living with her mother in a small cupboard hole, ventures out into the big room one day. She returns full of excitement, having discovered a more luxurious residence with stout cat-proof wires, and a supply of food. Her mother, older and more experienced, points out that several mice had previously enjoyed that luxurious accommodation, but had not been seen again. Not surprisingly, for the desirable residence was, of course, a mouse-trap.

'Letting I dare not wait upon I would'
William Shakespeare, *Macbeth*, I, vii (1606)

King Duncan of Scotland has just entered the castle of Macbeth, one of his lords. Both Macbeth and his wife have previously thought of achieving the throne by way of Duncan's murder. Now that the opportunity offers, Macbeth is inclined to draw back. But Lady Macbeth, as always, eggs him on, accusing him of cowardice. Will he, she demands, be content to wish for kingship but be afraid to take the necessary steps to seize it, 'Letting ... would / Like the poor cat i' the adage' – a cat that wanted fish but was afraid to wet its paw.

'The liberty of the individual must be thus far limited: he must not make himself a nuisance to other people'
J. S. Mill, *On Liberty*, ch. 3 (1859)

Mill points out that although opinions are rightly freer than actions, even opinions must be subjected to some restraint. For example, we should be free to write in the press, if we believe it, that corn dealers are starvers of the poor, but we should not be free to express the same opinion orally to an excited mob in front of a corn dealer's house. We should be free to carry our opinions into practice provided that they do not molest other people.

'Liberty, what crimes are committed in thy name!'
Jeanne Manon Roland (8 November 1793)

Mme Roland was married to a French minister of the crown who later became a revolutionary. Their salon was a meeting place for many supporters of the coming insurrection. But the Rolands opposed the excesses of the wilder revolutionaries, and in 1793 Mme Roland herself was arrested and guillotined. Before her execution she bowed mockingly before the statue of Liberty, erected in the Place de la Révolution, and uttered her now famous apostrophe to it.

'A lie which is half a truth is ever the blackest of lies'
Alfred Tennyson, *The Grandmother* (1859)

An old lady, whose eldest son has just died at nearly seventy, looks back at her early life, telling the story of it to her granddaughter. In particular she recalls her cousin Jenny coming to stay, and slandering her to Willy, the man the grandmother was engaged to. Exactly what the half-lie was she does not tell her granddaughter, but the thought of it still makes her angry. She had it out with Willy, and he proved loyal to her. 'So Willy and I were wedded.' That was seventy years ago, and now not only Willy but all her children are dead too.

'Life is not a crossword puzzle, with an answer settled in advance'
Aldous Huxley, *Do What You Will – Swift* (1929)

Huxley is disagreeing with those who expect life to be like a competition, with a prize for the right answer. There are many answers, just as there are many people; and the best answers are those that permit the answerer to live most fully. Any answer will do as a working hypothesis if it serves its purpose effectively. Savages who imagine they are blood brothers to parrots may live efficiently in this belief, and are they any more absurd than those who think men are brothers to imaginary angels?

'Life is real! Life is earnest!'
H. W. Longfellow, *A Psalm of Life* (1839)

There is little doubt about the poet's general message in this *Psalm*, which is that we must put our shoulders to the wheel and do the best we can with our lives, for our time is short. The poet gave his verse the subtitle 'What the Heart of the Young Man said to the Psalmist'. The second stanza runs:
    Life is real! Life is earnest!
    And the grave is not its goal;
    'Dust thou art, to dust returnest',
    Was not spoken of the soul.
This is clearly a firm reply to the Biblical, 'Dust thou art, and to dust thou shalt return.' The Young Man's heart was in the right place, but his Biblical reference was not, for the saying comes not from the Psalms but from Genesis (iii, 19).

'The light fantastic toe'
John Milton, *L'Allegro* (1632)

The poet has called upon the goddess of Mirth, Euphrosyne, to bring him pleasant, joyous activities and delights, among which was dancing. The goddess is invited to 'trip it as you go / On the light fantastic toe'. Milton may have had particularly in mind the courante, a lively dance performed largely on tiptoe with jumping movements. It developed into the minuet, which was originally a sprightly dance.

'Listen, my children, and you shall hear
Of the midnight ride of Paul Revere'
H. W. Longfellow, *Tales of a Wayside Inn* (1861)

Paul Revere was a passionate rebel in the days when American states were British possessions. He was one of the leaders of the Boston Tea Party, when a group of anti-British citizens showed their objection to the tea tax by seizing a consignment of tea and throwing it into the harbour. But his most famous exploit was a desperate midnight ride from Charleston to Lexington (18–19 April 1775) to warn the townspeople that British troops were approaching. Longfellow told the story in rousing verse, with (it has been said) 'little attention to exactness of fact'. All the same it is a lively poem with a fine galloping rhythm.

'Literature cannot be the business of a woman's life, and it
ought not to be'
Robert Southey, *Letter to Charlotte Brontë* (1836)

Supporters of Women's Lib may perhaps gnash their teeth at Southey's pronouncement, but Charlotte herself felt no such indignation. Nor is this surprising, for the professional poet was merely making a point that was generally accepted in those early nineteenth-century days. Charlotte, at the age of twenty, had asked Southey for a frank opinion on some of her verses. He gave it kindly and carefully. He also gave her what is excellent advice for any poet: 'Write poetry for its own sake, not with a view to celebrity.'

'A literary man – with a wooden leg'
Charles Dickens, *Our Mutual Friend*, Bk I, ch. 5 (1864–5)

This unusual figure is Mr Silas Wegg, whose chief literary qualification is that he is able to read. For years he had kept a very primitive stall in a London street where he sold oddments of fruit or gingerbread, together with a few halfpenny ballads. Mr Boffin, who has unexpectedly come into an inheritance but cannot read, invites Wegg to come and read to him regularly, for a fee. The offer is accepted, and Mr Boffin is delighted to take into employment so distinguished a figure as 'a literary man with a wooden leg'.

'The little black cat with bright green eyes
Is suddenly purring there'
Harold Monro, *Milk for the Cat*

A poem which has long delighted the noble army of cat-lovers with its acute and accurate picture of a cat's five-o'clock tea. Remarkably, she knows exactly when tea-time is due, and 'all her lithe body becomes / One breathing, trembling purr'. The white saucer descends like a full moon, and the cat is in ecstasy as she 'buries her chin in the creamy sea'. Then she curls up in the arm-chair to sleep. Harold Monro was an influential figure in the world of poetry, founder of the *Poetry Review* (1911) and the Poetry Bookshop in Bloomsbury (1912).

'A little learning is a dangerous thing'
Alexander Pope, *Essay on Criticism*, Pt II (1711)

The poet is warning readers and critics against allowing ignorant pride to lead them to think they know more than they do. They should read widely: 'Drink deep, or taste not the Pierian spring.' (Pieria at the foot of Mount Olympus was the birthplace of the Muses.) The more you know, the more you realize how much more there is to know, just as a climber in the Alps sees more and more hilltops the higher he climbs. The line is often misquoted as 'A little knowledge is a dangerous thing.'

'The little more, how much it is'
Robert Browning, *By the Fireside* (1855)

The narrator asks his wife to go back with him in imagination to the Alpine gorge where their young love had blossomed. Their shared interests might have brought no more than friendship if he had been afraid to risk ending it by expressing a word of love. But he ventured the little more, and the result was the great love that had developed between them.

'A little more than kin, and less than kind'
William Shakespeare, *Hamlet*, I, ii (c 1601)

This riddling utterance, Hamlet's first words in the play, are in keeping with his subtle nature. He is referring (aside) to his stepfather and uncle, King Claudius. He implies that although the relationship between them is close ('more than kin') it is neither friendly nor natural. Hamlet already suspects Claudius of foul play towards his father, and in the next scene his suspicions are confirmed by the father's ghost.

'The little rift within the lute'
Alfred Tennyson, *Idylls of the King – Merlin and Vivien* (1859)

A song sung by the wily, deceitful Vivien to King Arthur's magician, Merlin, invites him to give her complete trust. A holding back of love or trust in just one matter will lead to complete lack of love or trust. It is the little crack in the lute that will gradually grow wider and wider until the lute becomes completely silent. What the wicked girl is really after is to get Merlin to tell her a certain charm which will enable her to imprison him by magic. After some delay, he is fool enough to do just this.

'Look thy last on all things lovely,
Every hour'
Walter de la Mare, *Farewell* (1918)

In this short but profound lyric the poet counsels us to look intently at lovely things as though we were seeing them for the last time. They have surely absorbed some of the beauty that was enjoyed by those who came before us. Will their beauty, he wonders, form a link with us when we are dead by similarly giving joy to those who come after us?

'Lord, what would they say
Did their Catullus walk that way?'
W. B. Yeats, *The Scholars* (1919)

Yeats is thinking of the men who so often edit and annotate poetry. He is struck by the contrast between the intensity of emotion which inspires a young man's passionate love poems and the sober solemnity with which 'old, learned, respectable bald heads' write conventional comments upon them. He wonders what would happen if they were suddenly faced with the real thing instead of the remote written word. Catullus (84–54 B.C.) was the author of passionate, sometimes venomous, and obscene love poems to his mistress, Lesbia.

'Love and murder will out'
William Congreve, *The Double-Dealer*, IV, vi (1694)

Mr Brisk, a coxcomb but no fool, desires to seduce Lady Froth, an affected but not unattractive woman. It does not suit him to blurt out his passion openly, especially as she and her husband are on affectionate terms. He therefore contrives that she shall come upon him when he is seemingly daydreaming. As he hears her approaching from behind, he cries out her name three times. When she asks what is the matter, he pretends to have been uttering his feelings aloud unconsciously. 'Love and murder will out', he declares, and the delicate topic of sexual desire is satisfactorily introduced.

'Love is not love
Which alters when it alteration finds'
William Shakespeare, *Sonnet 116* (1609)

A tribute to constancy in true love, which does not grow less as time passes. It remains steady, like a fixed star. The coming of old age, even, does not affect it. In some sonnets a development of ideas is shown, but here a single theme is repeated in several ways. It concludes:
    If this be error, and upon me proved,
    I never writ, nor no man ever loved.

'Love is to be avoided, because marriage is at best a dangerous experiment'
T. L. Peacock, *Gryll Grange*, ch. 12 (1861)

This was the view of Mr Falconer, a wealthy young man living comfortably on his own, with seven delightful young servants to wait on him. He would like to shun love, lest it should destroy his present contentment, and he instances a number of men whose marriages have brought little satisfaction: Socrates, Euripides, Cicero, Marcus Aurelius, Dante, Milton, and even Shakespeare. Peacock's novels are concerned more with conversation than with character study or action. But by the end of the book Mr Falconer is duly married to the charming (if talkative) Miss Gryll.

'Love's the noblest frailty of the mind'
John Dryden, *The Indian Emperor*, II, ii (1667)

Cortés, Spanish commander of an expedition against Mexico, is begged (according to this unhistorical drama) by the Aztec Indian emperor's daughter, with whom Cortés has fallen in love, to call off an attack upon the Aztecs. At first he refuses, but at length Love wins the day, and he agrees to sacrifice honour and duty. 'Men can but say Love did his reason blind', he consoles himself. But his submission to Love has come too late, and he finds that the battle has already begun.

'Love the sense of right and wrong confounds'
John Dryden, *Palamon and Arcite*, Bk III (1699)

Arcite is apologizing for his behaviour in this much-repeated story of two friends, Palamon and Arcite, who compete for the same lady. Chaucer told it in *The Knight's Tale*, which was in turn taken from Boccaccio. Fletcher, possibly with Shakespeare's help, dramatized it as *The Two Noble Kinsmen* (1613). In Dryden's version Arcite wins a jousting contest for Emilia, but is fatally injured immediately afterwards when his horse is frightened and throws him. Before dying he confesses that he had unfairly plotted against Palamon, partly excusing himself on the ground that Love confused his sense of right and wrong.

'The lowest and vilest alleys in London do not present a more dreadful record of sin than does the smiling and beautiful countryside'
A. Conan Doyle, *The Adventures of Sherlock Holmes* (1892)

In the story *The Copper Beeches* Holmes is engaged to protect the interests of Violet Hunter, newly employed as a governess at a large country house near Winchester. As the train passes through Hampshire Dr Watson remarks on the beauty of the scenery. But to Holmes, whose mind is concerned solely with evil doing, the isolated houses suggest only 'the impunity with which crime can be committed there'.

'Loyalties cut up against each other sometimes'
John Galsworthy, *Loyalties*, II, ii (1922)

That is the theme of this very tense and convincing drama. Captain Dancy, a reckless officer, is accused by a wealthy young Jew, De Levis, of stealing £1,000. The result is a conflict of loyalties in various directions. When evidence suggests that he is in fact guilty, some of his friends, including his solicitor, find that other loyalties (social or professional) cut across personal loyalty. Dancy's young wife is furious that anyone should doubt him for a moment. But her own loyalty to the idea of his innocence restrains him from escaping justice by fleeing the country, and in the end destroys him.

'Mad, bad, and dangerous to know'
Caroline Lamb, in her *Journal* (1812)

Caroline Lamb, wild and undisciplined wife of the unfortunate Viscount Melbourne, hearing of Byron's bad reputation with women, decided that it would be most unsafe to know him. She then pursued him recklessly. The handsome young poet endeavoured for a while to act the appropriate part, but at last grew tired of the affair after some violent episodes. Caroline at length relinquished him, and for a mad moment tried to console herself with the Duke of Wellington.

'Mad dogs and Englishmen
Go out in the midday sun'
Noel Coward, *Words and Music* (1932)

There was no plot in *Words and Music*; it was a revue made up of songs and sketches. But this song, making good-humoured fun of a certain type of Englishman, was given a colonial setting, with a couple of very English types sitting at a table with their glasses of whisky. For no obvious reason a missionary arrives in a rickshaw and at once bursts into song, describing the curious behaviour of the English in the heat, as compared with other races. Whereas 'Hindoos and Argentines sleep firmly from one to two', Englishmen, like mad dogs, go out of doors. It is a remarkable habit, the missionary sings, and even 'the toughest Burmese bandit / Can never understand it'.

'Maken vertu of necessitee'
Geoffrey Chaucer, *The Canterbury Tales* (c 1387)

In this story from *The Knight's Tale* Palamon and Arcite, two friendly Theban knights, both fall in love with Emily, sister-in-law of Duke Theseus. They agree to engage in a vigorous but unmalicious jousting match, the winner to marry Emily. Although Arcite is the victor, he soon afterwards suffers a fatal fall from his horse. Palamon and Emily both grieve over his fate, but Theseus points out that death is ultimately the end to which everyone comes. Therefore they may just as well make the best of things ('maken vertu of necessitee') and reflect that Arcite died in his moment of triumph instead of having to sink into old age and oblivion.

'A man cannot be too careful in his choice of enemies'
Oscar Wilde, *The Picture of Dorian Gray*, ch. 1 (1891)

It would be a mistake to take too seriously any epigram uttered by one of Wilde's witty characters. The speaker here, Lord Henry Wotton, is very much Wilde's own mouthpiece with a strong liking for saying the opposite to what is expected. In the first chapter of this unusual novel Wotton is being particularly Wilde-like. He has been accused of not understanding friendship, and is meeting the accusation with affected indignation. He chooses his friends for looks, his acquaintances for character, and his enemies for intellect, as he wants them to appreciate his own intellectual gifts.

'Man is Nature's sole mistake'
W. S. Gilbert, *Princess Ida*, Act II (1884)

This is the battle cry of the Women's Libbers of a hundred years ago. Professor Psyche is advising students on their duties at their Women's University, and adding a few words on a coarse, plain, half-witted thing called Man. The play was based firmly but facetiously on Tennyson's *The Princess*. Gilbert called it 'a respectful perversion'. Oddly enough, when Tennyson dealt seriously with the theme, the idea of women at a university was almost a joke. When Gilbert dealt jocularly with the same theme, women's colleges had at least been seriously founded.

'Man is not a reasoning animal'
J. H. Newman, *The Tamworth Reading Room* (1841)

In 1840 Sir Robert Peel (1788–1850) had made a gift of a reading room and library to the town of Tamworth in Staffordshire, which borough he represented in Parliament. In his address at the opening of the institution he referred to the good effects of a secular education upon the working classes. (This was many years before the Education Act of 1870 spread the education net wider.) Cardinal Newman used the occasion for a series of articles in *The Times*, written under a pseudonym, stressing his belief that faith was more important than reason – though he relied on reason in attempting to prove his case.

'A man must serve his time to every trade
Save censure – critics all are ready made'
Lord Byron, *English Bards and Scotch Reviewers* (1809)

Byron's first book of poems, *Hours of Idleness* (1807), issued while he was still under twenty, was rather contemptuously reviewed in the *Edinburgh Review*. Incensed by such criticism, Byron set out to show that he could be equally severe if he chose. His satire, *English Bards and Scotch Reviewers* hit out vigorously and effectively (but rather indiscriminately) not only at critics such as Jeffrey, editor of the *Edinburgh*, but also at a variety of other writers. Byron later admitted that some of his criticisms were unjustified and on too personal a level.

'Man's inhumanity to man
Makes countless thousands mourn'
Robert Burns, *Man Was Made to Mourn* (1786)

This poem was one of the earliest of Burns's printed verses. On a chill November evening he meets an aged man who delivers himself of what the poet rightly calls a dirge. The theme is 'the miseries of man' in general, and in particular the treatment by the rich of the poor. This complaint may well have been justified, but the example of a wretch who fails to get 'a brother of the earth to give him leave to toil' is not particularly compelling. In death the poor are the gainers, for to them death brings relief, whereas the wealthy are cut off by it from their pleasures.

'Man's love is of man's life a thing apart,
'Tis woman's whole existence'
Lord Byron, *Don Juan*, I, cxciv (1818)

As we are in medieval Spain, it is no doubt quite true that whereas a man can forget a broken heart in the everyday life of the Court or military camp, the conventions of the time confine a woman's experience largely to affairs of the heart. After her elderly husband has caught her in the act with a young lover, Donna Julia is banished to a convent, and writes a sad farewell to the youth. She foresees sadly that he will proceed to love many other women, and since the lover is the youthful Don Juan her prophecy is not far wrong.

'A man's reach should exceed his grasp,
Or what's a Heaven for?'
Robert Browning, *Andrea del Sarto* (1855)

The Italian artist Andrea del Sarto (1486–1531), known as 'The faultless painter', is presented here as talking about his life and art to his wife, Lucrezia. His technical skill is superb, yet he feels his deficiencies. He lacks the inspiration of the greatest painters, whose work has more soul than his own technically perfect pictures. Many fine painters are affected by praise or blame, while he himself remains unmoved. His work remains on one level, but he ought to be striving to rise above that level.

'The man that lays his hand upon a woman,
Save in the way of kindness, is a wretch
Whom 'twere gross flattery to name a coward'
John Tobin, *The Honeymoon*, I, ii (1804)

The Duke of Aranza, doubtless drawing inspiration from *The Taming of the Shrew*, decides to subdue his proud young wife by subjecting her to some humiliating treatment immediately after the wedding. He tells her that he is not really a duke at all, takes her to a humble cottage as their home, and proposes to keep her confined there. She scathingly suggests that he will probably beat her if she tries to escape. He repudiates the suggestion, and explains that he will thrash her only with his tongue. His treatment, it turns out, is as successful as Petruchio's with Katharina a couple of hundred years earlier.

*'The man thinks he's a hero and looks like a fool, and the
woman goes about with that damn-conceited look of having
got something for nothing'*
Harold Chapin, *The New Morality*, Act I (1920)

Betty, exasperated at seeing her husband, Ivor, dancing
attendance on a woman from a neighbouring houseboat,
goes across one very hot day and abuses her. Ivor later
protests that the friendship was purely platonic. Betty
has a cynical disbelief in platonic friendships. 'There's no
sort of friendship between you and Muriel. She's simply
run you down and cornered you, and you are trying to
make the best of it by calling the affair romantic names.'
This witty comedy, posthumously produced, underlines
the sad loss suffered by the theatre through the early
death of the author in the First World War.

'Man to command and woman to obey'
Alfred Tennyson, *The Princess* (1847)

King Hildebrand had definite and old-fashioned views
on sex inequality. A woman's place, he believed, was in
the home. 'Man for the field and woman for the hearth.'
He was angry that Princess Ida, who since childhood had
been affianced to his son, Hilarion, now repudiated the
agreement, having established a Women Only community in her father's kingdom. The disagreement is
eventually settled by a fierce tournament between fifty
men led by Hilarion, and fifty led by Ida's brother (for in
spite of her feminist views she does not object to having
men fight for her). In the end the Prince loses the contest
but wins Ida's love.

*'Man wants but little here below
Nor wants that little long'*
Oliver Goldsmith, *The Vicar of Wakefield*, ch. 8 (1766)

This modest sentiment occurs in a ballad which illustrates the virtues of the simple life. The poem, *The
Hermit, or Edwin and Angelina*, tells of a youth seeking
shelter in the dwelling of a hermit. The latter, a vege-
tarian, preaches the value of simple tastes. The youth
turns out to be a girl in male clothes. She had trifled with
the affections of an honest man, who had since gone
away in despair. Full of remorse, the girl is desperately
seeking him, fearful that he may be dead. But the ballad,
unlike most, has a happy ending. The hermit reveals that
he is the missing lover.

*'Man was born to wait
On Woman, and attend her sov'reign pleasure'*
John Tobin, *The Honeymoon*, I, ii (1804)

The speaker is Juliana, the proud, overbearing young
woman whom the Duke of Aranza proposes to marry.
The Duke appears so mild and patient that she confidently expects to rule the ducal roost, and on the
morning of the wedding she complains of his 'disobedi-
ence' in not turning up promptly for the ceremony. But
the Duke has merely been biding his time. He has
'prepared a penance for her pride', and deceives her into
thinking that she has got to knuckle down to being an
ordinary wife in a very ordinary home.

'Man was for the Woman made
And Woman made for Man'
Thomas Otway, *The Soldier's Fortune*, V, iii (1681)

A snatch of song sung by Sir Jolly Jumble, an old pander, in this bawdy, rough-and-tumble Restoration comedy. Its main theme is the cuckolding of Sir Davy Dunce who, being an elderly merchant, is fair game for the young disbanded soldier, Beaugard. Fair game, too, for the young author, not yet thirty, who had himself recently returned from soldiering in Holland. To him, no doubt, a man of sixty-five had indeed reached 'nauseous old age and unwholesome deformity'. Sir Jolly has brought Beaugard and young Lady Dunce together for a brief evening's pleasure, pointing out in song that 'youth's a flower that soon does fade'.

'The man who boasts that he has not experienced fear in war
or on a mountain is a liar'
F. S. Smythe, *Adventures of a Mountaineer* (1940)

No one had a better right than Smythe to an opinion on mountaineering. Not only was he a leading climber; he was also perhaps the leading writer and photographer on the subject of mountain climbing. He had scaled mountain peaks in many parts of the world, and was a notable member of three Mount Everest expeditions. Here he is referring to a climb made in Wales when he was still a boy. Trying to make an ascent with small and insufficient handholds, he looked down, and 'for the first time in my life I knew the meaning of fear'.

'A man who eats like a pig ought to look like a pig'
H. G. Wells, *The Truth about Pyecraft* (1903)

Pyecraft was very fat and anxious to reduce his weight without reducing his meals. The narrator of this amusing short story knew an old Indian weight-reducing recipe. The remedy – a very unpleasant one – worked perfectly, but it achieved its result literally. It reduced Pyecraft's *weight* but left him as fat as ever, like a balloon. He now had to live near the ceiling, causing serious difficulties in his domestic arrangements. The narrator was not very sympathetic, as his quoted opinion shows, but he did suggest a way of overcoming the problem – lead weights attached to underclothes!

'A man who would woo a fair maid
Should 'prentice himself to the trade'
W. S. Gilbert, *The Yeomen of the Guard*, Act II (1888)

Colonel Fairfax undertakes to show the jester, Jack Point, how to woo Elsie, the jester's young partner. Point is proposing to offer her jests, jibes, and quips, but Fairfax shows a different method of wooing – 'how to flatter, cajole, and persuade'. He does it so successfully that Elsie falls into his arms, to the dismay of the jester. Fairfax, rather unkindly, advises him to apply elsewhere the lesson he has been taught. But the unkindness is less than it appears, for, unknown to herself, Elsie is in fact already secretly married to Fairfax, through a curious chance.

'Many a worthy heart beats within a dusky bosom'
M. G. Lewis, *The Castle Spectre*, II, iii (1797)

The sentiment may be true, but the speaker is soon inclined to change his mind. He is Earl Percy, a captive in his enemy's castle, guarded by two African servants. He offers them a well-filled purse if they will allow him to escape. They accept the offer and the purse, but that is the end of the matter. They then assure him that they have no intention of keeping their promise to release him, and every intention of remaining faithful to their wicked master. Percy's earlier (quoted) thought changes to a regret that 'the only merit of these villains should be fidelity'.

'Marriages are made in Heaven, and if we once set to work to repair celestial mistakes and indiscretions we shall have our hands full'
Henry Arthur Jones, *The Liars*, Act I (1897)

Ned Falkner, a gallant, serious-minded African explorer, is deeply in love with flirtatious Lady Jessica who is married to a mannerless boor. Falkner is being lectured by Sir Christopher Deering, intended by the author to be a sensible, honest, broad-minded friend, though to most modern readers he will doubtless seem also something of an interfering prig. A great deal of fuss is made about an assignation for dinner between Falkner and Lady Jessica at a Thameside hotel, and in the end Falkner allows himself to be dragged off to Africa by Deering. The bright dialogue belongs to a forward-looking period, the period of Shaw and Maugham, but the moral outlook is mid-Victorian.

'Married in haste, we may repent at Leisure'
William Congreve, *The Old Batchelor*, V, viii (1693)

Heartwell, the Old Batchelor, tricked into a mock marriage with a lady whom he immediately afterwards believes to be a whore, laments to a friend that he has been married for two hours. 'Thus Grief still treads upon the heels of Pleasure', the friend observes, and adds the quoted sentence. Another character promptly adds a rider of his own:
Some by Experience finds these words misplaced:
At Leisure marry'd, they repent in haste.

'Marrying to increase love is like gaming to become rich'
William Wycherley, *The Country Wife*, IV, i (1672)

The result is that 'you only lose what little stock you had before'. Pert maids in Restoration Comedy are apt to be as witty as the fine gentlemen whose bribes they take, and Lucy is no exception. But her advice to her mistress is sincere and shrewd. She hates to see Alithea throw herself away on a foolish coxcomb. Alithea feels bound to honour her engagement to Sparkish, though she does not love him and rather doubtfully hopes that love will grow after marriage. Lucy scoffs at the idea, and wants her to throw over Sparkish, whose lack of jealousy is almost a disease, and to marry the fine gentleman, Harcourt, who keeps pressing her to do so.

'The maximum of danger means the minimum of pay'
F. W. Harvey, *Gloucestershire Friends – Ballad of Army Pay* (1917)

Most of the verses in this little book were written in a German prisoner-of-war camp. To their credit the prison authorities sent the manuscript back to England without alteration or obliteration. Many of the poems are simple reflections of Harvey's Gloucestershire days, but the present one has more than a touch of irony. The quoted line, repeated in each verse, stresses that the men undergoing the horrors of trench warfare are far worse paid than those doing executive and clerical jobs, or making munitions, or singing 'Keep the home fires burning' in music halls.

'May there be no moaning of the bar
When I put out to sea'
Alfred Tennyson, *Crossing the Bar* (1889)

Tennyson expresses the hope that all will be calm and quiet when he leaves port, and his ship crosses the sandbank across the harbour mouth. The theme is symbolical. He goes on to express the wish that there will be 'no sadness of farewell' when he crosses the bar of life and sees 'my Pilot face to face'. The sixteen-line poem was written during a ferry crossing from Lymington to Yarmouth, Isle of Wight. Tennyson expressed a wish that it would be placed at the end of all future editions of his works. Some years earlier Charles Kingsley had used the line, 'Though the harbour bar be moaning' (*The Three Fishers*). This might have been in Tennyson's mind.

'Men are but children of a larger growth'
John Dryden, *All for Love*, IV, i (1678)

In Dryden's version of the Mark Antony story, Antony, married to Octavia but enamoured of Cleopatra, has now decided to give up his mistress and return to his wife, thus bringing to an end the conflict between himself and Octavius Caesar (Octavia's brother). Afraid to tell Cleopatra himself of his decision, he deputes the task to his friend Dolabella. Yet even in the act of rejecting her he feels himself still drawn to Cleopatra, and almost changes his mind. Dolabella muses that men's feelings are as changeable as children's.

'Men may come and men may go,
But I go on for ever'
Alfred Tennyson, *The Brook* (1855)

The brook itself is speaking, describing how it perpetually winds its way down hills, under bridges, and through the fields 'to join the brimming river'. The thirteen stanzas making up the poem are usually printed in anthologies as if *The Brook* was a poem on its own, but in fact it belongs to a blank verse narrative poem about a young village girl and her simple love affair. She lived at 'Philip's farm where brook and river meet'.

'Men must work, and women must weep'
Charles Kingsley, *The Three Fishers* (1851)

After preaching a political sermon which was publicly repudiated by the local vicar, Kingsley calmed his angry spirit by composing a poem. His strong social conscience shows itself in a great deal of his work – here with the hardships endured by the seafaring folk of Devon, where he had spent his childhood. In verse 1 three fishermen go out to sea despite bad weather, 'for there's little to earn, and many to keep'. In verse 2 their wives watch and wait anxiously through the stormy night. In verse 3 'three corpses lay out on the shining sand'.

'The men that were boys when I was a boy
Shall sit and drink with me'
Hilaire Belloc, *The South Country* (1910)

These are the last two lines of a hymn of praise to Sussex. Belloc rejects the Midlands, the North, and the West of England, and turns his thoughts southward. Sussex is his home; he smells it in the pines, and loves its splendid scenery:
> And along the sky the line of the Downs
> So noble and so bare.
Fearing to be left on his own as he grows older, he determines to return to Sussex and gather his friends from Sussex men, who will share his interests and his affection for the Downs. Belloc, incidentally, was not a native of Sussex but was born in France.

'Men! The only animal in the world to fear'
D. H. Lawrence, *Mountain Lion* (1923)

By 'to fear' the poet means 'to be feared'; the poem is a condemnation, in very free verse, of man's slaughterous habits. While travelling in South America Lawrence meets two men in the lonely desert. Will they be friendly or dangerous? Luckily they are the former, but he reflects that if the meeting had been with a four-footed animal he would have had no cause for concern, for even wild ones rarely attack without provocation. Man is the only unprovoked killer. One of the men carried a dead mountain lion, and Lawrence, later seeing the animal's empty lair, was revolted at the senseless killing of a lovely living creature that was harming nobody.

'Merely corroborative detail, intended to give artistic
verisimilitude to an otherwise bald and unconvincing
narrative'
W. S. Gilbert, *The Mikado*, Act III (1885)

Believing that the Mikado, Emperor of Japan, is coming to the town of Titipu to find out why no executions have taken place recently, the local executioner (Ko-Ko) gets another official (Pooh-Bah) to support him in pretending that they have just executed a visitor named Nanki-Poo. Pooh-Bah graphically describes how the severed head politely bowed to him. When it turns out that Nanki-Poo is in fact the heir to the throne, and that they have made themselves guilty of a fearful crime, Ko-Ko turns on Pooh-Bah for his ridiculous story of the severed head. But Pooh-Bah defends himself with the quoted sentence.

'The mirth and fun grew fast and furious'
Robert Burns, *Tam O'Shanter* (1791)

Nowadays the line is likely to be applied to a lively evening party, but in Burns's poem it has a more sinister application. It describes the dancing antics of devil-worshipping witches in the churchyard at Kirk Alloway one midnight. Tam, half drunk, steals upon them and watches their activities. Excited by the appearance of a young witch in a 'cutty sark' (short shift), he foolishly disturbs them with a shout, and only just escapes their clutches. His horse is less fortunate and loses its tail.

'Moon-washed apples of wonder'
John Drinkwater, *Moonlit Apples* (1917)

This is a simple descriptive poem skilfully conveying a strange, almost eerie atmosphere. The apples are lying in rows on the attic floor. Everyone is asleep as the moon's rays pour through the skylight and dapple the apples 'with deep-sea light'. A cloud momentarily blots out the light; but soon the apples once more gather 'the silver streams' from the moon. There is no sound in the house except for a brief scratching of mice. 'Deep is the silence / On moon-washed apples of wonder.'

'The most goodliest Prince that ever reigned over the Realme of Englande'
Edward Hall, *Chronicle* (1542)

This high praise relates, ironically, to one of the vilest of English kings. Hall's *Chronicle* (so-called for short) had a lengthy title page indicating that his purpose was to show how the union of the families of York and Lancaster had culminated in the reign of wonderful King Henry VIII. As that infamous monarch was still alive, and pretty free with the axe, Hall was no doubt wise to be thus eulogistic. The quoted passage described Henry as he had appeared at the meeting of the French and English kings at the notable Field of the Cloth of Gold in 1519, at which early time the young king had (however misleadingly) truly seemed to be the personification of splendour and charm.

'Most of our world are at present possessed of an opinion that visions and miracles are ceased'
Izaak Walton, *The Life of Dr John Donne* (1640)

Walton's rather reluctant admission was occasioned by a story that he tells about Donne. Donne's wife was pregnant at a time when he was morally obliged to leave her for a couple of months to accompany a very generous friend to Paris. Two days after their arrival Donne was said to have seen a vision of his wife walking past with a dead child in her arms. It turned out (according to the possibly embellished tale) that Mrs Donne was delivered of a dead child at that very hour. Wisely, perhaps, Walton, though a believer himself, comments: 'I am well pleased that every reader do enjoy his own opinion.'

'Mouths without Hands, maintain'd at vast Expense;
In peace a charge, in War a weak Defence'
John Dryden, *Fables Ancient and Modern* (1700)

Dryden is using ancient fables to have a smack at modern political opponents. This story is adapted from Boccaccio. Cymon has been captured by the people of Rhodes, whose army, however, appears to bear a close resemblance to the militia of seventeenth-century London. The poet satirically portrays this body as more of a liability than a defence. They trained once a month, and were always at hand – except when needed.

> Drawn up in Rank and File they stood prepar'd
> Of seeming Arms to make a short Essay,
> Then hasten to be Drunk, the Business of the Day.

'The Moving Finger writes; and having writ, moves on'
E. Fitzgerald, *The Rubáiyát of Omar Khayám* (1859)

Fitzgerald's very free translation, or transmutation, of the Rubáiyát (quatrains) of an eleventh-century Persian poet has become one of the great classics of English verse, clothing a spirit of sceptical rationalism in superb rhythmical language. The quotation (from Stanza 51) asserts that whatever Fate has in store for us must be accepted, and that nothing can alter what has already taken place. Neither virtue nor intelligence can cancel what has been written in the book of Fate, 'Nor all thy tears wash out a word of it'.

'Much have I travelled in the realms of gold'
John Keats, *On First Looking in Chapman's Homer* (1816)

Keats compares his reading of literature to the adventures of an explorer in South America, where a great deal of gold was discovered. When he came to read Homer (in the translation by the Elizabethan poet George Chapman) it was as if he had discovered a wonderful new land – just as 'stout Cortez' must have felt when he first discovered the Pacific Ocean and gazed upon it, 'silent upon a peak in Darien'. Keats was better at poetry than at history, for it was not Cortez himself but one of his men (Balboa) who first saw the Pacific, nor was he silent on the occasion.

'The multitude, that seldom know anything but their own
opinions, speak that they would have'
Beaumont and Fletcher, *Philaster*, I, i (c 1610)

The belief that mobs are both ignorant and prone to wishful thinking is put forward by Dion, a lord at the Sicilian court. He is under the impression that the citizens are in favour of a match between the King's daughter and the Prince of Spain. He himself is opposed to the match and hence scornful of the 'multitude'. But towards the end of the play the citizens, in fact, take the Prince of Spain prisoner, and show themselves hostile to the intended match. Dion then speaks of them as 'brave fellows ... my fine dear countrymen'. Though not intended by the authors as such, he appears to be a typical politician.

'Murder will out, that see we day by day'
Geoffrey Chaucer, *The Canterbury Tales* (c 1387)

The Nun's Priest's Tale relates how Chauntecleer, a handsome cock, tells his chief wife, Pertelot, of the dreams he has been having. He takes them to be a warning not to leave his safe perch and strut around the yard. In an effort to convince her he reminds her of a well-known story of a man who dreamt that his friend had been murdered and his body hidden in a cart near a certain gate. He went to the spot, saw a similar cart, and insisted on searching it. The body of his murdered friend was discovered there. Pertelot, alas, dismissed his belief that dreams were shown to be prophetic, and thus led him to be caught by a lurking fox.

'The muscles of his brawny arms
Are strong as iron bands'
H. W. Longfellow, *The Village Blacksmith* (1842)

Blacksmiths are now a dying breed, but not so many years ago every village had its smithy. No one typified honest skilled labour more than the powerful smith, or performed his work more openly.

Children coming home from school

Look in at the open door.

Longfellow's blacksmith is a religious man who goes to church every Sunday and listens to his daughter singing in the choir. Brawny and muscular though he is, he is also a sentimental fellow, wiping a tear from his eye when he thinks how much her voice resembles that of her dead mother.

'Music has charms to soothe a savage breast'
William Congreve, *The Mourning Bride*, I, i (1696–7)

This is the opening line of the play, spoken by the heroine, Almeria. But in spite of its power to soothe savages, music (which is sounding softly as the curtain rises) is unable to assuage her grief. This is hardly surprising for, among other troubles, she believes her husband to have been drowned on the very day of their secret wedding. The soft music at the rising of the curtain would have been played by violins, which then formed the main part of the orchestra at both of the two London theatres.

'My blood is up, and I have the strength of ten such men
as you'
Charles Dickens, *Nicholas Nickleby*, ch. 13 (1838–9)

This is the speaker's response to the intended flogging of a wretched lad named Smike at Mr Squeers's dreadful school. Squeers starts to thrash him savagely when his young assistant, Nicholas, cries 'Stop!' This interference is rewarded by a blow with the cane across the young man's face, whereupon he seizes the cane and proceeds to thrash the schoolmaster. The episode is a joy, but one cannot help wishing that the great novelist had allowed his hero to talk in language less like that of an actor sending up the old Lyceum melodramas: 'Look to yourself, for by Heaven I will not spare you!'

'My first impressions of people are never wrong'
Oscar Wilde, *The Importance of Being Earnest*, Act II (1895)

There is amusing dramatic irony in Gwendolen Fairfax's self-assured assertion. Her first impression of young Cicely Cardew is favourable. ('I like you already more than I can say.') A few minutes later, however, her impression has drastically changed, for it appears that Cicely and Gwendolen are both engaged to the same man. The breach is healed only by the discovery that there has been a mistake in identity, and that the man loved by Cicely is not, after all, Gwendolen's fiancé. The trouble has arisen because both men (for different reasons) have called themselves Ernest, whereas one is really Jack and the other Algernon.

'My heart aches, and a drowsy numbness pains
My sense, as though of hemlock I had drunk'
John Keats, *Ode to a Nightingale* (1819)

The poem was suggested by the continued song of a nightingale that had built its nest close to the house where Keats was living. The birdsong often put him into a trance of delight as he listened to it. It was as though he was being drugged by the lovely notes of the bird as it 'singest of summer in full-throated ease'. Benjamin Haydon, the artist, recorded that 'as we were walking one evening in the Kilburn meadows, he repeated it to me, before he put it to paper, in a low, tremulous undertone, which affected me extremely'.

'My name is Norval: on the Grampian hills
My father feeds his flocks'
John Home, *Douglas*, Act II (1756)

But his name is not really Norval, nor is the shepherd his father. Norval is really a Douglas, who had been abandoned as an infant by his wicked grandfather, and found and adopted by a shepherd. The Douglas family were certainly not favoured by Fate. Norval is killed by his stepfather after a misunderstanding, and his mother then throws herself over a cliff. This Scottish play created a tremendous sensation in Edinburgh, where an enthusiastic playgoer bawled, 'Where's your Wully Shakespeare the noo!' It remained a popular play for many years.

'My name is Ozymandias, king of kings:
Look on my works, ye mighty, and despair!'
P. B. Shelley, *Ozymandias* (1817)

Ozymandias is one of the Greek names for Rameses II of Egypt. The object to be looked upon is the ruin of a colossal statue. The lines are a paraphrase of an inscription on a ruined Egyptian temple recorded by a Greek scholar of the first century. The ironic contrast between the former grandeur and later ruination so impressed Shelley that he took the paraphrase as the basis for a sonnet that is one of the most straightforward he ever wrote, and one of the best. The sonnet concludes:
Nothing beside remains. Round the decay
Of that colossal wreck, boundless and bare,
The lone and level sands stretch far away.

'My object is not to make fanatics, but to train up the lower classes in habits of industry and piety'
Hannah More, *Letter to the Bishop of Bath and Wells* (1801)

Some people may feel indignant at the quoted statement, but Miss More's activities must be seen against her own background, not against ours. She was explaining to a prominent prelate that her desire to offer some simple religious and practical instruction to poor children was not inspired either by a desire to undermine the influence of the clergy or by a wish to imitate the excesses of the recent French Revolution. She had been accused of both objectives, and was strongly opposed by those people who did not want the poorer classes to have any education at all.

'My sand is sinking, and I shall traverse old love's domain never again'
Thomas Hardy, *At Castle Boterel* (1913)

Hardy has revisited the place where he had met his first wife forty years earlier. They had just alighted from the chaise, and the brief feeling of ecstasy, though it lasted but a minute, would remain in his mind 'till hope is fled'. He knows he will never again visit the spot, for his time is running out, as the sand runs through an hourglass. It is perhaps symbolic of Hardy's attitude to life that it was drizzling with rain on his early visit to Castle Boterel (Boscastle) and raining again on his last.

'My sole object in writing was to preach to boys'
Thomas Hughes, *Tom Brown's Schooldays*, Preface to Second Edition (1861)

Some readers of Hughes's famous school story, although admiring the book, had complained that the great fault of it was 'too much preaching'. Hughes refused to accept the criticism as valid. 'I can't see that a man has any business to write at all unless he has something which he thoroughly believes and wants to preach about.' Hughes wished to show up school abuses and at the same time hold up the headmaster as a great Christian figure. A novel thus setting out to be a sermon could very easily have become as soggy as a lump of dough. Yet *Tom Brown's Schooldays*, while achieving its aim, remains after more than 120 years one of the most robust and readable books ever written on school life.

'My soul, like to a ship in a black storm, Is driven, I know not whither'
John Webster, *The White Devil*, V, vi (1608)

Vittoria Corombona is the White Devil in this wild but powerful play, though she is in fact less devilish than the chief male villains. Indeed, there is little to choose between the supposedly black and the supposedly white. Vittoria has just been stabbed, along with her brother and her maid, and her soul is about to start on its journey from the body – presumably downward. Their murderer is promptly shot, and the play ends with a character uttering the appropriate words: 'Remove the bodies'. Six of the chief male characters are corpses, and three out of four of the women. (The fourth goes mad.)

'Mysteriously united in spite of all their differences, they had taken arms against a common peril'
John Galsworthy, *The Man of Property*, ch. 1 (1906)

The Forsytes were a family of mixed characters and attitudes, but a curious family feeling gave them a certain unity, especially when someone alien to the group was present. The first chapter of the novel portrays an 'At Home' at the house of Old Jolyon, the senior member of the family, to celebrate the engagement of his grand-daughter June to Philip Bosinney, a young architect with views and temperament utterly different from those of the careful upper-middle-class Forsytes. Many of the Forsyte characteristics were shrewdly taken from members of the author's own family of uncles, aunts, and cousins.

'Nature red in tooth and claw'
Alfred Tennyson, *In Memoriam*, lvi (1850)

The allusion is to the savagery found in all Nature. The poet's mood here has a note of despair in it. 'Are God and Nature then at strife?' he wonders, brooding on Nature's seeming indifference towards man. Is Man, 'with such purpose in his eyes', doomed after all to disappear from the earth, and become of even less significance than the prehistoric monsters which once occupied it? The poet longs for the voice of his dead friend, Arthur Hallam, to set his doubts and fears at rest.

'Never in the field of human conflict has so much been owed by so many to so few'
Winston Churchill, speech to the House of Commons (20 August 1940)

The 'few' were the R.A.F. fighter pilots in the Second World War who broke up the heavy air attacks on Britain though the German bombers and fighters were far more numerous. The 'many' were the people of Britain. In his speech Churchill (recently made Prime Minister) voiced 'the gratitude of every home in our island'. It is worth noting that his famous words were spoken not, as is often supposed, at the close of the Battle of Britain but in its early stages. The battle lasted roughly from 8 August to 31 October, the most crucial day being 15 September.

'Never send to know for whom the bell tolls; it tolls for thee'
John Donne, *Devotions* (1624)

The bell is the funeral bell, and Donne is indicating that it tolls not merely for the dead person but for all mankind. After a serious illness in 1623 Donne wrote a series of *Devotions*. In one of these ('Meditation 17') he puts forward the view that men are not separate but are joined in a common humanity. 'No man is an island; every man is a piece of the continent.' Just as Europe is diminished if a small part of it is washed away, so mankind is diminished when one man dies, for we are all involved in mankind.

'New words had terror and fascination for him'
H. G. Wells, *The History of Mr Polly*, ch. 1 (1910)

Mr Polly was something of a modern Malaprop. He found it hard to resist the attraction of fine words, but equally hard to know how to pronounce them. He therefore developed the habit of deliberately mixing up words and mispronouncing them, so that people would think the habit was due not to ignorance but to whim. He was inclined, too, to think of fine but muddled phrases to attach to people and happenings. 'Eloquent Rhapsodooce', 'The High Egrugious', 'choleraic disposition', 'the Shoveacious cult' – these are specimens of his 'urgent loogooobuosity'.

'A niece is so safe – however good you are at statistics, you can't really prove anything'
A. A. Milne, *Belinda*, Act I (1918)

As there are two men paying court to Belinda and one of them is a statistician (a horrible word to pronounce, as Belinda discovers) the point is of some significance. Belinda may look no more than thirty, but when her almost-grown-up daughter arrives from finishing-school the pretence is hard to maintain. So Delia agrees to be a niece instead, in this thin but pleasing comedy.

'The night we went to Birmingham by way of Beachy Head'
G. K. Chesterton, *The Rolling English Road* (1914)

The curiously winding nature of the country lanes of England suggested to Chesterton, a humorous lover of wine and beer, that they must have been planned by 'a rolling English drunkard', staggering from side to side. With cheerful exaggeration he pictured a journey to the Sussex Downs that first wandered up to the Midlands. Even greater exaggerations follow ('The night we went to Bannockburn by way of Brighton Pier'), but the keynote of the poem is an optimistic outlook on life.

> But there is good news yet to hear and fine things
> to be seen,
> Before we go to Paradise by way of Kensal Green.

Kensal Green is a north-western suburb of London notable for its two adjoining cemeteries.

'No aspirant was ever more eager to go to Court than More was to avoid it'
Erasmus, *Letter to Ulrich von Hutten* (23 July 1519)

This distinguished Dutch scholar writes a long letter giving a detailed account of Sir Thomas More, the great humanist of Henry VIII's time. Erasmus knew him well and calls him 'the sweetest of all friends'. After describing his appearance, he refers to More's natural and easy manner, his dislike of formality, his cheerful disposition, and his integrity as a judge. Although More was reluctant to be too much involved in public life, he was dragged to the Court by the King who liked to be surrounded by intelligent men. Of More, Henry was 'so fond that he will scarcely ever let him go'. Erasmus was not to know that sixteen years later the affectionate King would have his favourite beheaded because More's integrity would not be broken to suit Henry's pleasure.

'The noble King of Brentford
Was old and very sick'
W. M. Thackeray, *The King of Brentford's Testament* (1855)

The King was in fact so sick that he sent for his lawyer
and made his will. The ballad tells us that he had two
sons. The elder, Thomas, was sober, cautious, and
industrious. The younger, Ned, was careless, extravagant, and idle. The King died and his will was duly read: it
stated that he had confidence in Tom but none in Ned,
and that the whole estate was therefore left to Thomas.
But then came the sting:

> I leave to you, my Thomas –
> To you IN TRUST for Ned . . .
> Poor Edward knows but how to spend,
> And thrifty Tom to hoard;
> Let Thomas be the steward then,
> And Edward be the lord.

'Nobody told him anything, he had to find out everything
for himself'
John Galsworthy, *The Man of Property*, ch. 3 (1906)

James Forsyte, seventy-five years of age, father of
Soames (the Man of Property), was a natural worrier,
always tending to foresee trouble, and always suspecting
that other members of his family were keeping information from him. 'Nobody tells me anything' was his
frequent complaint, and a slight deafness accentuated
his uncertainties. In this chapter he is greatly concerned
at what looks like the possible break-up of his son's
marriage, a scandal that would be hard for a Forsyte to
bear. Yet neither his daughter-in-law nor Soames mentioned the matter. He was left in the dark to worry about
it. 'Nobody tells me anything.'

'No dishonest desire to be a woman of the world'
William Shakespeare, *As You Like It*, V, iii (c 1599)

In Elizabethan times a woman of the world was not, as
might be thought, a courtesan but simply a married
woman. Audrey, the country wench, is about to be
married to Touchstone, the court jester, and makes no
secret of her desire for the married state. There is nothing
dishonest (immodest) in her longing for a wedding ring,
but she has not chosen her husband very wisely, for
Touchstone was looking for an escape route from matrimony even before the wedding ceremony.

'No kind of traffic would I admit'
William Shakespeare, *The Tempest*, II, i (1611)

Gonzalo, a worthy lord and a bit of a bore, is holding
forth about the sort of land he would rule if he ruled the
magic island where he and his companions have been
cast away. He is not, however, talking about vehicle
congestion in a crowded city. To Elizabethans, 'traffic'
meant the buying and selling of goods, and in Gonzalo's
Utopia that kind of thing is barred. Some of his regulations seem a little strange (no use of metal, corn, and
wine), while others are somewhat idealistic ('riches,
poverty, and use of service none'). Gonzalo had doubtless been reading Montaigne's *Essays*.

'No limit but the sky'
Cervantes, *Don Quixote*, Pt I, Bk iii, ch. 3 (1605)

Nowadays we say 'the sky's the limit' to mean that there
are no limitations to a given undertaking. Cervantes,
however, used the term in a very literal sense. Don
Quixote and his 'squire', Sancho Panza, had stayed at an
inn. They romantically regarded it as a noble castle and
refused to pay on leaving, for there was no record of the
Knights in days of Romantic Chivalry having to pay for
hospitality. Some lodgers at the inn had a less romantic
way of looking at the matter. They dragged Sancho off
his ass and put him in a blanket. Since the place they
were in had too low a roof for their purpose, they took
him out into the yard, 'which had no limit but the sky',
and there they tossed him to their heart's content.

'"No love," quoth he, "but vanity, sets love a task like that"'
Leigh Hunt, *The Glove and the Lions* (1836)

The task was set by a lady of the Court of Francis I of
France in the sixteenth century. The cruel sports of the
time included lion fights, and the lady, to test the valour
of her lover the Count de Lorge, deliberately dropped
her glove into the arena. The Count boldly sprang into
the midst of the lions to retrieve it, but instead of
handing it to her with a polite bow he threw it in her
face. Francis I thoroughly approved of the action, as the
last (quoted) line of the poem indicates.

'No man is a match for a woman, except with a poker and a pair of hobnailed boots. Not always even then'
George Bernard Shaw, *Man and Superman*, Act IV (1903)

The basic theme of Shaw's brilliant comedy is that the
Life Force, expressing itself through woman's desire to
mate and reproduce, inevitably domesticates man, overcoming the male desire for freedom. The quoted speech
illustrates this theme. It also reveals the fear of Jack
Tanner, the eloquent hero of the play, that this fate is
about to happen to him, and that the charming but
devious Ann Whitefield will ultimately entrap him. He
indicates to Ann's simple-minded mother, half seriously,
half cynically, that male dominance cannot really match
feminine subtlety.

'No Mask like open truth to cover Lies'
William Congreve, *The Double-Dealer*, V, iv (1694)

Maskwell, the double-dealer of the play, has an ingenious way of hiding his villainies. He openly tells his
victims what he proposes to do, but presents the truth in
such a way that they fail to understand it. In this brief
scene (a soliloquy rounded off with a couplet) he is about
to trick the hero, Mellefont, who believes him to be a
sincere friend, into helping Maskwell to run off with
Cynthia, to whom Mellefont himself is engaged. But by
the end of the play the truth no longer serves to hide
villainy, and Maskwell is at length unmasked.

> ### 'No monarch but would give his crown
> ### His arms might do what this has done'
> Edmund Waller, *On a Girdle* (1645)

The girdle has encircled the waist of his sweetheart. Give me that which that girdle enclosed, the poet says charmingly but extravagantly, and you can have whatever else the world holds.

> Give me but what this ribband bound,
> Take all the rest the sun goes round.

Many of Waller's best verses, including this, were addressed to 'Saccharissa', who was Lady Dorothy Sidney (a descendant of the great Sir Philip). They were addressed in vain, however, for she married somebody else – and so did he.

> ### 'None but the brave deserves the fair'
> John Dryden, *Alexander's Feast* (1697)

The poem was written for a musical society in honour of St Cecilia, the patron saint of music. In the late seventeenth century it was the custom in London to have an annual service on her day (22 November), followed by entertainment. The ode written by Dryden for the occasion in 1697 was his second ode in her honour. It opens by portraying Alexander the Great ('Philip's warlike son') sitting in state with his beautiful courtesan at his side. The musician Timotheus proceeds to sing:

> Lovely Thais sits beside thee,
> Take the good the gods provide thee!

Alexander accepted the advice, and 'at length with love and wine at once opprest' he 'sunk upon her breast'.

> ### 'No one can learn by the experience of another, because no
> ### circumstances are quite the same'
> W. Somerset Maugham, *The Circle*, Act III (1921)

Lord Porteous is talking to Lady Kitty, with whom he had eloped thirty years earlier, braving the disapproval of the Society of those days. Since Kitty had been married to another man, and since Lady Porteous refused to divorce her husband, Porteous and Kitty had been unacceptable to London Society and had had to live abroad, among broader-minded but less distinguished people. It was in many ways an unsatisfactory life, and when Elizabeth, the wife of Kitty's son, proposes to do just what Lady Kitty did, the latter and Lord Porteous try to dissuade her. Their attempt fails, and Porteous then sensibly reflects that no two situations are really alike.

> ### 'No one ever wished it longer than it is'
> Samuel Johnson, *Lives of the Poets – Milton* (1779)

Johnson paid many tributes to Milton's epic, *Paradise Lost*. 'He has interwoven the whole system of theology with such propriety that every part appears to be necessary ... There is perhaps no poem, of the same length, from which so little can be taken without mutilation ... In Milton every line breathes sanctity of thought.' Having praised the poem highly, Johnson then honestly admitted that he found the perusal of it a duty rather than a pleasure; and only passionate Miltonians, perhaps, would disagree with his quoted verdict.

'No Right! No Wrong! All's perfect, evermore'
John Betjeman, *The Planster's Vision* (1945)

A satire on the totalitarian attitude to humanity, a
'planster' (a word of Betjeman's own, doubtless formed
by analogy with 'punster') being a person who carries
planning to excess. 'Cut down that timber' is his first
demand, the ruthless felling of woods being a characteristic activity of those who plan vast new estates. There
are too many churches, too many small cottages. 'In
future,' the planster seems to say, 'the people will live in
enormous blocks of flats where they can be kept under
control, and they will be constantly reminded by boom-
ing radio voices that they now live in a perfect world'.

'No sooner are we ... acquainted with the laws of nature, than we frame to ourselves the idea, by the aid of some invisible ally, of suspending their operation'
William Godwin, *Lives of the Necromancers – Preface* (1834)

Godwin, father-in-law of Shelley and an influential
writer on social and political ideas, is here dealing with
the supernatural. The purpose of his book, he says, is 'to
exhibit a fair delineation of the credulity of the human
mind', and he tells briefly the stories of numerous
conjurors and sorcerers. The term 'necromancers' is
incorrectly used, for it strictly applies only to magicians
specializing in calling up spirits of the dead. Godwin
covers a much wider field, including almost anyone
connected with magic or witchcraft, from the ancient
oracles to the end of the seventeenth century.

'Nothing is so delightful as to sit down in a country village in one of Miss Austen's delicious novels'
M. R. Mitford, *Our Village* (1824)

Miss Mitford was praising the virtues of books covering a
strictly limited locality, in order to show why her own
sketches of simple village life need not be scorned. Jane
Austen's novels, all quite recent, gave good support to
her theme. Her other literary instances were Gilbert
White's Selborne, Robinson Crusoe's desert island, and
the magic island of Prospero. Whether or not we agree
that 'nothing is so tiresome as to be whirled half over
Europe at the chariot-wheels of a hero', Miss Mitford's
own confined locality (Three Mile Cross, near Reading)
offered excellent material for a series of admirable essays.

'Nothing is so good as it seems beforehand'
George Eliot, *Silas Marner*, ch. 18 (1861)

This is such a quotable aphorism that it is a pity it was
not more relevant to the occasion. Nancy Cass is talking
to her husband, Godfrey, son of the squire. Godfrey has
just confessed that before they were married he had been
secretly married to another woman (who had died before
the marriage to Nancy). It was a most unsuitable match
into which he had been drawn as a youth. He points out
to Nancy that if she had known about this earlier
discreditable marriage she would probably not have
agreed to marry him. Nancy gives the quoted reply,
which was perhaps more meaningful to her (and
perhaps to her author) than it is to the reader.

'Nothing looks more formidable and impressive than an armoured train; but nothing is in fact more vulnerable'
Winston Churchill, *My Early Life* (1930)

No one could have been better qualified than Churchill to discuss the weakness of armoured trains, for it was a journey in one of these powerful-looking weaklings that led to his capture during the South African War. As war correspondent for the *Morning Post* he joined an armoured train of six trucks rashly sent out to reconnoitre. A handful of Boers put an obstacle on the line, and the train was derailed on its attempted return. The occupants were successfully ambushed and, despite heroic efforts, those left alive were compelled to surrender. Churchill himself soon afterwards made a dramatic escape from prison to safety.

'Nothing on earth [is] so easy as to forget, if a person chooses to set about it'
R. B. Sheridan, *The Rivals*, I, ii (1775)

Mrs Malaprop has ordered her young niece, Lydia, to forget Beverley, the man she loves, in order to receive a new suitor. Lydia replies that memories cannot be controlled at will. She is at once contradicted by her aunt, who maintains that she herself has forgotten all about her late husband, as if he had never existed. This is not hard to believe, but Lydia does not find it a convincing argument.

'No time like the present'
Mrs Manley, *The Lost Lover* (1696)

Nowadays we use the phrase as an incitement to immediate action. In its original sense, however, it was intended to convey that the charms of a lady no longer young are even greater than when she was more youthful. The speaker is Sir Amorous Courtall, the object of his flattery Lady Young-Love, 'an old conceited lady'. This short play was Mrs Manley's only comedy, but she wrote a few serious dramas, and was at one time editor of *The Examiner*, succeeding Swift in 1711.

'Not to be sneezed at'
G. Colman (the Younger), *The Heir-at-Law*, II, i (1800)

Sneezing has long been regarded superstitiously as an ominous sign, indicating that evil spirits are hanging around. (Hence we say, 'Bless you' after a sneeze, in order to keep them away.) An extension of this belief makes sneezing an expression of dislike or contempt, and this was doubtless in Colman's mind when he first coined the phrase. The heroine has been reduced to £200 a year, but her faithful retainer reasonably points out that £200 is not to be despised. Alas, she loses it through the knavery of her man of business, but luckily a missing sweetheart makes a timely reappearance to marry her.

'Not to know me argues yourselves unknown'
John Milton, *Paradise Lost*, Bk IV (1668)

The line is ambiguous. It could mean: 'You know me as well as you know yourselves'. Or it could mean: 'If you don't recognize anyone as well-known as myself you must be very insignificant members of your society.' The Speaker (none other than Satan) has been asked to identify himself by a couple of angels who were on guard duty in the Garden of Eden, and had come upon the Devil preparing to offer temptation to the sleeping Adam and Eve. Satan appears to be disgusted at being asked his name, and scornfully calls his interlocutors 'the lowest of your throng'.

'Nowadays a broken heart will run to many editions'
Oscar Wilde, *The Picture of Dorian Gray*, ch. 1 (1891)

Basil Hallward, artist, has been telling his friend, Lord Henry Wotton, that he will never exhibit his portrait of the beautiful youth, Dorian Gray, for he has put much of himself into the painting, and he will not bare his soul to the shallow, prying eyes of the outside world. Cynical Lord Henry (Oscar Wilde) remarks that Basil's attitude is very different from that of most poets, who are only too ready to expose their inmost feelings for publication, and who find it very profitable to write about their private passions.

'Now am I slap-dash down in the Mouth'
William Congreve, *The Old Batchelor*, IV, ix (1693)

Words change their significance in the course of three centuries, and here there is a double transformation. 'Slap-dash' does not mean careless, and 'down in the mouth' does not indicate misery. Sir Joseph Wittol, a foolish coxcomb, and his braggart friend, Captain Bluffe, are proposing to chat up two fine ladies in St James's Park. Bluffe is the first to address them, and is received with such contempt that Wittol loses his self-confidence. He is, he murmurs to himself, suddenly ('slap-dash') at a loss for words ('down in the mouth'). After a pause he summons up sufficient boldness to make a remark about the weather.

'Now as I was young and easy under the apple boughs'
Dylan Thomas, *Fern Hill* (1946)

Fern Hill was the farm where Dylan's aunt lived, and where he spent many happy hours during his childhood, playing in the apple trees, and the hayricks, and the barns, and beside the brooks.

In the sun born over and over,
I ran my heedless ways.

Images and phrases merge into each other breathlessly as he relives these early days.

'Now hast thou but one bare hour to live'
Christopher Marlowe, *Doctor Faustus*, V, ii (*c* 1588)

This is Faustus's final appearance. His twenty-four-year compact with the Devil is up, and on the stroke of midnight his body and soul will be claimed. This last soliloquy of Faustus is a remarkably daring piece of writing, for in the space of not quite sixty lines the author has to suggest the passing of sixty minutes. By variety in length of lines and skilful choice of phrases, the feeling of time slowly but remorselessly moving on is well conveyed. As the clock strikes the fatal twelve strokes, devils appear and drag Faustus off stage as he gasps his last half-incoherent words:

Ugly Hell, gape not! Come not Lucifer!
I'll burn my books! – O Mephostophilis!

'Now he belongs to the ages'
John Drinkwater, *Abraham Lincoln*, VI (1918)

The scene is the small lounge behind the boxes of an American theatre, with the doors of three boxes visible. In the centre box (the door being open) can be seen President Lincoln, his wife, and Edwin Stanton, a member of the Cabinet. The President rises in his box to address the audience, who have been applauding him. He sits down and the door is closed. A figure now creeps across the lounge, flings open the door, and fires directly at the President. Soon afterwards Stanton emerges, uttering the historic epitaph.

'Now may the good God pardon all good men!'
Elizabeth Barrett Browning, *Aurora Leigh*, Bk IV (1857)

The lovely Lady Waldemar has been secretly scheming against Romney Leigh's prospective marriage with a lowly bred but charming girl. When Aurora (Romney's cousin) hears Romney unsuspectingly referring to Lady Waldemar as good, she reflects on the frequency with which the term 'good' is misapplied. So many people thought to be good produced effects that were actually harmful. There were 'good' friends who preyed on you; 'good' critics who destroyed a poet's work; 'good' statesmen who ruined their country; 'good' Christians who damned those who did not share their views. All such goodness needed pardon rather than blessing.

'Now they are all on their knees'
Thomas Hardy, *The Oxen* (1915)

The poet refers to a legend, told to him as a child, that on Christmas Eve at midnight the animals in their stables all kneel in honour of the birth of Jesus. He believed it then, though few people would do so now. Yet if someone invited him to go along to the barton (farmyard) that they knew in childhood to see if the legend was true

I would go with him in the gloom

Hoping it might be so.

Hardy was an agnostic but was not antagonistic to the Christian religion. Though he no longer believed the Church's doctrines, he would still have been happy to see a charming but unlikely religious legend proved true.

'O brave new world
That has such people in't!'
William Shakespeare, *The Tempest*, V, i (1611)

Prospero, the rightful Duke of Milan, has been dispossessed of his dukedom by his brother. For many years he has lived on a virtually uninhabited island, and where his daughter Miranda has grown up. Prospero uses his magic art to create a storm which brings his brother and friends to the island. Miranda has never seen any person except her father, and when she first beholds the wrecked courtiers her reaction is one of wonder and admiration. Aldous Huxley (1894–1963) used the phrase *Brave New World* as the title of a now-famous satirical novel (1932) portraying a future in which science has solved all human problems.

'O Captain! my Captain! our fearful trip is done'
Walt Whitman, *O Captain! My Captain* (1866)

The Captain has steered his ship through many perils and has almost reached port. On shore people are already cheering, and bells are ringing out. But in the very moment of triumph the Captain falls dead and bleeding, while the narrator walks the deck 'with mournful tread'. This is not, as it appears to be, based on a true story of the sea. It is an allegory, written not long after the assassination of the American President (1865). He is the Captain, and the port which the ship has reached after a perilous voyage is the port of Peace, attained after the miseries of the late Civil War.

'O'er rough and smooth she trips along,
And never looks behind'
William Wordsworth, *Lucy Gray* (1798)

It is the ghost of Lucy that trips along in this rather sad story. The tale had its origin in an incident which Wordsworth's sister told him about. A little girl from Halifax got lost in a snowstorm. Later her footprints were tracked by her parents to the middle of a canal lock. Wordsworth turned the canal lock into a plank bridge over a river. The girl goes out with a lantern to light her mother home, but loses her bearings in the snow. The poem concludes with a hint of the supernatural.

Some maintain that to this day

She is a living child

who can still be seen roaming the moors.

'Off with his head!'
William Shakespeare, *King Richard III*, III, iv (1597)

This bloodthirsty command is often associated with the sharp-tempered Queen in *Alice in Wonderland*, but priority belongs to Shakespeare's Richard III, who was a great one for separating heads from bodies. Lord Hastings was the victim here. Finding that this Lord was unwilling to support his unjust claim to the throne, Richard of Gloucester (as he then was) took an early opportunity to pick a quarrel. 'Thou art a traitor: off with his head!' There were servants ready to obey Richard's command, and Hastings' head duly left his shoulders. The Duke of Buckingham suffered the same fate a little later.

> *'O for the touch of a vanished hand*
> *And the sound of a voice that is still'*
> Alfred Tennyson, *Break, Break, Break* (1842)

The vanished hand and silent voice belonged to Tennyson's dear friend Arthur Hallam, who died in 1833. The poem was written soon afterwards on the Lincolnshire cliffs as the poet watched the waves breaking on the shore below and the stately ships sailing 'to their haven under the hill'. Hallam was also the subject of Tennyson's *In Memoriam*.

> *'O Fountain, dost thou never run with blood?'*
> J. Elroy Flecker, *Hassan*, III, i (1922)

Hassan, a simple confectioner, has been taken into great favour by the Caliph of Baghdad because of a service Hassan has rendered. The Caliph offers friendship, and proceeds in a good-humoured way to discuss poetry and beauty. Hassan admires a splendid fountain in the garden, and the Caliph tells him why it remains unique: when the sculptor was asked by the Caliph's father if he could make more as fine, he had replied delightedly that he could, and was promptly impaled. In spite of himself Hassan cannot help exclaiming against such cruelty, and it is touch and go whether he shares the sculptor's fate.

> *'Of whom to be dispraised were no small praise'*
> John Milton, *Paradise Regained*, Bk III (1671)

Christ is in the wilderness, being tempted by Satan. 'Collecting all his serpent wiles', the Devil tries to flatter Christ into a desire to achieve 'fame and glory'. However, Christ rejects his proposals, mainly for the not-very-Christian reason that glory is merely 'the people's praise', and the people are a pretty poor lot not worth bothering about:
> A miscellaneous rabble, who extol
> Things vulgar.

The attitude is perhaps more Miltonic than Christ-like.

> *'Oh, I am a cook and a captain bold,*
> *And the mate of the* Nancy *brig,*
> *And a bo'sun tight, and a midshipmite,*
> *And the crew of the captain's gig'*
> W. S. Gilbert, *The Yarn of the 'Nancy Bell'* (1869)

The narrator of this *Bab Ballad* meets an old sailor who proceeds to make the strange claims expressed in the quotation. His justification is that he had eaten the characters referred to! When the *Nancy Bell* was wrecked, the survivors drew lots as to which of them should be eaten. Eventually only the old sailor and the cook were left. While the latter was sniffing at the big cooking-pot, his companion seized his legs and tipped him in. It may be that Gilbert was casually making fun of that other teller of sea yarns, Coleridge's Ancient Mariner.

'Oh, I have slipped the surly bonds of earth'
John Magee

This poem, widely read and spoken during the Second World War, was written by a nineteen-year-old American fighter pilot who scribbled the lines on the back of a letter. He was killed soon afterwards. The verse, in loose sonnet form, praises the delights of flying – climbing, wheeling, soaring, 'high in the sunlit silence', reaching 'where never lark, or even eagle, flew'. He has even in the 'high untrespassed sanctity of space, / Put out my hand and touched the face of God'.

'Oh, never, never, never, since I joined the human race
Saw I so exquisitely fair a face'
W. S. Gilbert, *Trial by Jury* (1875)

The Judge presiding at a breach-of-promise case is unable to control his susceptibility. He is first attracted by one of the bridesmaids (witnesses for the plaintiff), but when the plaintiff herself appears, he transfers his affections. After giving voice to the quoted admiration of her beauty, he feels ready to start an impartial hearing of the breach-of-promise case. In the course of this the lovely plaintiff receives tender consolation, first from her Counsel, then from the foreman of the jury, and finally from the Judge, who invites her to sit with him on the bench.

'Oh, to be in England
Now that April's there'
Robert Browning, *Home Thoughts from Abroad* (1845)

Probably writing in Italy in 1838, Browning nostalgically conjures up a picture of the English Spring as he remembers it. The chaffinch sings in the orchard, the trees are beginning to be in leaf; then in May the whitethroat and the swallow build their nests, and the thrush sings and repeats his song in the leaning pear-tree. Buttercups will be growing in the fields, happily gathered by children; the Italian melon-flower is gaudy by comparison. Not a few people have noted that the typical April rainstorms appear to have escaped the poet's memory.

'Oh, wad some power the giftie gie us
To see oursel's as others see us'
Robert Burns, *To a Louse* (1786)

The louse had most inconsiderately settled itself on the bonnet of a fine lady in church, instead of seeking out some humbler person. If the lady only realized the situation, Burns comments, she would be less ready to give herself airs.

> *'Oh! ye lords of ladies intellectual,*
> *Inform us truly, have they not hen-peck'd you all?'*
> Lord Byron, *Don Juan*, I, xxii (1818)

Byron is having a swipe at blue-stocking ladies. His immediate concern is the mother of Don Juan, Donna Inez, 'a learned lady famed / For every branch of every science named'. The poet is also, like a juggler, displaying his skill – in this case his skill with words, showing his ability to make a seemingly impossible rhyme.

> *'Old Cato is as great a rogue as you'*
> Alexander Pope, *Moral Essays*, Epistle III (1731–5)

The words are spoken indirectly to a group of courtiers. Pope is dealing with the use of riches for bribery, and suggesting that even men (like Cato) noted for their patriotic integrity are capable of being bribed. He is referring, rather maliciously, to a specific incident. A highly regarded old patriot, said to be Sir Christopher Musgrave, was seen to emerge from the back door of William III's closet. As he descended, a large bag burst in his arms and a stream of golden guineas trickled down the stairs. (Cato, incidentally, was *not* guilty of accepting bribes.)

> *'The oldest man he seemed that ever wore grey hairs'*
> William Wordsworth, *Resolution and Independence* (1807)

Wordsworth describes how, amidst the beauties of Nature, which usually uplift him, he is suddenly stricken with a feeling of dejection. He becomes, as he later put it, 'overwhelmed by the thoughts of the miserable reverses which have befallen the happiest of all men, viz. poets'. He is rescued from his despair by meeting a very old man, bent double, who earns a precarious livelihood by catching leeches and selling them to doctors for drawing blood from patients. The sturdy independence of the old man, 'carrying with him his own fortitude', proved an inspiration to the poet.

> *'The old Lie: Dulce et decorum est*
> **Pro patria moi'**
> Wilfred Owen, *Dulce et Decorum Est* (1920)

Wilfred Owen is attacking the sentimental glorification of war. He was one of the leading poets of the First World War, in the last week of which he was killed. Although the vile realities of war had largely pierced the veil of sentimentalism by 1918, traces of the earlier attitude still lingered here and there. He describes a group of exhausted men subjected to a sudden gas attack. One man is too bewildered to don his gas mask, and dies in terrible agony, 'his hanging face, like a devil's sick of sin'. In the face of such horrors how false it is, Owen avers, to say, 'It is sweet and fitting to die for one's country'.

'The old order changeth, yielding place to new'
Alfred Tennyson, *The Passing of Arthur* (1869)

Sir Bedivere, the only one of King Arthur's Knights remaining after a great battle, tells the mortally wounded King that now that the Round Table is dissolved he feels lost without his companions. Arthur replies that change is the natural order of things. He implies that truth is given to the world in new forms to prevent it from becoming disregarded through familiarity. This is not very persuasive consolation, but as Bedivere watches the barge bearing the King's body disappear from sight, at least 'the new sun rose bringing the new year'.

'O leave this barren spot to me!
Spare, woodman, spare the beechen tree'
Thomas Campbell, *The Beech-Tree's Petition* (1805)

The tree points out that it has stood on its barren spot for sixty years. Children have played under it, and beneath its shade lovers have pledged their vows and carved their names on its trunk.

By all that Love has whispered here,
Or Beauty heard with ravish'd ear;
As Love's own altar honour me.
Spare, woodman, spare the beechen tree!

The result of this persuasive entreaty has not been recorded, but the American writer George Morris was later inspired to make a similar and better-known plea.

'Once people start on all this Art
Farewell moralitee'
A. P. Herbert, *Ballads for Broadbrows* (1930)

The title of this ballad is 'Lines for a Worthy Person who has drifted by accident into a Chelsea Revel' (perhaps the Chelsea Arts Ball). Herbert is poking good-humoured fun at elderly and rather straitlaced people who disapprove of 'those who write or paint or act'.

Let Dagoes paint and write and sing,
But Art is not an English thing!

Such persons as artists have an unsatisfactory moral tone; moreover, they have strange hairstyles and wear eccentric clothing.

Not these the kind of people who
Were prominent at Waterloo.

'One foot in the grave'
Beaumont and Fletcher, *The Little French Lawyer*, I, i (1619–20)

This unkind reference to old age is spoken by the hero to an elderly gentleman, who is told that as he will soon be dead it is quite wrong for him to want to save money! It must be added that the hero was somewhat bitter at the time because the elderly man's daughter, whom he loves, has been given in marriage to somebody else – an old man wealthy enough not to require a dowry.

'One of the has beens'
William Hone, *The Everyday Book* (22 June 1826)

Hone was an assiduous collector of miscellaneous information on customs, etc. Here he is dealing with an eighteenth-century mock election which used to be held in what was then the village of Garratt, long vanished, but still recalled by the Garratt Lane which links the London suburbs of Wandsworth Town and Tooting. When Hone visited Garratt he was invited to meet 'old Jack Jones', the only surviving person in the village to have been elected to the mock office of 'Master of the Horse'. In his day he had been tall and strong, but now he hobbled about with the aid of walking-sticks and was very much 'one of the *has* beens'.

'One impulse from a vernal wood
May teach you more of man,
Of moral evil and of good,
Than all the sages can'
William Wordsworth, *The Tables Turned* (1798)

One day a friend (William Hazlitt) asked Wordsworth why he just sat for hours on a rock beside Esthwaite Water in the Lake District instead of employing his time reading a useful book. Wordsworth was not the man to take this lying down. He decided to turn the tables on Hazlitt by producing a poem exhorting a friend (unnamed) to stop poring over books and to go into the country to learn from Nature. In one of his essays Hazlitt briefly refers to the occasion: 'I got into a metaphysical argument with Wordsworth ... in which neither of us succeeded in making ourselves perfectly clear and intelligible.' (*My First Acquaintance with Poets*)

'One swallow does not make a Spring'
Aristotle, *Nicomachean Ethics* (4th cent. B.C.)

Examining the nature of happiness, Aristotle advises that the good of man consists in the active exercising of the soul's faculties in conformity with virtue. But this is a long-term process: one day's virtuous exercise no more makes for supreme happiness than one swallow makes a Spring. That great sixteenth-century proverb collector, John Heywood, turned Spring into Summer to suit the English climate, and created a popular adage that warns us not to expect too much from a single piece of good luck. Nicomachus was the son of Aristotle; he may have edited the *Ethics*.

'On Linden, when the sun was low,
All bloodless lay the untrodden snow'
Thomas Campbell, *Hohenlinden* (1801)

The French Revolution brought France into conflict with the German States, which included Austria. Campbell was in Germany in 1800 and saw some of the fighting. Although he had left the Bavarian village a little while before the Battle of Hohenlinden took place (3 December 1800) the news of the conflict made a great impression on him, as his lyric suggests. The Austrian army tried to cut off the French, but hampered by the driving snow were repulsed with heavy losses.

'The only way to get rid of a temptation is to yield to it'
Oscar Wilde, *The Picture of Dorian Gray*, ch. 2 (1891)

Wilde's only novel has been called 'the most complete expression of Wilde's personality that we possess'. Certainly one of the chief characters, Lord Henry Wotton, is an excellent portrait of the author. His witty, artificial approach to life was precisely that of Wilde himself. Here he is endeavouring to persuade the handsome youth, Dorian Gray, that we should not be afraid of our desires. To resist temptation is to make the soul sick with longing for things it has forbidden itself. 'Every (natural) impulse that we strive to strangle broods in the mind, and poisons us.'

'On the stage he was natural, simple, affecting; 'Twas only that when he was off he was acting'
Oliver Goldsmith, *Retaliation* (1774)

Not long before he died Goldsmith was the victim of a good-humoured literary attack. The details are uncertain, but it seems likely that a group of friends at the literary club, inspired by the actor David Garrick, conspired each to write an epitaph on Goldsmith. The one that stuck most was Garrick's 'Who wrote like an angel, and talked like poor Poll'. Goldsmith took an opportunity to respond, writing satirical epitaphs on several of those who had written on himself. It was perhaps fitting that Garrick should receive the brunt of the friendly attack, and the shrewd description of the actor is the best-known of the sketches.

'Oon ere it herde, at the other out it wente'
Geoffrey Chaucer, *Troilus and Criseyde*, Bk IV (1380–6)

This does not here imply inattention or forgetfulness, as in modern usage, but a refusal to listen. Troilus, a distinguished Trojan warrior, had fallen desperately in love with Criseyde, daughter of a Trojan prophet who had deserted to the Greek enemy. When the Trojan parliament insisted on sending Criseyde to join her father, Troilus was so overcome that he spent nearly twenty Chaucerian stanzas bemoaning his lot. Pandare, Criseyde's uncle, tried to cheer Troilus up by reminding him that 'the town is full of ladies'. All in vain. The lovesick Troilus would not listen.

'Open my heart and you will see Graved inside of it, "Italy"'
Robert Browning, *De Gustibus* (1855)

This explicit declaration of love is reinforced in many of Browning's poems. He lived in Italy for many years after his marriage to Elizabeth Barrett (1846). When asked if he had been to Oxford or Cambridge he would reply, 'Italy was my University'. In this poem there are two sections: the first deals with his love of England, the second with his love of Italy. The rather curious title is an abbreviation of the Latin saying: *De gustibus non est disputandum* (there is no disputing about tastes).

'The oracles are dumb'
John Milton, *On the Morning of Christ's Nativity* (1629)

Milton's youthful poem pictures exuberantly the birth of
Christ immediately silencing pagan gods and causing
havoc to their oracles, the most famous of which was at
Apollo's Delphic shrine at the foot of Mount Parnassus.
The classical household gods were also driven away, and
the moon goddess was no longer worshipped. Even the
great Egyptian deities, Isis and Osiris, were put to flight.
The Christian triumph is complete, and the Babe 'Can in
his swaddling bands control the damned crew'. To many
people today Milton's attitude to other religions will
seem somewhat intolerant.

'Others abide our question. Thou art free'
Matthew Arnold, *Sonnet* (1849)

In most respects Arnold was an acute critic of literature,
but this sonnet is a typical example of the bardolatry
which swept over English literary criticism in the nineteenth century. Shakespeare was seen not as a practical
working dramatist, getting on with his job of providing
plays for the Lord Chamberlain's company and doing it
remarkably well, but as a giant among men 'making the
heaven of heavens his dwelling-place'. Such exaggerated
tributes carried Shakespeare's undoubted pre-eminence
among his fellow playwrights to ridiculous lengths,
turning him from a wonderfully gifted but by no means
faultless dramatist to a kind of god.

'Our England is a garden, and such gardens are not made By singing: "Oh, how beautiful" and sitting in the shade'
Rudyard Kipling, *The Glory of the Garden* (1911)

The poem is an allegory, indicating that it is necessary for
all to work for the good of the country no matter in what
capacity. The garden metaphor is closely followed.
'Some can pot begonias and some can bud a rose', but
everyone, however weak or sad, can find 'some needful
job that's crying to be done'. The poem first appeared in
a children's history of England written in collaboration
with the historian C. R. L. Fletcher.

'Our knowledge of the universe is really very limited'
Patrick Moore, *Can You Speak Venusian?*, ch. 1 (1972)

Moore's book deals with what he calls 'Independent
Thinkers' – people whose scientific views are unconven-
tional, though he kindly differentiates them from
'cranks'. While he himself does not accept the peculiar
views of such people, he points out the limitations of
accepted scientific beliefs. The size of the Earth, its
distance from the Sun, the number of stars in our Galaxy
– all these are known to scientists. But we do not know
how the Earth and the rest of the Universe came into
being. 'Modern science is strong on details, weak on the
essential fundamentals.'

'Out, damned spot!'
William Shakespeare, *Macbeth*, V, i (1606)

Macbeth, egged on by his wife, stabs the sleeping King Duncan in order to gain the throne of Scotland. Overcome by his own action he unwittingly brings away the bloody dagger and is afraid to return to the bedroom to replace it. Lady Macbeth, emotionally tougher, takes the dagger from him and returns it, confident that she can easily wash any blood from her hands. Years later, however, her toughness begins to dissolve. While sleepwalking she is subconsciously worried by an imaginary spot of blood on her hand, and she tries unsuccessfully to wipe it away.

'Out of the jaws of death'
William Shakespeare, *Twelfth Night*, III, iv (1601)

Antonio, a sea-captain, has saved young Sebastian from drowning. Later, in the land of Illyria, Antonio finds himself arrested for a former offence. He is amazed and disgusted when Sebastian appears to be repudiating him, and indignantly describes how he had snatched the youth 'out of the jaws of death'. His indignation, though understandable, is unjustified for the youth he takes for Sebastian is (somewhat improbably) Sebastian's twin sister in male disguise, who has never seen Antonio before.

'Out of the strong came forth sweetness'
Bible, Judges, xiv, 14 (c 600 B.C.)

One suspects that Samson would have been quite at home in Al Capone's Chicago. At his wedding he bet thirty companions that they could not explain the riddle: 'Out of the eater came forth meat, and out of the strong came forth sweetness'. (Samson had earlier killed a lion cub, and a swarm of bees had settled in its carcass.) Unable to guess the answer, the thirty men blackmailed Samson's wife by threats to reveal it. She yielded, and Samson had to pay up. He did this, in true gangster fashion, by murdering and robbing thirty innocent people.

'O wanderer from a Grecian shore'
Matthew Arnold, *Philomela* (1853)

The poem is addressed to the nightingale, 'the tawnythroated'. In Greek mythology Philomela was a woman raped and subsequently transformed into a nightingale. The bird's song, therefore, was supposed always to be a sad one.

> Still nourishing in thy bewildered brain
> That wild, unquench'd, deep-sunken, old-world
> pain –
> Say, will it never heal?

Though finely expressed, this attitude to the nightingale's song is perhaps rather artificial. To most people the nightingale's notes suggest sheer delight rather than the tragedy of remote legend.

> *'O what a tangled web we weave*
> *When first we practise to deceive'*
> Sir Walter Scott, *Marmion*, VI, 17 (1808)

By having certain papers forged, Lord Marmion has caused his rival, de Wilton, to flee as a supposed traitor. Marmion has also had his own mistress, Constance, shut up in a nunnery so that she can no longer interfere with his intention to marry the lovely and wealthy Lady Clare, betrothed to de Wilton. Marmion has just realized that a palmer who has recently been in his company is in fact de Wilton in disguise. He foresees difficulties ahead in carrying out his scheme regarding Clare, and says so in the quoted couplet.

> *'O what can ail thee, knight-at-arms,*
> *Alone and palely loitering?'*
> John Keats, *La Belle Dame Sans Merci* (1819)

This narrative in ballad form tells of a knight-at-arms wandering alone on a hillside, pale and haggard. He had met a lovely and loving lady who took him to her home, where he fell asleep. Then he dreamt that other victims cried to him that he was under the enchantment of a fairy, and when he awoke she had vanished and he was alone on the hillside. Although the dead of winter had driven all life away, he felt himself impelled to continue wandering there. The title (The Beautiful Lady without Pity) was taken from a medieval French poem by Alain Chartier.

> *'O what is that sound that so thrills the ear?'*
> W. H. Auden, *O What is that Sound* (1932)

The sound is the drumming of a troop of soldiers as they march steadily forward. Each verse of this ballad asks an anxious question, spoken by a wife (or mistress) and parried by a euphemistic reply from the husband (or lover). But the tension grows as the men come nearer and nearer to the house, not pausing at the doctor's, the parson's, or the farmer's. Finally they reach the husband's own house, and he must depart with them.

Their boots are heavy on the floor
And their eyes are burning.

> *'O woman! in our hours of ease*
> *Uncertain, coy, and hard to please ...*
> *When pain and anguish wring the brow*
> *A ministering angel thou'*
> Sir Walter Scott, *Marmion*, VI, 30 (1808)

Lady Clare has been gravely wronged by Marmion, an English nobleman. He has temporarily disposed of her lover by trickery, and has taken her in charge, hoping to force her into marriage. During the bloody battle of Flodden he leaves her near the battlefield in the care of his squires. He himself is mortally wounded during the fight, and cries desperately for water. It is Clare who hears him, and despite her wrongs she fills his helmet from a nearby stream, brings it to him, and tends his wounds. The poet prepares us for this incident by the quoted couplet.

'Passing rich with forty pounds a year'
Oliver Goldsmith, *The Deserted Village* (1770)

This is a description of the village parson, probably based on the poet's brother, whose salary was precisely forty pounds a year. Although this was only a moderate income for an educated man, even in the eighteenth century, 'the village preacher', like the Reverend Henry Goldsmith, was absurdly generous with his relatively thin purse. The village, which Goldsmith called 'sweet Auburn', was a composite of English and Irish villages that he had known. The poem was inspired by the depopulation which he believed to be sadly affecting rural England.

'Patriotism is not enough. I must have no hatred or bitterness towards anyone'
Edith Cavell, Last words (12 October 1915)

When the First World War broke out, Nurse Cavell was matron of a hospital in Brussels. Besides tending wounded on both sides, she sheltered and helped some English and French soldiers to reach the neutral Dutch border. Despite neutral protests, she was sentenced to death by the Germans. Just before being shot she uttered her now famous last words to the British chaplain. After the war she was buried in Norwich Cathedral, and among other memorials is a statue near Trafalgar Square, London.

'Patriotism is the last refuge of a scoundrel'
Samuel Johnson, in Boswell's *Life of Johnson* (1791)

A quotation often misunderstood and misapplied. Johnson, an intensely patriotic man, was not asserting that genuine patriotism was a vice, but indicating that a scoundrel often tried to hide his self-interest under a cloak of false patriotism. Boswell himself adds: 'He did not mean a real and generous love of our country, but that pretended patriotism which so many, in all ages and countries, have made a cloak for self-interest.' No doubt Johnson had in mind those 'patriot throats / That ask no questions but the price of votes' (*The Vanity of Human Wishes*).

'Peace hath her victories
No less renowned than war'
John Milton, *To the Lord General Cromwell* (1652)

After recalling some of Cromwell's great military victories against the Scots and Royalists at Dunbar and Worcester, Milton points out in this sonnet that there are more peaceful victories remaining to be won. What he has particularly in mind is the need to avoid shackling religious freedom by linking the State with any religious organization.

'The pen is mightier than the sword'
E. G. Bulwer-Lytton, *Richelieu*, II, ii (1839)

Cardinal Richelieu (1585–1642), the great French statesman of Louis XIII, was originally intended for the
military profession, and never lost his interest in it. In
this scene the Cardinal, no longer young, attempts to
show how the enemies of France should be treated,
grasping one of the great two-handed swords used in the
Middle Ages and trying to wield it. His strength is no
longer equal to the task. He lets the weapon fall and
picks up a pen, 'the arch-enchanter's wand'. This, he
indicates, is more powerful than a sword, for a message
written by it can have tremendous consequences.

Take away the sword –

States can be saved without it!

'People always live for ever where there is any annuity to be paid to them'
Jane Austen, *Sense and Sensibility*, ch. 2 (1811)

John Dashwood had promised his father, at the latter's
deathbed, that he would do his best for his stepmother
and three half-sisters. His first intention was to give
these sisters £1,000 apiece. His wife protested that this
was robbing his own son of his inheritance, so he
decided to make the sum £500 each. Then he wondered if
an annuity of £100 a year to the mother might not be a
better idea. His wife then points out that 'if Mrs
Dashwood should live fifteen years we should be completely taken in', for it would amount to more than
giving the sisters £500 each. In the end he decides not to
give any of them anything.

'A perfect and an upright man'
Bible, Job, i, 8 (c 5th century B.C.)

The author of the Book of Job portrays Job as a prosperous man who praised God for all his blessings. But one
day Satan said to God (in effect), 'I bet I can make Job
curse you.' God disagreed, and gave Satan a free hand to
torment Job. Thereupon his cattle, servants, and children
were suddenly destroyed (presumably they did not
matter), while Job himself was afflicted with terrible
boils. Job still remained uncomplaining, so Satan lost his
bet. The story may be (as has been claimed) a poetical
masterpiece, but it reveals a curious idea of Divinity.

'Perhaps ours is the only little corner of the British Empire which is thoroughly, wisely, and strongly ruled just now'
Thomas Hughes, *Tom Brown's Schooldays*, ch. 8 (1856)

That particular 'corner' was the small section of the
Midlands known as Rugby School, governed by the
notable Thomas Arnold. His quiet reforms at the school
had a considerable influence on education. The speaker
was not given a name in Hughes's novel, but was
referred to only as the Young Master. He was in fact
based on the Reverend Mr Cotton, like Arnold a real
figure among a host of fictitious ones. He subsequently
became headmaster of Marlborough School, and within a
few years raised that quite new establishment from one
of the worst public schools to one of the best.

'A person on business from Porlock'
S. T. Coleridge, *Kubla Khan – Preface* (1816)

This person was one of the most notorious characters in literary history, for he unwittingly destroyed what might have been one of the great English poems. Coleridge had fallen asleep while reading about a great palace built by Kubla Khan (1214–94). As soon as he awoke he recollected clearly two or three hundred lines of a fine poem he had composed in his sleep. He started to write them down, but when he had completed only a few he was interrupted by 'a person from Porlock', who stayed for an hour. At the end of that time Coleridge found that he had forgotten the rest of the poem.

'A place for everything and everything in its place'
Samuel Smiles, *Thrift*, ch. 5 (1875)

Smiles was a competent biographer and a busy writer of moral homilies which were very much to the taste of Victorians. Though his style of work is out of favour today, there are a good many precepts which we might profitably make a note of. One of these is his advice on orderliness, which he claims is the secret of wealth. 'Disorderly people are rarely rich, and orderly people are rarely poor.' It's an interesting theory, and he may be right.

'Play up! play up! and play the game!'
Henry Newbolt, *Vitaï Lampada* (1892)

There was a breathless hush in the Close (at Clifton College) as the last man came to the wicket with ten runs needed for victory. The team captain proceeded to thump him on the shoulder and exhorted him to play the game – which was surprisingly vague and unhelpful advice to give to a No. 11 batsman. However, the poem shows the familiar words being applied as a rallying cry in other situations. The title appears to be taken from a line by Lucretius, where *vitae lampada* means 'the torch of life'. This was Newbolt's earliest-written published poem.

'Please do not shoot the pianist. He is doing his best'
Oscar Wilde, *Impressions of America* (1883)

This uncharacteristic quotation comes from a lecture given by Wilde after a visit to America in 1882. At the mining city of Leadville, Colorado, 'reputed to be the richest city in the world – also the roughest', he saw a notice bearing the quoted words above a piano in a dance saloon. 'It was,' Wilde commented, 'the only rational form of art criticism I have ever come across.'

'Please, sir, I want some more'
Charles Dickens, *Oliver Twist*, ch. 2 (1837–8)

Oliver is brought up in a workhouse where the boys are almost starved. They draw lots to decide which one shall ask the master for a second helping. Oliver is chosen, and 'desperate with hunger, and reckless with misery' he approaches the master to make his request. The master aims a blow at Oliver's head, pinions him, and screams for the beadle, who in turn goes rushing to the governors to cry, 'Oliver Twist has asked for more!' The novel has some fine scenes, but one cannot help feeling that the irony here is even more heavy-handed than the master.

'Pleasure's a sin, and sometines sin's a pleasure'
Lord Byron, *Don Juan*, I, cxxxiii (1818)

The poet, digressing from his story, is discussing human behaviour in general. But he probably has particular reference to 'first and passionate love'. When he returns to the story it is to describe the scene when the pleasurable sin of the youthful Juan (barely sixteen) with the lovely Donna Julia, is unhappily interrupted by the untimely return of her husband, Don Alfonso. Juan has no time to escape from her bed and therefore has to hide inside it, curled round, and disguised by the bedclothes half thrown back in a heap.

'A poet could not but be gay'
William Wordsworth, *I Wandered Lonely as a Cloud* (1807)

In Wordsworth's time the word 'gay' had not been given its curious modern extension of meaning, and the line merely indicates his poetic enthusiasm at the sight of 'a host of golden daffodils' near Lake Ullswater, 'fluttering and dancing in the breeze'. The sight so filled his mind that he could recall it almost at will, 'and then my heart with pleasure fills / And dances with the daffodils'. A similar scene excited his sister Dorothy to express equal enthusiasm in excellent prose in her *Journals*.

'The poetry of earth is never dead'
John Keats, *On the Grasshopper and Cricket* (1817)

One day Keats and his friend Leigh Hunt agreed to have a competition, each to write there and then a sonnet comparing the grasshopper of the field and the cricket of the hearth. Keats finished first, and each then read the other's poem. Hunt, always generous, at once awarded the palm to his young friend. Keats dealt first with the grasshopper, singing 'from hedge to hedge about the new-mown mead', and then with the cricket's shrill song from the stove 'on a lone winter evening, when the frost has wrought a silence'. 'That's perfect,' Hunt observed; and posterity has approved his judgment.

'The Poet's eye, in a fine frenzy rolling'
William Shakespeare, *A Midsummer Night's Dream*, V, i (1600)

Duke Theseus has been told, off stage, of the strange incidents that have occurred to four lovers in the nearby woods. He remarks cynically that tales told by madmen, lovers, and poets can never be believed. In particular, the poet's imagination wanders where it will, and entirely transforms the things and ideas of everyday life.

> Turns them to shapes, and gives to airy nothing
> A local habitation and a name.

'The policeman's lot is not a happy one'
W. S. Gilbert, *The Pirates of Penzance* (1880)

The policemen of Penzance are about to march against the pirates. But in Gilbert's topsy-turvy world they are very reluctant to do anything that might deprive a fellow creature of his liberty. Apart from his wrongdoing, the police sergeant reflects, the criminal may have 'a capacity for innocent enjoyment', loving the sounds of the gurgling brook and the merry village chimes. To have to arrest such a person makes a policeman's life a distressing one.

> Our feelings we with difficulty smother
> When constabulary duty's to be done.

'A poor excuse for picking a man's pocket every twenty-fifth of December'
Charles Dickens, *A Christmas Carol* (1843)

The excuse that Christmas comes only once a year was offered to the miser, Scrooge, by his inoffensive clerk, Bob Cratchit, when apologetically asking to have Christmas Day off. Scrooge grudgingly allows the free day, asserting that he himself is being ill-used through having to pay a day's wages for no work. 'Be here all the earlier next morning.' Cratchit meekly promises that he will – and Scrooge for the present remains ignorant of his coming change of heart.

'Preserved they lie
In tombs that open to the curious eye'
George Crabbe, *The Library* (1781)

Crabbe was not much given to making jokes, but perhaps he was here indulging in a kind of pun. The 'tombs' to which he is referring are really books, or tomes. Through books the dead can still speak to us, just as though they were alive. Indeed, they are not really dead.

> 'The dead,' methinks a thousand tongues reply;
> 'These are the tombs of such as cannot die!'

Books can give 'new views to life'. They can admonish fools and 'confirm the wise'. Moreover, they shun nobody, and offer their contents to everyone alike, poor or proud, subject or king.

> *'A primrose by the river's brim*
> *A yellow primrose was to him,*
> *And it was nothing more'*
> William Wordsworth, *Peter Bell*, Pt I (1819)

Wordsworth is trying to indicate that Peter Bell is a thoroughly worthless fellow with no appreciation of Nature. But his criticism of Bell is off target. A primrose is just a yellow primrose to most Nature lovers; it is only introspective poets who regard flowers as preachers or teachers. The real trouble with Peter Bell was that the primrose was *not* to him a yellow primrose but an object of no more significance than a stone or a bit of mud. His insensitivity led him to belabour a stolen ass, but a change of heart occurs in the last stanza of this overlong narrative poem.

> *'A problem without a solution may interest the student, but*
> *can hardly fail to annoy the casual reader'*
> A. Conan Doyle, *The Case-book of Sherlock Holmes – The Problem*
> *of Thor Bridge* (1927)

Strange as it may seem, Sherlock Holmes was not always successful. Dr Watson had in his files notes of several cases which remained unsolved, and which were therefore never recorded in narrative form. He instances, for example, the case of the man who returned to his house for an umbrella and was never seen again; the ship which disappeared in a patch of mist; the man who was found insane, staring at a matchbox containing an unknown insect. Dr Watson did not know the answers to these cases – and we may be pretty sure that Conan Doyle was just as much in the dark.

> *'Procrastination is the thief of time'*
> Edward Young, *Night Thoughts*, I (1742)

This long, didactic blank verse poem, largely about death and related themes, was once very popular. It contains some shrewd and neatly expressed thoughts, though the total effect of it is like being repeatedly struck over the head with a heavy book. In this passage a certain Lorenzo, perhaps representing the poet's son, is warned against the danger of allowing good intentions to fail through delay. 'Be wise today; 'tis madness to defer.' We tend to think of ourselves as enjoying a comparatively permanent existence, but death can come very suddenly.

> *'A project for extracting sunbeams out of cucumbers'*
> Jonathan Swift, *Gulliver's Travels*, III, ch. 5 (1726)

The land of Balnibarbi is one where impractical activities are normal, and rational action is abnormal. In the Grand Academy of the chief city all kinds of fantastic experiments were carried out. One of these was a plan for getting sunbeams out of cucumbers and putting them in hermetically sealed vessels. Then, if the summer should prove cold, warm air from the vessels could be let out. This and other fanciful ideas were smacks at the gullibility of society, and at the absurdities of those so-called scientists whose activities were still linked with alchemy and magic. Swift was perhaps following similar satires by Rabelais (1494?–1553).

'The proper study of mankind is man'
Alexander Pope, *Essay on Man*, Epistle II (1732–4)

The poet asserts that man should be aware of his limitations. He should not try to put himself in the place of God and judge the fitness or unfitness of what God ordains. He is an imperfect being, a 'chaos of thought and passion, all confused', and should study to understand himself, not question the workings of Providence.

'A prophet is not without honour, save in his own country'
Bible, Matthew, xiii, 57 (c A.D. 80–100)

After touring the land, preaching and narrating parables, Jesus returned to Nazareth where he was brought up. But he could make little impression in his own village, where most of the inhabitants had known him since childhood as the local carpenter's son. (According to Mark vi, 3, Jesus himself was also a carpenter.) The fact that the villagers knew his brothers and sisters seemed to make it difficult to believe in his ability to perform wonders, and had an inhibiting effect on his activities. Who were these relations? Mary was unlikely to have been their mother. Perhaps they were Joseph's children by a former marriage.

'Proud man still seems the enemy of all'
John Clare, *Summer Evening*

Walking in the country, Clare notes how all living creatures are afraid of his approach. The frog, the mouse, the hare, the bird, even the grasshopper, all show alarm until he has passed. 'Thus nature's human link and endless thrall ... still seems the enemy of all.' (Thus man, who binds and enslaves all other living things, seems to be their constant enemy.)

'The Puritan hated bearbaiting, not because it gave pain to the bear, but because it gave pleasure to the spectators'
T. B. Macaulay, *History of England*, ch. 1 (1848)

The quotation, sometimes regarded as a witticism, is a simple statement of fact. The Puritans found equal offence in maypoles, theatres, dancing, wrestling matches, and other public amusements. Under Puritan rule Christmas ceased to be a season of joy and was ordered (not always successfully) to be a time of fasting. The spirit behind these regulations was that man was a sinful creature, born of original sin, and should spend his time bemoaning his unworthiness instead of enjoying happiness.

'A quenchless hope of happiness to be'
F. D. Hemans, *Arabella Stuart* (1828)

There is sad irony in the quoted phrase (expressing Arabella's thoughts) for there was little happiness in her life and her hopes were presently crushed altogether. It was her fate to have a slender claim to the throne, which in the sixteenth and seventeenth centuries was very dangerous indeed. All she wanted was domestic happiness with William Seymour, whom she managed to marry in secret, but they were both hastily imprisoned by James I. They both escaped, and hoped to be reunited in France. But Arabella was captured near Calais, and imprisoned in the Tower, where she went mad and died soon afterwards. Mrs Heman's poem, included in a volume (Records of Woman) with a strong feminine content, deals with Arabella's thoughts during her first imprisonment.

'Quick wits commonly be apt to take, unapt to keep'
Roger Ascham, *The Schoolmaster* (1570)

Ascham was a remarkable man, being Latin Secretary to three successive monarchs in a contentious age – Edward VI, Mary I, and Elizabeth I. He was also tutor to Elizabeth when she was Princess. Ascham had thought a great deal about education, and was persuaded to put his thoughts in writing. These views were published by his widow two years after his death at the age of fifty-three. He is here stressing the need for schoolmasters to exercise patience and to bear in mind that pupils who were slow to learn might none the less be surer of their learning in the long run.

'Quoth the Raven, "Nevermore"'
E. A. Poe, *The Raven* (1845)

This was Poe's favourite poem, 'shining above them all (his other poems) as a diamond of purest water'. It was not the product of any flash of inspiration, however, but was carefully and deliberately planned. He wanted a single word containing a long ō and the consonant r, and 'nevermore' came to mind. In order to have the word repeated he thought of 'a non-reasoning creature capable of speech'. A parrot was his first idea, but his second thought, a raven, seemed better suited to the gloomy theme of a lost love (Lenore) whose death meant that she would nevermore be seen.

'Railing at life, and yet afraid of death'
Charles Churchill, *Gotham*, Bk I (1764)

In this poem Churchill has reduced the Seven Ages of Man to five (infancy, childhood, youth, manhood, and old age). Here he is dealing with the last stage, which in the eighteenth century was looked upon without much respect. The old (and sixty was old in those days) were seen as tiresome to their friends, short-tempered, failing in memory, and given to praising the days of their youth. Their only justification for existence, seemingly, was that they united with robuster ages in praising Churchill's invented Utopia.

'The race is not to the swift, nor the battle to the strong'
Bible, Ecclesiastes, ix, 11 (*c* 200 B.C.)

The moral of this two-verse section of the preacher's sermon (Ecclesiastes = preacher) appears to be that chance plays a big part in life. Clever and able people do not necessarily get their desserts. And just as fishes are suddenly caught up in a net, and birds trapped in a snare, so man can never be sure that the same kind of thing will not happen to him.

'Rattle his bones over the stones;
He's only a pauper, whom nobody owns'
Thomas Noel, *Rhymes and Roundelays* (1841)

This verse, entitled 'The Pauper's Drive', offers an ironical social comment on the poverty too often prevailing in early-nineteenth-century England. The poet implies that when the friendless pauper is dead he at last has a chance to ride in a coach! Other paupers are invited to note the privilege enjoyed by the corpse in the hearse, and to reflect how lucky they are that one day they will have the same respect paid to them. Noel, who graduated at Merton College, Oxford, in 1824, was not a very prolific author, but he wrote a few well-known songs.

'A really sympathetic race would not so much as know the
meaning of happiness'
Aldous Huxley, *Crome Yellow*, ch. 16 (1921)

Mr Scogan, middle-aged, highly intelligent, very talkative, is holding forth to his male companions after dinner, reflecting on the frightful horrors that are taking place in the world all the time. 'People are being crushed, slashed, disembowelled, mangled.' In spite of this we continue to enjoy life, for sympathy and imagination are very limited. And a good thing too, he insists. Anyone who had 'an imagination vivid enough and a sympathy sufficiently sensitive really to comprehend and to feel the sufferings of other people' would never have a moment's peace of mind.

'The real war will never get in the books'
Walt Whitman, *Specimen Days* (1882–3)

During the American Civil War, Whitman acted as helper in military hospitals and saw some of the realities of war at close hand. The sufferings and deaths of so many men, it seemed to him, presented the essence of the war more truly than the formal accounts of campaigns and battles, and the 'surface-courteousness' of the generals. No doubt he had in mind the chivalrous way in which General Grant received the sword of surrender from General Lee.

'Regained my freedom with a sigh'
Lord Byron, *The Prisoner of Chillon* (1816)

The castle of Chillon stands at one end of Lake Geneva. Francois de Bonnivard, a Swiss patriot, was confined there by the Duke of Savoy from 1530 to 1536. Byron's poem is written from the prisoner's point of view. At first he is chained in a dungeon with his two brothers. When they die he has to endure his imprisonment alone. As time passes he is left unchained and able to peer from the window at the mountains, the sails of ships on the lake, and the birds. He grows so accustomed to his strange life that he is almost reluctant to leave his cell when freed. Bonnivard himself lived for over thirty years after being released.

'Remarkably nice young men, were the crew of the Hot Cross Bun'
W. S. Gilbert, *Poll Pineapple* (1869)

Nice they were indeed. They never swore, and though they were not very efficient, their commander Lieutenant Belaye decided that 'it *is* such a treat to sail with a gentle well-bred crew'. However, when he brought a wife back to his ship the secret of his crew's niceness was revealed. Every one of them was really a girl in disguise who had enlisted for love of the Lieutenant! Gilbert's humorous *Bab Ballads* were published over a century ago. No doubt in a unisex age the crew would be less nice than Lieutenant Belaye's.

'The remedy is worse than the disease'
Francis Bacon, *Essay, Of Seditions and Troubles* (1612)

Sedition was a very real threat to rulers in the sixteenth and seventeenth centuries, and a shrewd and experienced politician such as Lord Bacon was just the man to deal with the subject. Among other suggestions, he recommends that the ruler should have one or more 'military persons' always at hand, ready and able to put down revolt as soon as it shows itself. On second thoughts, however, he adds that there is a danger that the 'military person' might turn out to favour the wrong side, and might thus foment trouble instead of repressing it.

'Remote from busy Life's bewildered way'
Thomas Campbell, *The Pleasures of Hope*, Pt II (1799)

'Remote . . . way', the lover of Nature, 'free on the sunny slope, or winding shore', enjoys the woods and waves, the sunrises, the call of the cuckoo, and other rural delights. A love of Nature was beginning to show itself in late-eighteenth-century poetry, but it had not really shaken itself free from the artificial verbiage which offended such poets as Wordsworth and Keats. Such poetry with its 'Idalian bowers', and its 'enamoured Fancy', was also 'remote from Life's bewildered way'.

'Riches are for spending'
Francis Bacon, *Of Expense* (1597)

Lord Bacon was accused of taking bribes, but he was no miser with his possibly ill-gotten gains. He believed that money should be spent, not hoarded, and spent for 'honour and good actions'. None the less, he favoured spending with a canny regard for sound economy. A man might reasonably spend up to half his income. Even a hoarder ought to spend about a third. Though spending is good, laying out money in all directions is bad. Lavish payments in one direction should be balanced by saving in another. Spend on food, save on dress; be plentiful in the hall, be saving in the stable.

'Ride, ride together, for ever ride'
Robert Browning, *The Last Ride Together* (1855)

An unsuccessful lover begs the lady who has rejected him to take a last ride with him. She consents, the result being a Browning monologue, speculating profitlessly on what might have been, and finally hoping that the instant might be made eternal, and that they would go on riding together for the rest of time. An amusing parody of this poem was written by the nineteenth-century humorist, J. K. Stephen, giving an account of the ride from the lady's point of view.:

I spoke of the weather to Mr B.:
But he neither listened nor spoke to me . . .
He never smiles and he never speaks:
He might go on like this for weeks.

'Rides in the whirlwind, and directs the storm'
Joseph Addison, *The Campaign* (1704)

The Campaign relates to the Battle of Blenheim (1704), likened here, no doubt aptly, to a hurricane. Just as an angel might direct a hurricane from the very heart of it, so John Churchill, Duke of Marlborough, directed the course of the Battle of Blenheim from the centre of the conflict. This notable campaign brought the war against France to a successful end, and the Government wished the event to be commemorated by a poem. Addison was given the commission, and he turned out a poem which in the circumstances was a commendable literary effort. It was equally commendable politically, and won him an appointment as Commissioner of Appeals.

'The Right Divine of Kings to govern wrong'
Alexander Pope, *The Dunciad*, Bk IV (1727)

Looking back a century or more, Pope is dragging James I into his net, along with other supposedly dull people. The goddess of Dulness had asked for a pedant king, and James seemed to fill the bill. Henry of Navarre had dubbed him 'the wisest fool in Christendom'. But although James was something of a pedant – he loved to correct the Latin of his councillors and even of foreign ambassadors – he was no fool, and too shrewd to be a dullard. Pope was on firmer ground when he mocked James's belief in the Divine Right of Stuart kings to do whatever they pleased.

'Ring out, wild bells, to the wild sky'
Alfred Tennyson, *In Memoriam*, cv (1850)

On New Year's Eve the poet cries to the bells to ring out
the death of the old year, with all its evils. He longs to
see the end of grief for those who have died (his friend
Arthur Hallam was very much in his mind), of class
hatred, of political strife, of disease, of greed for money.
In their place he hopes the bells will ring in 'nobler
modes of life', and 'the common love of good'. Putting it
in religious terms he concludes:

Ring out the darkness of the land,
Ring in the Christ that is to be.

'A Robin Red breast in a cage
Puts all Heaven in a rage'
William Blake, *Auguries of Innocence* (1803)

The poem consists mainly of couplets condemning the
cruelty of man to humbler creatures. An overfilled
dovecote, a starved dog, an ill-used horse, a hunted
hare, an injured skylark or wren – these are examples of
abuses which drew forth Blake's protests. To achieve
eternity, man must show an all-embracing love, and
even the humblest creatures must be treated with consideration. The whole poem asserts Blake's belief that
'everything that lives is Holy'. His attitude of mind is
shared with St Francis of Assisi, and is akin to Albert
Schweitzer's 'Reverence for Life'.

'A rose-red city – "half as old as Time"!'
J. W. Burgon, *Petra* (1845)

The city is Petra in Jordan, which dates back to the fourth
century B.C. and was once a famous capital. Its ruins
have the rosy hue of sunrise. The poem won the
Newdigate prize at Oxford in 1845 but, rather unfairly,
only one line has managed to survive the onslaught of
Time – and half of that line was borrowed from Samuel
Rogers's *Italy* (1822). Burgon became Dean of Chichester
in 1876.

'The rub and scrape of a city's feet
Prepare your canvas'
James Kirkup, *Pavement Artist* (1957)

The artist draws his pictures on pavement slabs worn
smooth by passersby. On that 'canvas' he shows such
scenes as The Pyramids, or Daybreak on the Alps, or
rather sentimentalized domestic animals, or portraits of
well-known personalities. Politicians, TV stars, sporting
heroes, and royalty are all brought to pavement level.
Later, however, the feet that made the slabs smooth
enough to draw upon begin to erase the pictures as
home-going pedestrians tread carelessly over the works
of art.

'Rule, Britannia, rule the waves:
Britons never will be slaves'
James Thomson, *Alfred: a Masque*, Act II (1740)

These notable lines were almost certainly by Thomson,
though the masque was written in conjunction with
David Mallet who later adapted it for the regular theatre.
It was created originally to please the Prince of Wales
(father of George III), and first performed for him at
Cliveden House. Thomson was often inspired by patriotic fervour, as his poem *Britannia* (1729) had shown. On
this later occasion the fervour might also have been
encouraged by a pension which the Prince had recently
awarded him. 'Rule, Britannia', set to music by Dr Arne,
was sung by a sailor to bring the masque to a triumphant
conclusion, while other sailors joined in a lively dance.

'Russell let me always call you Edwin, and call me Eric'
F. W. Farrar, *Eric, or Little by Little*, ch. 4 (1858)

Eric, the young hero of Dean Farrar's novel, is swearing
eternal friendship with the school's good boy, Edwin
Russell, at the end of Eric's first term. There are not a few
sentimental, over-emotional passages in the story, and it
has long been the fashion to laugh, if not sneer, at this
novel as the work of an old fogey in a cathedral close,
sadly ignorant of boys and schools. It is worth noting
that Farrar was in fact a brilliant and experienced teacher,
remarkably successful in his handling of his pupils.
Despite certain sentimentalities, excessive religiosity,
and some over-writing, *Eric* gives a great deal of valuable
insight into public school life in the mid-nineteenth-
century.

'A sadder and a wiser man'
S. T. Coleridge, *The Rime of the Ancient Mariner*, Pt VII (1798)

A wedding guest has been stopped on his way to the
feast by an old sailor, determined to relate the story of his
remarkable sea adventures. Unable to get away, the
wedding guest has listened to the end. Now, in a daze,
he turns away from the wedding party, too bewildered
(and perhaps too late) to enjoy the festivities, 'a sadder
and a wiser man'. His sadness may be due to his having
missed the feast, but his increased wisdom is doubtless
due to his having received, though at secondhand, a
very vivid emotional experience.

'Sail on, O Ship of State'
H. W. Longfellow, *The Building of the Ship* (1849)

The poem is both a simple story and an allegory. It tells
of the building of 'a goodly vessel, that shall laugh at all
disaster', by a master shipbuilder. Helping him is a
youth who hopes to marry the master's daughter. The
ship is at length completed and launched, 'the bride of
the old grey sea', and the young man and girl are duly
married aboard her. To the poet the vessel also represents the Ship of State, the union of States formed by
Washington and his colleagues in 1775. 'Our hearts, our
hopes, are all with thee.' Sixteen years after the poem
was written the hearts and hopes of all Americans
suffered the heavy blow of a terrible Civil War.

'Satan finds some mischief still
For idle hands to do'
Isaac Watts, *Divine and Moral Songs for Children* (1715)

Watts, a clergyman, was a very successful eighteenth-century author of improving verses for children, and also of some well-known hymns (he wrote 'O God, our help in ages past'), which secured for him a memorial in Westminster Abbey. He is here inviting his readers to contemplate the activities of 'the busy bee', which improves each shining hour by ceaselessly gathering honey. The child, Watts insinuates, should be equally busy at 'books, work, or healthful play'.

'The satisfied grunt of the **Daily Mail**, the abandoned gurgle of the **Sunday Times**, and the shrill enthusiastic scream of the **Daily Express**'
Noel Coward, *Hay Fever*, Act I (1925)

Judith Bliss, recently retired actress, is describing the thrill of first nights. Ardent playgoers would be wishing for a success, and even the critics would be 'emitting queer little inarticulate noises' at lines which amused them. Coward's relations with the Press were somewhat mixed. They were kind to one or two of his early plays, but the notices of *Fallen Angels* were 'vituperative to the point of incoherence'. This play and *Hay Fever* (written in three days) were composed much about the same time, and Coward sometimes liked to meet his critics head-on. Here he is giving them a good-humoured punch in the ribs.

'Scots wha hae wi' Wallace bled'
Robert Burns, *Scots Wha Hae* (1794)

Edward I, at first aiming to bring Scotland into union with England, found himself ultimately trying to conquer it. He had a limited success, defeating William Wallace and hanging him. But he died before he could deal with the next Scottish leader, Robert Bruce, and Edward II was a very different man from his father. In 1314 Bruce routed an English force at Bannockburn, near Stirling, and the idea of conquering Scotland was abandoned. Nearly five hundred years later Burns imagined himself as a Scottish leader in Bruce's day, exhorting his countrymen to fight fiercely for freedom in the coming battle at Bannockburn. 'Scots, who have bled with Wallace, and who have often been led by Bruce, go forward either to die in battle or to achieve victory.'

'Seated one day at the organ,
I was weary and ill at ease'
Adelaide A. Procter, *The Lost Chord* (1858)

Sitting sadly at her instrument, the organist lets her fingers roam idly over the keys. Suddenly she hears a splendid chord 'like the sound of a great Amen'. It was like a call from Heaven, setting at rest all her griefs and perplexities. Unfortunately she fails to write it down, and try as she may she can no longer find the right notes. So she supposes she will have to wait until she reaches Heaven to hear the chord again. (She appears to have no doubt that this is her destination.) Sir Arthur Sullivan did not find the lost chord, but he found a tune that made Miss Procter's lyric one of the best-known songs of all time.

'Seeing his evil prisoned thus, I knew
For the first time, the wonder man can do'
John Masefield, *Wonderings* (1943)

As a child Masefield heard terrifying tales of the fearful things a bull could do. One had gored its master. Another had chased and tossed a small boy, leaving him insane. The clothes of another were left clinging to the bull's horns. One day he crept into the barn where the farm bull was stabled, frightened yet irresistibly drawn towards it. He climbed up into the loft. Suddenly he saw the beast close beneath him, tremendously powerful, yet fastened with 'a cringle (ring) in his snout', and the boy was filled with amazement that so fearsome a creature could be thus confined.

'See the conquering hero comes'
Thomas Morell, *Judas Maccabaeus* (1746)

Judas was a Jewish ruler in the second century B.C. who led a revolt against the Syrians and recaptured Jerusalem. The story was told as an oratorio by Morell, a classical scholar (1703–84), with music by Handel. Two books of the Maccabees are included in the *Apocrypha*. The chorus of praise to Judas is sung by Israelite youths, after which a chorus of virgins endeavours to go one better with 'See the godlike youth advance!'

'Set your faces like a flint'
John Bunyan, *The Pilgrim's Progress*, Pt I (1678)

After Christian and his friend Faithful had made their way through the Valley of the Shadow of Death, they met the good preacher, Evangelist. He encouraged them to continue their journey to the Celestial City and exhorted them to preserve flint-like faces against the Devil's wiles, particularly as they were approaching the evil place known as Vanity Fair. Here the two travellers were imprisoned. Both men maintained faces of stone, as advised, but their fates were unequal. Christian escaped but Faithful was put to a cruel death.

'Several excuses are always less convincing than one'
Aldous Huxley, *Point Counter Point*, ch. 1 (1928)

To add to an excuse is to admit that you are not convinced by it. This is precisely the case with Walter, who wants to attend an evening party on his own but is being pressed not to go by the woman with whom he is living. He feels both irritated and guilty. Trying to find a reason for going, he suggests that he thinks he may meet his father there. It is not an ideal excuse, and he does not strengthen it by hurriedly adding a second. She is convinced that he is going to meet another woman – and she is perfectly right.

'The shades of night were falling fast'
H. W. Longfellow, *Excelsior* (1842)

A youth carrying a banner bearing the word 'Excelsior' (the motto of the United States: 'aim ever at higher things') goes climbing in the Alps. He ignores warnings ('Beware the awful avalanche') and even a maiden's invitation to stay and rest 'thy weary head upon this breast'. Next day he is found dead in the snow. The moral is intended to be the value and importance of continuing to strive. But this admirable precept tends to be obscured by the feeling that the youth was a bit of a fool to go mountaineering in adverse conditions and without taking any precautions.

'Shall anything bolder be found than united woman'
Thomas Hardy, *Under the Greenwood Tree*, ch. 6 (1872)

Though the cause of female rights was very much in the air when Hardy wrote this early novel, this reference is much more parochial. 'United woman' here refers to a small group of Sunday-school girls in Mellstock Church, led (without any intention of deliberate provocation) by the new schoolmistress. On one memorable Christmas morning they astounded the choir and orchestra in the gallery by innocently joining in the singing so vigorously that the official choristers were almost out-sung. Such a thing had never happened before, and Mellstock Church gallery was soon buzzing with indignant whispers, Mr Spinks, the speaker here, being prominent among the protesters.

'Shall fold their tents, like the Arabs, And as silently steal away'
H. W. Longfellow, *The Day is Done* (1844)

In this song the poet asks for his evening melancholy to be cleared away by the recital of some simple narrative poem that will soothe him and drive away 'the cares that infest the day'. Like the nomadic Bedouins, his worries will then gradually disappear, for

Such songs have power to quiet
The restless pulse of care.

'Shall I strew on thee rose or rue or laurel'
A. C. Swinburne, *Ave Atque Vale* (1868)

Written shortly after the death of Charles Baudelaire (1821–67), this elegy pays tribute to the French poet whose work Swinburne greatly admired. *Ave Atque Vale* (Hail and Farewell) was not published until ten years later. The flowers to be strewn were all emblematic. The rose was for love, the rue for remembrance, the laurel for poetry. Alternatively, Swinburne suggests offering 'half-faded fiery blossoms, pale with heat / And full of bitter summer'. Baudelaire's most famous work was *Les Fleurs du Mal* (Flowers of Evil).

'She is the darling of my heart'
Henry Carey, *Sally in Our Alley* (1737)

The line comes from one of the best-known of all ballad songs. The young singer tells of his love for his sweetheart, Sally, who lives with her street-seller parents in the same alley as himself. He is looking forward to the end of his seven-year apprenticeship, by which time he will be free to marry.

O then we'll wed, and then we'll bed –

But not in our alley!

The song was inspired by the simple sight of a London girl out walking with her sweetheart one holiday. It became so popular that Carey, primarily a writer of burlesques, was often called 'the alley poet'. He wrote the music for many of his own songs, including *Sally*.

'She must be seen to be appreciated'
Harrison Ainsworth, *Old St Paul's*, ch. 3 (1841)

The woman is the lovely wife of a captain in King Charles II's army. He has been gambling recklessly with a dissipated young nobleman, Parravicin, and has lost every penny. Parravicin then challenges him to stake his wife by handing over the key of his house, if he loses, so that the nobleman can enter that night and enjoy her. Parravicin wins, and asks a companion, who claims to know the lady, whether she is as beautiful as reputed. He is told that 'words are too feeble to paint her charms'. However, Parravicin is disappointed after all: the wife has caught the plague.

'She pleased by hiding all attempts to please'
Charles Churchill, *The Rosciad* (1761)

Churchill's main purpose in this poem was to offer sincere praise to Garrick by damning all other actors, but since actresses did not compete with the great little actor, they too were allowed their merits. Very justly in the case of Kitty Clive, who was generally accepted by audiences and actors alike as Queen of Comedy. Even so stern a critic as Johnson had a high opinion of her comic powers. Fielding called her 'the best daughter, the best sister, and the best friend' – a tribute which few actresses could have earned.

'She's as headstrong as an allegory on the banks of the Nile'
R. B. Sheridan, *The Rivals*, III, iii (1775)

One of the best known of Mrs Malaprop's sixty language errors, an allegory, of course, being confused with an alligator. She is apologizing to young Captain Absolute for the apparent refusal of her niece, Lydia, to accept him as her suitor. But the situation is in fact even more confused than Mrs Malaprop's language, for Lydia believes Absolute to be her lover, Beverley, pretending to be Absolute, whereas Mrs Malaprop knows him as Absolute pretending to be Beverley.

'She sat like Patience on a monument'
William Shakespeare, *Twelfth Night*, II, iv (1601)

Viola, disguised as a boy page to the Duke Orsino, whom she secretly loves, is comparing men and women as lovers. Denying Orsino's assertion that men's passions are stronger than women's, Viola describes her own secret love for him. She pretends (speaking as a youth) that she had a sister who loved a man deeply but was unable to confess her love, and pined away, sitting 'like Patience on a monument, / Smiling at grief'. The figure of Patience was often used as a statue on church-yard monuments.

'She smooths her hair with automatic hand, And puts a record on the gramophone'
T. S. Eliot, *The Waste Land*, III (1922)

A typist has just been seduced by an estate agent's clerk, but her mood is one of indifference. Unlike the eighteenth-century heroine of Goldsmith's lyric whose seduction leads to thoughts of suicide, the less sensitive girl of the 1920s finds the whole business rather a bore. This joyless unromanticism of spirit (drying combinations were hanging from the window, while stockings, slippers, camisoles, and stays were piled on the divan bed) typified the disillusionment felt by many intellectuals in the period just after the Great War. The poem's obscure, cynical aridity quickly established Eliot's reputation among the élite.

'She would show an image of the times'
Ben Jonson, *Every Man in His Humour – Prologue* (1598)

Jonson is giving a very explicit statement of his views on what comedy ('she') ought to be and do. He has just mocked some of the traditional stage conventions: a life span covered in a couple of hours, great battles represented by 'three rusty swords', a chorus wafting the audience overseas, imitation thunder, and the like. In place of such artificialities he wants 'deeds and language, such as men do use'. Although he carried out his intention effectively, plays of the type he mocked continued to flourish, and one not insignificant writer of them cheerfully acted in Jonson's play and may even have recommended it: William Shakespeare.

'Ships that pass in the night'
H. W. Longfellow, *Tales of a Wayside Inn – Elizabeth* (1873)

Normally the phrase applies to two people who meet each other for a brief while and are then separated for good. But in this particular tale the metaphorical ships ultimately dock together. Elizabeth, a Quaker, after many years met a Quaker friend of her childhood days. She told him that she loved him. He replied, 'I have yet no light to lead me' (which, it may be thought, was a convenient way of saying that he could not make up his mind). After a long journey he decided to accept her proposal ('the light shone at last', the poem phrases it), and fortunately he found her still willing.

> *'Shoot, if you must, this old grey head,*
> *But spare your country's flag'*
> J. G. Whittier, *Barbara Frietchie* (1863)

In the early years of the American Civil War an elderly woman in Maryland boldly flew the United States flag from her window as the Southern forces were approaching. The Southern States were trying to secede from the Union, and to fly the United States flag was a defiant gesture towards the South. The flag was promptly shot down, but the woman (Barbara Frietchie) picked it up and invited the Southerners to shoot her if they wished but to spare the flag. The Southern leader, General Jackson, was so impressed by her courage that he ordered his men not to harm her.

> *'Shut up the world at large, let Bedlam out;*
> *And you will be perhaps surprised to find*
> *All things pursue exactly the same route'*
> Lord Byron, *Don Juan*, XIV, lxxxiv (1819–24)

Departing as ever from his thin story, Byron is satirizing the society of his day, suggesting that if the lunatics of the London Bethlehem Hospital (Bedlam) were let out and allowed to run the country, there would be no noticeable difference. He calls ironically on William Wilberforce, who has been campaigning for the freedom of *black* people, to turn his attention to *whites*, and in particular to curb the reckless extravagances of George IV, including the Brighton Pavilion.

> *'Sighed, and looked unutterable things'*
> James Thomson, *The Seasons – Summer* (1727)

This would seem to be an idyllic picture of blissful young love. The pastoral lovers, idealized in description as in name, are Celadon and his Amelia, 'a matchless pair'. They spend their days in innocent enjoyment of each other's company, as the quotation indicates. But a summer storm disturbs the peace, and Amelia becomes frightened. 'Fear not,' Celadon tells her protectively. The guilty, he asserts, may well feel terror, but her innocence will protect her – and so it should in this charming pastoral. But Thomson suddenly changes tack: 'That moment, to the ground, / A blackened corpse, was struck the beauteous maid.'

> *'A sight to dream of, not to tell'*
> S. T. Coleridge, *Christabel*, Pt 1 (1797)

The lovely maiden, Christabel, finds Geraldine, an equally lovely damsel, in distress. Christabel takes her home with her, and the two share a bedroom. When Geraldine disrobes, Christabel sees 'a sight to dream of, not to tell'. Many readers imagine that this implies that her body was too lovely for words to describe. In fact Coleridge intended an opposite meaning. Geraldine was really a witch. In his original manuscript the preceding lines read: 'Full in view / Behold! her bosom and half her side, / Hideous, deformed, and pale of hue.' Later Coleridge struck out the last line, leaving the rhyme scheme incomplete and the meaning ambiguous. Second thoughts are not always best.

'Silence gives consent'
Oliver Goldsmith, *The Good-Natured Man*, Act II (1768)

Miss Richland's silence, however, does not indicate consent but craftiness. Her guardian, Mr Croaker, wants his son to marry her, thereby securing her fortune. If she openly refuses him she will lose half of it, according to the terms of the will. She therefore decides to say nothing, knowing that Leontine himself has no desire to marry her as he is in love with another girl – and knowing, doubtless, that complications of this sort are bound to sort themselves out in this kind of eighteenth-century comedy.

'Silence more musical than any song'
C. G. Rossetti, *Rest* (1849)

Christina Rossetti, sister of Dante Gabriel, was a deeply religious woman whose beliefs permeated most of her poetry. Like Donne, she refuses to accept a realistic view of death. But where Donne is defiant ('Death be not proud'), Christina is joyous. In this sonnet ('O earth, lie heavily upon her eyes') she sees death as a beautiful release from the weariness of life, a perfect peace, which will be disturbed only by a glorious Resurrection. Carried away by mystical dreams she sees the darkness of the grave as 'more clear than noonday' and its silence as 'more musical than any song'.

'The silk stockings and white bosoms of your actresses excite my amorous propensities'
Samuel Johnson, in Boswell's *Life of Johnson* (1791)

During and after the rehearsals of his play *Irene* (1749), produced by his friend David Garrick, Johnson got into the habit of frequenting the 'Green-Room' of Drury Lane theatre, finding the lively personalities and cheerful conversation of the players an agreeable diversion. But his sense of domestic virtue was so strong that he felt compelled to desist when he found the sexual attraction of the actresses, especially Kitty Clive, too powerful for his sense of propriety. He told Garrick that he would come no more behind the scenes. Garrick passed the story on to David Hume, the historian, who helped it on its way to Boswell.

'Simplicity and spotless innocence'
John Milton, *Paradise Lost*, Bk IV (1668)

The phrase refers to Adam and Eve, who wandered naked about the Garden of Eden, not even bothering with fig leaves.

> Nor those mysterious parts were then concealed;
> Then was not guilty shame.

Gazing on this happy pair, Satan decided, with kindly reluctance, that he must offer them and their offspring the hospitality of Hell.

'Simplify, simplify'
H. D. Thoreau, *Walden*, ch. 2 (1854)

Thoreau was an educated American rebel and individualist who believed strongly in self-sufficiency and the simple life. 'Our life is frittered away by detail,' he complained – not without reason. The idea of the simple life has appealed to many of us without actually leading us into the wilds. Thoreau put it into practice by going to live alone in a self-erected hut in a remote spot, observing nature and reading. However, his sojourn lasted only for two-and-a-half years. The excellent book he wrote about it was printed and published by the despised urban machinery.

'Sing me a song of a lad that is gone,
Say, could that lad be I?'
R. L. Stevenson, *Songs of Travel*, XLII (1895)

The poet looks back to the days of his boyhood when he travelled in his boat among the Western Isles of Scotland – Mull, Rum, and Eigg. In those days he was merry of heart as he sailed over the sea to Skye, and he longs to recapture the same spirit of youth and eagerness.
Give me the eyes, give me the soul,
Give me the lad that's gone.
In spite of a long and failing struggle against ill-health, he maintained his courage and spirit to the end of his varied life, cut short all too soon (1850–94).

'Sing the glorious day's renown'
Thomas Campbell, *The Battle of the Baltic* (1801)

In 1801 the Russians, Swedes, and Danes formed an alliance to hinder British trade in the Baltic Sea. This was not to be tolerated, so a British fleet attacked Copenhagen. It was during the conflict between British and Danish ships that Nelson distinguished himself by putting the famous telescope to the famous blind eye and refusing to see the signal to withdraw. The result was a resounding victory for Britain, and 'a glorious day's renown', though there were many casualties to mar the rejoicing.

'Sir Patrick Spens is the best sailor
That ever sailed the sea'
Ballad, *Sir Patrick Spens*

According to the ballad, the Scottish King was advised that the best sea-captain to undertake a difficult voyage was Sir Patrick Spens. So Spens (Spence) is directed to sail to Norway to bring back the King's daughter, Margaret. Sir Patrick duly sets forth, and picks up the Maid of Norway. They run into bad weather on the return, however, and the ship founders with all aboard her. Two separate events, in fact, are unhistorically combined in the ballad. One Margaret was conveyed to Norway to marry King Eric, and many lords were drowned on the return journey. Twenty years later another Margaret, the Maid of Norway, was drowned on the voyage to Scotland.

'Sleep after toil, port after stormy seas'
Edmund Spenser, *The Faerie Queene*, Bk I, ix (1589)

This restfulness, which sounds so soothing and agreeable, is in fact an invitation to suicide, put forward by the villainous creature Despair to the gallant Red Cross Knight. He insinuates that since death is inevitable and since dire punishment awaits those who have sinned, it is best to cut life as short as possible lest prolonging it should mean committing more sins and incurring worse punishments. The knight is almost convinced, and is saved from taking his own life only by the intervention of the lady he loves.

'Slow and steady wins the race'
Robert Lloyd, *The Hare and the Tortoise* (1757)

Lloyd was a very minor writer of Cowper's time (they were schoolmates) who, like too many other minor writers, then and later, threw up his job to become a full-time author. He was subsequently imprisoned as a debtor. Here he has adapted Aesop's very famous fable to make a moral tale in verse, proving the virtues of perseverance. His tortoise is sufficiently educated to refer to classical history – 'I'll win, like Fabius, by delay' – before achieving victory. Alas, the moral did little to help Lloyd himself: he died in the Fleet Prison.

'Slowly and sadly we laid him down'
Charles Wolfe, *The Burial of Sir John Moore* (1817)

Moore, a notable British general, was forced by circumstances to retreat during the Peninsular War. He was mortally wounded at the battle of Corunna (1809) despite the defeat of the French enemy. His burial in the early hours at Corunna was a silent one. 'Not a drum was heard, not a funeral note.' Charles Wolfe, an Irish clergyman, originally published his poem anonymously. It was at one time attributed to Byron, among other poets; but Wolfe eventually moved into the limelight to enjoy his solitary success. It is the only poem of his ever to overcome oblivion.

'So daring in love, and so dauntless in war'
Sir Walter Scott, *Marmion*, V (1808)

A ballad is sung to entertain the English lord, Marmion, at the court of James IV of Scotland. It tells of the exploit of 'young Lochinvar' who has ridden desperately to Netherby Hall to meet the girl he hopes to marry, despite parental opposition, and finds that she is just about to be wed to another man. He appears to accept the situation, drinks the bride's health, and asks permission to dance a measure with her. He duly whirls her round the room, but as soon as they are near the doorway he swings her up on to the saddle of his horse (after 'one word in her ear') and provides a romantic finish to the tale.

'Somebody *must play the bad parts in this world, on and off the stage*'
A. W. Pinero, *Trelawny of the 'Wells'*, Act I (1898)

A theatrical landlady is offering consolation to one of her lodgers, the actor Tom Wrench, a born loser. As a mediocre actor he has to put up with all kinds of minor parts. He is also in love with the leading actress of the company, Rose Trelawny, knowing that he stands no chance, for her affections are firmly placed elsewhere. The character was partly based on Tom Robertson, author of *Caste* (1867). Like Wrench, Robertson was a moderate actor with a gift for playwriting. Unlike Wrench, however, Robertson sensibly married the young actress he fell in love with. The 'Wells' is Sadler's Wells theatre in North London, which had been in existence since 1765 (rebuilt 1931).

'*Some conjurers say that the number three is the magic number, and some say number seven. It's neither, my friend. It's number one*'
Charles Dickens, *Oliver Twist*, ch. 43 (1837–8)

Fagin, an old Jew who employs a gang of young pickpockets, is explaining to a new recruit that a person's business is to look after himself (number one), who is every man's best friend. But he adds: 'In a little community like ours, my dear, we have a general number one.' In other words, they were all so dependent upon one another that they needed to cling together.

'*Somehow I never seemed to enjoy so much doing things with other people*'
Francis Chichester, *The Lonely Sea and the Sky*, ch. 27 (1964)

Chichester was one of the greatest of all loners. He flew solo from London to Sydney (1929–30), and in the following year made the first solo flight across the Tasman Sea. Soon afterwards his innovatory solo flight from Australia to Japan ended in near-disaster, caused by some exceptionally high telephone wires. Nearly thirty years later he started a new career as a single-handed sailor. In 1960, after a serious illness, he won the first solo Atlantic race, and in 1967 he completed the most famous of all his feats – the first solo circumnavigation of the world.

'*Some mute inglorious Milton here may rest*'
Thomas Gray, *Elegy Written in a Country Churchyard* (1751)

Gray, writing his fine elegy among the Stoke Poges gravestones, is here reflecting that one of the inhabitants of the small village might have been a great poet if he had been given the education and opportunity. It is an interesting thought, but one which allows of no proof whatever either way. Circumstances as well as nature help to make a poet, and so, if a man's circumstances do not enable him to produce poetry, it is perhaps rather futile to think of him as a mute Milton.

'Something between a hindrance and a help'
William Wordsworth, *Michael* (1800)

Michael was an old shepherd whose only son was born when the father was getting on in years. Despite his 'stern unbending mind' he loved to have the child in view while he was at work watching or shearing the sheep. As soon as the boy was five years old Michael made him a little shepherd's crook. Equipped with this he would try to help his father tend the sheep, standing at a gap or gate to act as a watchman 'to stem or turn the flock'. At this rather premature employment he was, as the quotation suggests, a mixed blessing.

'Sometimes I've believed as many as six impossible things before breakfast'
Lewis Carroll, *Through the Looking-Glass*, ch. 5 (1871)

Alice, asked to believe that the White Queen is 101 years 5 months and 1 day old, says, 'One *can't* believe impossible things.' The Queen disagrees and asserts that when she was Alice's age she used to believe impossible things regularly for half an hour every day. The secret, she disclosed, is to 'draw a long breath, and shut your eyes'. It seems an easy way of achieving credulity, and perhaps it explains the popularity of (for instance) Flying Saucers and Uri Geller.

'So near and yet so far'
Alfred Tennyson, *In Memoriam*, xcvii (1850)

In Memoriam is a series of poems (written 1833–50) inspired by the poet's great sense of loss on the death of his young and talented friend Arthur Hallam (1811–33). Tennyson deeply admired the intellect of his friend. In section xcvii of the poem he reveals his humility by comparing his spiritual relationship with Hallam to that of a wife whose husband is vastly superior to her in intellect but whose love for him remains true. 'He seems so near and yet so far' but 'she dwells on him with faithful eyes.'

'So sit two kings of Brentford on one throne'
William Cowper, *The Task*, Bk I (1785)

Invited to write a blank verse poem about the sofa in his room, Cowper offered good measure, turning out an epic poem in six books. He began by describing the evolution of the sofa from a humble stool to the soft settee on which two people sit comfortably side by side, like the 'two kings of Brentford'. These were a kind of Tweedledum and Tweedledee created by the Second Duke of Buckingham for his burlesque play, *The Rehearsal* (1671), making fun of Restoration heroic tragedy. The kings reigned jointly, going about hand in hand. Precisely who or what they parodied remains uncertain: possibly characters in a play that was mocked into oblivion. The chief character parodied Dryden.

'Splendour, splendour everywhere'
John Betjeman, *Seaside Golf* (1954)

Betjeman was so inspired one day by the sea breezes on a cliffside golf course that he managed to hole out in three. His drive from the tee carried the ball over a bunker. From the fairway a strong iron shot took it to the green, only a couple of yards from the hole. A steady putt completed the triumph – the only time he had ever achieved such a feat. It left him with a wonderful sense of well-being, linked in his mind with the smell of seaweed, the sound of waves slapping the cliffs, and the song of the lark. 'Splendour, splendour everywhere' – that feeling that most of us have occasionally experienced, though not necessarily on the golf course.

'Spurn not the nobly born'
W. S. Gilbert, *Iolanthe*, Act I (1882)

Mid-Victorian plays and novels often dwelt on social distinctions, with an aristocratic hero or heroine being compelled because of family pressure to reject a mate of humble birth. Gilbert characteristically reverses the convention, and gives us a couple of noble lords begging a simple country girl not to reject them because of their rank. As Earl Tolloler points out:

Hearts just as pure and fair
May beat in Belgrave Square
As in the lowly air
Of Seven Dials!

His plea is rejected, for Phyllis loves somebody else.

'A square person has squeezed himself into the round hole'
Sydney Smith, *Sketches of Moral Philosophy* (1850)

This witty and agreeable clergyman was inviting his hearers (for the sketches were originally lectures) to think of people as being of certain distinctive shapes – triangular, circular, oblong, and square. Their chosen activities might also be regarded as similarly shaped holes. All too often, he suggested, we find that 'the triangular person has got into the square hole, the oblong into the triangular, and a square person has squeezed himself into the round hole'. Common usage has seized upon this last graphic image and turned it into 'a square peg in a round hole'.

'The stag at eve had drunk his fill'
Sir Walter Scott, *The Lady of the Lake*, c. I (1810)

The stag, indeed, needed all the drink he could take, for he was about to supply Scott's rather long-winded opening to this narrative poem by being chased to the point of exhaustion. At length only one hunter is left, having ridden his unfortunate horse to death. He now meets the Lady of the Lake (not to be confused with the mysterious Lady of Arthurian legend). Scott's Lady is the charming Ellen Douglas who lives on an island in Loch Katrine. The hunter, known for the nonce as James Fitz-James, encounters her at the lakeside, and the adventures begin.

'Stand between me and his wit'
William Congreve, *The Way of the World*, II, iv (1700)

Millamant, the heroine, is asking her maid, Mincing, to stand between herself and Witwoud, the fop who is one of her followers and who prides himself on his wit. Unlike most fops in Restoration comedy he shows a strain of genuine wit in his folly – enough to make plausible Millamant's tolerance of him. He has been offering would-be witty similes at every stage of the conversation, and Millamant pretends that his mind is so sharp that she needs a shield to protect her from it. Or, as Witwoud himself expresses it: 'Like a screen before a great Fire. I confess I do blaze today.'

'Stands the church clock at ten to three? And is there honey still for tea?'
Rupert Brooke, *The Old Vicarage, Grantchester* (1912)

From his temporary Berlin residence the poet is looking back longingly to the Cambridge village where he resided after taking his degree. He rented three rooms at the Old Vicarage, where his landlord kept bees and supplied home-made honey. The church clock at Grantchester was said to be a local joke as a timekeeper. Brooke's poem, half seriously, half humorously praising Grantchester, and contrasting it not only with Germany but with other Cambridge villages, closes with the quoted couplet.

'The stately Homes of England How beautiful they stand'
F. D. Hemans, *The Homes of England* (1828)

This is not, as might be thought, a poem about stately homes. It is a patriotic poem dealing with various types of English home, and prefaced by a quotation from *Marmion*:
Where's the coward that would not dare
To fight for such a land.
Each stanza of Mrs Hemans's verse deals with a different type of home: the stately homes; the merry homes ('gladsome looks of household love'); the blessed homes ('the holy quietness'); the cottage homes ('smiling o'er the silvery brooks'); the free, fair homes (a summing up). This slightly gushing praise of English domestic residences first appeared in *Blackwood's Magazine*.

'Stern daughter of the Voice of God'
William Wordsworth, *Ode to Duty* (1807)

This well-known but uncharacteristic poem was modelled on Gray's *Hymn to Adversity* – the sort of personified abstraction that Wordsworth normally criticized. Milton had a hand in it too: 'Sole daughter of his voice' (*Paradise Lost*, IX). Thus inspired and encouraged, Wordsworth calls upon Duty to guide his steps in future.
I myself commend
Unto thy guidance from this hour.
It was rash to make his submission public. Privately he later admitted that he was often twitted by his wife and sister for 'having forgotten this dedication of myself'.

'Stick close to your desks and never go to sea,
And you all may be rulers of the Queen's Navee'
W. S. Gilbert, *H.M.S. Pinafore*, Act I (1878)

Sir Joseph Porter, K.C.B., First Lord of the Admiralty, is
explaining (in song) how he came to achieve his exalted
office. His advancement, as Gilbert satirically makes him
explain, was in no way due to seafaring experience but to
his assiduous work as office boy, clerk, and partner in a
lawyer's office. The actual First Lord of the Admiralty in
Disraeli's government, when *Pinafore* was first produced,
was W.H. Smith, founder of the bookstall business. The
point was not lost on the public, and the unfortunate
First Lord soon became known as 'Pinafore Smith'.
Disraeli was not amused.

'Still the wonder grew
That one small head could carry all he knew'
Oliver Goldsmith, *The Deserted Village* (1770)

Goldsmith is perhaps giving an imagined picture of a
typical village schoolmaster. It is certainly not based on
Goldsmith's own experiences as an usher, which were
dismal. This schoolmaster is contented and successful,
severe enough to have his pupils under complete control, but not so severe as to earn their dislike.

    Yet he was kind; or if severe in aught,
    The love he bore to learning was in fault.

His intellectual accomplishments are sufficient to put
him at least on a level with the parson and the doctor;
while the less-educated villagers are amazed at the width
of his learning.

'Stitch! stitch! stitch!
In poverty, hunger, and dirt'
Thomas Hood, *The Song of the Shirt* (1843)

Hood was primarily a humorous poet, but his own life
was often full of problems occasioned by ill-health and
poverty. It is not surprising that he should look with
indignation on the evils of early-nineteenth-century
slave labour. His *Song of the Shirt* portrays the miserable
conditions in which underpaid seamstresses had to work
in order to produce cheap clothing.

    Oh God! that bread should be so dear,
    And flesh and blood so cheap!

'Stone walls do not a prison make,
Nor iron bars a cage'
Richard Lovelace, *To Althea, from Prison* (1649)

In April 1642, when England was on the brink of civil
war between Charles I and Parliament, Lovelace presented a Kentish petition to the House of Commons
asking for the restoration of the King's rights. Parliament's answer was to commit him to the Gatehouse
prison, Westminster. During the two months of his
imprisonment he composed this well-known poem,
published seven years later. The identity of Althea (if she
existed) remains unknown. He wrote no other poems to
her.

> *'Storied windows richly dight*
> *Casting a dim religious light'*
> John Milton, *Il Penseroso* (c 1632)

The poem, directly contrasted with *L'Allegro*, deals with the more serious pleasures of life. One of these pleasures was 'to walk the studious cloisters', and then to gaze at the richness of stained-glass windows – perhaps in the wonderful chapel of King's College, Cambridge, not far from Milton's own Christ's College, and noted both for its 'high embowed roof' and for its windows 'richly dight' (adorned). Here, too, he would listen to 'the pealing organ blow'. Ironically, in later and grimmer years Milton's political colleagues, the Cromwellians, were noted for their destruction of ecclesiastical stained glass because they claimed it was idolatrous.

> *'Strange to see what delight we married people have to see*
> *those poor fools decoyed into our condition'*
> Samuel Pepys, *Diary* (25 December 1665)

The diarist had been to church on Christmas morning and had found a wedding taking place. The young people were very merry with each other, and all the other married couples were looking on and smiling, which prompted Pepys to his quoted reflection. Despite his somewhat denigrating attitude towards marriage, his was by no means an unhappy one, though he was sometimes at odds with his young, attractive, illiterate, incompetent, and charming Elizabeth. His eye (and not only his eye) frequently strayed elsewhere, however, and even at this Christmas Day service he notes appreciatively: 'Here I saw again my beauty Lethulier'.

> *'Striped like a zebra, freckled like a pard'*
> John Keats, *Lamia*, Pt 1 (1820)

In addition to zebra stripes and leopard spots there were peacock-eye designs barred with crimson, and circles of many brilliant colours – vermilion, gold, green, and blue. The finishing touch was a series of lustrous silver moons. A human being thus attired would have been somewhat overdressed, but a serpent can carry such gorgeous decoration. Moreover, this was a very unusual serpent, having a face with feminine mouth and eyes. It was none other than the witch, Lamia. Touched by the magic wand of Hermes she assumed a woman's form.

> *'The summer springs so fresh and green and gay'*
> Anon, *Old May Song*

It has long been the tradition to celebrate the first day of May. In earlier days the celebrations included the erection of a maypole, and some cheerful folk-dancing; while groups of villagers would serenade the larger houses with traditional songs. This is one such ditty, the quoted line forming the second line of each verse – very convenient, for any villager could join in the chorus lines even if he did not know all the words of the song. The verses salute in turn the master, the mistress, and the children, with an extra one for the house itself. The serenaders then move on to the next house.

'Surely never before in the whole history of excavation had such an amazing sight been seen'
Howard Carter, *The Tomb of Tut-ankh-Amen* (1923)

An electric torch poking through a spyhole just made in a blocked doorway revealed a room which had remained undisturbed for over three thousand years. The gilded sides of three elaborately carved couches; two life-sized statues; inlaid caskets; strange black shrines; a golden throne; beautifully carved chairs; a translucent alabaster cup. 'Such were some of the objects that lay before us.' After a while they realized that there was another sealed doorway on the further side. The room they were looking at was merely the antechamber to the room that held the body of the Pharaoh!

'Sweet are the uses of adversity'
William Shakespeare, *As You Like It*, II, ii (*c* 1599)

Duke Senior, banished to Arden Forest by his usurping brother, makes the best of the situation, finding 'sermons in stones, and good in everything'. He even convinces himself and his fellow exiles that life in the open air is better 'than that of painted Pomp' at Court. 'I would not change it' he declares. All the same, he does change it as soon as the opportunity arises.

'Sweetest love, I do not goe For wearinesse of thee'
John Donne, *Song* (*c* 1611)

Donne is leaving his wife to go on a journey, and assuring her that he is not seeking another woman. He adds that since he will ultimately be parted from her by death, it is not a bad plan to get used to the idea of parting: 'by fain'd deaths to die'. The sun, he goes on, disappears every day, yet reappears the next. Donne himself with more occasion to hurry back, will do so just as surely as the sun does. It is a nice thought, but Donne died twenty years later whereas the sun still reappears each day.

'The sweet fruition of an earthly crown'
Christopher Marlowe, *Tamburlaine the Great, Pt 1*, II, vii (1587)

The play was based on the activities of a supposed descendant of Genghis Khan (1162–1227) named Timur the Lame, who terrorized and conquered huge areas of the East and Middle East in the fourteenth century. Marlowe turned the story into rousing, thunderous dramatic verse. In the play Tamburlaine is a Scythian shepherd whose personality makes him an unbeatable warrior. In this scene he has just won the first of his many crowns – that of the Persian King – by bold fighting and unscrupulous treachery. Tamburlaine was devoid of conscience, and to him the crown was 'perfect bliss and sole felicity'.

'Sweets to the sweet'
William Shakespeare, *Hamlet*, V, i (c 1601)

Rejected by Hamlet, Ophelia loses her reason, and in her madness has seemingly drowned herself. As a suspected suicide she is not supposed to be buried in consecrated ground, and only the royal command has overswayed that mark of disrespect. None the less, the burial rites are curtailed. But when the corpse is borne towards the grave, Queen Gertrude scatters flowers on it, observing (rather belatedly) that she had hoped Ophelia would be her daughter-in-law.

'Take care, if you please. Somebody's sharp'
Charles Dickens, *David Copperfield*, ch. 2 (1849–50)

Young David has been taken for a ride to Lowestoft by Mr Murdstone, who is hoping to marry David's mother, an attractive young widow. When two of Mr Murdstone's friends start discussing her in front of the boy Mr Murdstone pulls them up abruptly, realizing that the child is listening. To put David off the scent, when asked who is sharp Murdstone replies 'Brooks of Sheffield' – the name of a well-known maker of steel knives. The reply serves its purpose. The friends are warned (and amused) and David is deceived.

'Take care of him. He bites'
Charles Dickens, *David Copperfield*, ch. 5 (1849–50)

When he was unjustly thrashed by his stepfather, Mr Murdstone, David bit the hand that was holding him. Consequently, the boy was made to wear a placard bearing the above notice when he was sent away to boarding school. His fears that his schoolfellows would send him to Coventry in disgust were not realized. Some could not at first resist pretending that he was a dog, but when the head boy, Steerforth, took David's part, the matter was ended as far as the boys were concerned.

'Take her up tenderly,
Lift her with care'
Thomas Hood, *The Bridge of Sighs* (1844)

In early Victorian times a girl who had lost her honour and was then deserted often became desperate, especially if her own family disowned her. In this poem Hood deals sympathetically with 'one more unfortunate/ Weary of breath' who has drowned herself. The original Bridge of Sighs was in Venice, gaining its name from its proximity to a former place of execution. The name was later applied sometimes to Waterloo Bridge in London (not the present one, completed in 1944), from which suicides all too often leapt to their deaths.

'Take my drum to England, hang it by the shore,
Strike it when your powder's running low'
Henry Newbolt, *Drake's Drum* (1896)

When Drake died, his drum, used in those days for
signalling orders to the crew, was brought back to his
home at Buckland Abbey. A legend grew up that if
England was ever in grave danger and the drum was
struck, then Drake's ghost would leave Heaven to come
to his nation's help by driving off the enemy.

 An' drum them up the Channel as we drummed
 them long ago.

'"Take some more tea," the March Hare said to Alice, very
earnestly. "I've had nothing yet," Alice replied in an offended
tone, "so I can't take more."'
Lewis Carroll, *Alice's Adventures in Wonderland*, ch. 7 (1865)

Alice has joined the Mad Hatter's tea party, but has had
nothing to eat or drink. She is quick to point out that she
therefore cannot take *more*. The Hatter replies that she
must mean she cannot take *less*, for it is easy to take *more*
than nothing! It is a reply typical of Wonderland,
seemingly logical, but less than sensible.

'A tale which holdeth children from play, and old men from
the chimney-corner'
Philip Sidney, *An Apologie for Poetrie* (c 1580)

Sidney's *Apologie* (also known as *Defence*) was written to
counter an attack on poets and playwrights written by
Stephen Gosson (1579), a former actor who later became
a parson, and who had unwisely dedicated his book to
Sidney. Sidney defended all creative writing, not necessarily verse, though verse was then the most obvious
medium of expression. He maintained that it was
through tales such as those about Hercules, Achilles, and
Aeneas that people of all ages were drawn to appreci-
ative virtue.

'Tall oaks from little acorns grow'
David Everett, *Lines Written for a School Declamation* (c 1790)

Everett, an American, had a varied career as school
teacher, lawyer, and journalist. While acting in the first
capacity he wrote some lines for a seven-year-old pupil
to declaim. Referring to his diminutive size, the young
reciter offered the comforting thought that just as oak
trees develop from tiny acorns, so the greatest men were
once small boys.

'A teacher who is consistently fair, kindly and honest – whatever his religious convictions – does more moral good in a school than a year of religious assemblies'
'Balaam', *Chalk in My Hair*, ch. 1 (1953)

The author, a teacher of wide experience in many types of school, set down his impressions in a book which was generally accepted as giving a truthful and sometimes amusing portrait of school life from the point of view of the practising teacher as opposed to the theorizing educationist. He is here making the point that conventional religious assemblies in school have little or no effect on the moral attitudes of the pupils, who learn far more from precept than from 'the singing of a hymn, a few Biblical verses which they don't understand, and a prayer or two'.

'Tears, idle tears, I know not what they mean'
Alfred Tennyson, *The Princess* (1847)

A lyric sung to the harp by a young undergraduette of Princess Ida's Women Only College. The man-scorning Princess has just listened to a rather solemn evening song, and has asked for something in a lighter vein. She is unlucky, for this song is more melancholy than the other. Looking at Autumn fields, it says, causes tears to rise in the hearts of those who think 'of the days that are no more'. The song is so poignant that tears do indeed steal down the singer's cheeks. The Princess is by no means pleased at this nostalgic sentimentality. 'Let the past be past,' she commands.

'Tears such as angels weep'
John Milton, *Paradise Lost*, Bk I (1668)

Satan, after being driven out of Heaven, gathers his followers around him to give them consolation in their defeat. The sight of his beaten army eagerly waiting to hear the words of their dread Commander so affects him that at first he can hardly speak, and in spite of himself can do nothing but choke with 'tears such as angels weep'. At length, mastering his feeling, he assures them that although they were beaten they put up quite a good show ('that strife was not inglorious'). 'Now that we know the true force of our opponents,' he says in effect, 'we know how to proceed. We must use guile in future.'

'Telling the truth is about as healthy as skidding round a corner at sixty'
J. B. Priestley, *Dangerous Corner*, Act I (1932)

This dramatic play, somewhat contrived but ingenious, illustrates the dangers of telling the truth. A small group of family and business friends are provoked by a careless remark into telling a long and devastating series of truths about their relations with each other. The disclosures are such that the circle is irrevocably broken. Then, towards the end of the last Act, the stage is darkened. The beginning of the play is now repeated, but this time the careless remark is passed over, and the dangerous corner is smoothly negotiated. Truth is hidden, and everyone remains cheerful – at least on the surface.

'Tell me, for Heaven's sake, the method ... by which you have been enabled to fathom my soul'
E. A. Poe, *The Murders in the Rue Morgue* (1841)

This could very well have been Dr Watson baffled at Sherlock Holmes's skill in reading his thoughts. But it was in fact a predecessor of the Baker Street genius doing precisely the same thing and producing exactly the same effect on his bewildered listener. M. Dupin startled the narrator of this early detective story by remarking, 'He is a very little fellow, it's true' – which was just what the narrator was thinking at that precise moment. Like his famous successor, Dupin proceeded to explain, step by step, the chain of reasoning which had led him to read his companion's thoughts. (The 'little fellow' was an undersized actor who had undertaken a role too big for him.)

'Thank you for nothing'
Cervantes, *Don Quixote*, Pt I, Bk iii, ch. 1 (1605)

Having been beaten up by a gang of teamsters, Don Quixote and his squire, Sancho Panza, are left for dead. Quixote tries to console Sancho with stories of knights in romantic legend being similarly afflicted without feeling disgraced. A remedy for their misery exists. 'There is no pain to which death will not put a period,' says Don Quixote sententiously. 'Thank you for nothing,' replies his more realistic squire. 'What worse could befall us than to have only death to trust to?'

'That is no country for old men'
W. B. Yeats, *Sailing to Byzantium* (1927)

Regarding himself as old, Yeats decided that he had no place in the Ireland of his young manhood. He had now come to enjoy the serenity that he believed existed in old Byzantium – where artists, artificers, and architects 'spoke to the multitude and the few alike'. Yeats was little more than sixty when he wrote this, and senior citizens who are well past this milestone would not be too pleased to be regarded as 'a tattered coat upon a stick', which is how he describes himself.

'That man's silence is wonderful to listen to'
Thomas Hardy, *Under the Greenwood Tree*, Pt II, ch. 5 (1872)

The man is Geoffrey Day, gamekeeper and beekeeper, father of the chief character in the novel, the schoolmistress Fancy Day. The villagers of Mellstock regard him as a clever man because he is so sparing of speech with them. However, he is not notably silent in his own home, and he was almost eloquent in explaining to young Dick Dewy why he was not a good enough match for Fancy. Fortunately for Dick, Fancy disagreed.

'That no mourners walk behind me at my funeral and that no flours be planted on my grave and that no man remember me'
Thomas Hardy, *The Mayor of Casterbridge*, ch. 45 (1886)

The closing items of perhaps the saddest and bitterest last will in all literature. Michael Henchard, once the Mayor of Casterbridge and a prosperous merchant, has sunk into distress, partly through misfortune, partly through folly. Finally, rejected by his stepdaughter who was the only person who really touched his affection, he dies of hopelessness and despair. A man of powerful feeling and character, his mood is one of self-hatred rather than of self-pity. In the anguish of his dying he scribbles the pencilled will which, as he has nothing to leave, asks only for his death to go unnoticed and his memory to be obliterated.

'That's my last Duchess painted on the wall, looking as if she were alive'
Robert Browning, *My Last Duchess* (1842)

The Duchess was the Duke of Ferrara's former wife. The Duke's monologue unwittingly reveals his character. His charming wife, wonderfully painted by the artist, was gracious to everyone. This offended the self-centred Duke, who wanted her smiles to be for himself alone. 'Who passed without much the same smile? This grew; I gave commands; then all smiles stopped together.' Whether she died or was murdered, the grasping Duke is now about to marry again, clasping an ample dowry as well as a fair wife to his cold bosom.

'That's one small step for a man, one giant leap for mankind'
Neil Armstrong, On first stepping on to the Moon (21 July 1969)

Just before 4 a.m. B.S.T. on the morning of Monday 21 July 1969, Neil Armstrong put his left foot on to the moon's dusty surface, and uttered his historic words. Nearly five days earlier, on 16 July, he and two companions had started on their incredible journey in the spacecraft Apollo 11. The lunar module (*Eagle*) had to be steered over a large crater before a suitably smooth landing site was found. Then the words 'The *Eagle* has landed' were heard, and the most remarkable scientific feat in the world's history had been accomplished – watched by some five hundred million TV viewers.

'That which is everybody's business is nobody's business'
Izaak Walton, *The Compleat Angler*, Pt I, ch. 2 (1653)

Walton, whose special interest was fishing, naturally applies his precept in that direction. He is annoyed by fishermen who risk the destruction of fishing grounds by using nets when fish are spawning. We do not need to share his love of angling to approve of his indignation. He points out that there are statutes forbidding such practices, but they are not adequately enforced because 'everybody's business is nobody's business'. The comment is not very apt – enforcing the statutes was the business of the conservators concerned – but it is none the less a good epigram.

'That which is not fit to be uttered before women is not fit to be uttered at all'
William Cobbett, *Advice to Young Men* – Letter 2 (1829–30)

During the eighteenth and nineteenth centuries, and even later, it was the custom for women to retire to the drawing room after dinner, while the men continued to sit at the table, passing the decanter around. Cobbett, no lover of drink, was no admirer of the custom. If men cannot talk easily without plying themselves with drink, he maintained, so much the worse for their conversation, particularly if it was the indecency of their talk that made it desirable for women to leave the dining room. He advised young men to follow the ladies, and 'prefer their company to that of the sots who are left behind'.

'The theatre cat made a mess in the middle of the stage, which everybody said was lucky, but which, to me, seemed nothing so much as sound criticism'
Noel Coward, *Present Indicative*, Pt 6 (1937)

The reference is to the dress rehearsal of *The Vortex*. The play brought Coward his first success, partly through its intensity, and partly through the cocktail-drinking decadence of its rather unpleasant smart-set characters. Coward had some difficulty in persuading the theatre censor to accept it. The dress rehearsal lived up to theatrical tradition by going very badly, and the theatre cat's opinion was justified, as Coward notes. But the first night was triumphant. 'There it was, real and complete, my first big moment.'

'Their's not to reason why,
Their's but to do and die'
Alfred Tennyson, *The Charge of the Light Brigade* (1854)

In October 1854, during the Crimean War, the British and their allies, based at Balaclava, were besieging the Russians at Sevastopol. In the course of an attempt by Russian forces to relieve the city, an utterly reckless charge was gallantly made by the British Light Brigade owing to a misunderstanding for which the Brigade Commander, Lord Cardigan, was not personally responsible. Terrible losses were needlessly suffered. Tennyson's famous poem was inspired by an account in *The Times*.

'Then Denmark blessed our chief
That he gave her wounds repose'
Thomas Campbell, *The Battle of the Baltic* (1801)

The Danes were utterly defeated by the British navy in 1801 after trying to restrict British trade. Part of the English fleet, led by Nelson, forced its way up the intricate straits in front of Copenhagen, silenced the batteries, and captured or sank the Danish ships. Nelson ignored the withdrawal signals of the commander-in-chief, Sir Hyde Parker, who remained outside the danger area. After the battle Nelson sent the Danish wounded ashore in safety. His kindness was gratefully recognized by cheering Danes when he landed to arrange surrender terms.

'Then he will talk – good gods, how he will talk!'
Nathaniel Lee, *The Rival Queens*, I, iii (1677)

The big mouth belongs to none other than Alexander the
Great. But Statira, one of his two wives, is not complaining of his loquacity but praising his ability to flatter.

He speaks the kindest words, and looks such
    things,
Vows with such passion, swears with so much
    grace,
That 'tis a kind of heaven to be deluded by him.

Nevertheless, she sees nothing heavenly in the news
that he has been enjoying himself with his other wife,
and vows never to see him again.

'Then to the well-trod stage anon,
If Jonson's learned sock be on'
John Milton, *L'Allegro* (1632)

Dealing with the joys of life, this poem describes first the
pleasures of the country, and then passes to the delights
of the town. 'Towered cities please us then / And the
busy hum of men.' Among these delights is the theatre.
Ben Jonson's comedies were among the most popular
contemporary plays, and he was the leading literary
figure of the day, still alive when Milton's poem was
most probably written. The sock was a low-heeled shoe
worn by comic actors in classical times, and Jonson was
steeped in the classics and almost every other sort of
learning.

'There are few more impressive sights than a Scotsman
on the make'
J. M. Barrie, *What Every Woman Knows*, Act II (1908)

The statement may be true, but the example is not very
convincing. David Wylie is describing the progress in
public life made by the Wylie's protégé, John Shand.
After being helped by them to a university education (in
days long before government grants), he first entered
business, and then began to take part in politics. His
success at the polls is about to be announced. One would
expect a Scotsman on the make to do better for himself
than a seat in Parliament; and in any case Barrie tries to
persuade us that Shand's success was entirely due to the
little wife.

'There are few who would not rather be taken in adultery
than in provincialism'
Aldous Huxley, *Antic Hay*, ch. 10 (1923)

Mr Boldero, a businessman with a finger in all kinds of
pies, is talking of the advertising skills that manage to
persuade people that they are committing a pitiful
solecism by failing to do something or wear something.
He is referring in particular to an American advertising
campaign which convinced advertisement readers that it
was essential to have different types of spectacles for
different occasions: tortoiseshell rims for business, gold-
mounted rimless for full evening dress, and so on. Lots
of people were induced to buy four new pairs of
spectacles for fear of being thought provincial or sub-
urban.

'There are more things in heaven and earth ... than are dreamt of in your philosophy'
William Shakespeare, *Hamlet*, I, v (*c* 1601)

The ghost of his father has appeared to Hamlet and told him that he was murdered by his brother (Hamlet's uncle), now King. After this dramatic interview Hamlet is asking his friends not to disclose anything they may have seen and heard. Horatio finds the whole affair 'wondrous strange'. Hamlet reminds him that the world is full of mysteries that cannot be understood.

'There are people whom one would like very well to drop, but would not wish to be dropped by'
Samuel Johnson, in Boswell's *Life of Johnson* (1791)

Johnson's frank admission was occasioned by the action of Mrs Elizabeth Montagu, a prominent hostess of the day, regarded as one of the leading bluestockings. She was on friendly terms with him for some years, but in his *Lives of the Poets* (1779–81) Johnson made critical as well as favourable references to Lord Lyttelton, one of her friends. She herself, indeed, had contributed a section to one of his books, about which *Lives of the Poets* was lukewarm. Henceforth Johnson was no longer invited to Mrs Montagu's gatherings.

'There are people who simply can't live without danger'
John Galsworthy, *Loyalties*, II, ii (1922)

Margaret Orme, a friend of Captain Dancy, is discussing him with another friend. He has been accused of a daring theft, and Margaret is by no means sure that he is incapable of it. The period is just after the First World War when a certain type of officer was left without much outlet for recklessness. 'If there's no excitement going, they'll make it.' Dancy might do the maddest things for no reason but the risk. She has analysed his character accurately, except that in this instance there was a real reason, besides risk, for his wanting the money. He needed to pay off a former mistress.

'There are some opinions in which a man should stand neuter'
Joseph Addison, *The Spectator*, no. 117 (1711)

On the matter of witchcraft Addison tended to hedge his bets. He was sufficiently influenced by the superstitions of his time to believe in the existence of evil spirits, but too intelligent to accept the stories of witchcraft that actually came to his notice. 'I believe in general that there is, and has been, such a thing as witchcraft; but, at the same time, can give no credit to any particular instance of it.' But on the whole Addison's typical good sense was on the side of the unbelievers, for most of his essay is devoted to kindly ridicule of the witch-fearers.

'There can be very few people at the present day who are really without a working knowledge of bad language'
Harold Chapin, *The New Morality*, Act II (1920)

The dry comment is made by a suave barrister whose sister, Betty, has had an outburst during a houseboat holiday. Furious at the way her dignified husband has let himself be beguiled by an attractive neighbour into being her undignified errand-boy, Betty has gone to the neighbour's houseboat and unleashed all her pent-up indignation, using words she never realized she knew. The comedy deals brilliantly with the consequences of this off-stage episode, and with her decent but unsubtle husband's attempts to put the matter in perspective.

'There is a garden in her face'
Thomas Campion, *Fourth Book of Airs* (1610)

'Cherry-ripe – come and buy' was one of the cries of Old London, used by fruit sellers as they roamed the streets. The poet adapts it for his fanciful love lyric, in which he portrays the face of a pretty girl as resembling a garden, the pink and white of her cheeks being respectively roses and lilies. When she smiles, the lips enclosing her white teeth suggest 'rosebuds filled with snow'. And her eyes are like angels guarding the cherries, which no one may buy until she cries 'Cherry-ripe'. In other words, you must have her permission before you venture to kiss her.

'There is no happiness in love, except at the end of an English novel'
Anthony Trollope, *Barchester Towers*, ch. 27 (1857)

The beautiful, intelligent, but unfeeling Signora Neroni was the crippled daughter of a prebendary of Barchester Cathedral, and wife (or possibly ex-wife) of an obscure and objectionable Italian. She is talking to Mr Slope, the self-confident, unpleasant, and well-hated chaplain of the new Bishop of Barchester. She had successfully set out to captivate him, as she captivated most other men, and was maintaining that true lovers were never happy. To support her argument she cites Juliet, Imogen, Desdemona, Ophelia, Dido (loved but forsaken by Aeneas), and Haidee (loved and left by Juan). Mr Slope finds it difficult to answer her convincingly.

'There is no such word as fail'
E. G. Bulwer-Lytton, *Richelieu*, II, ii (1839)

The great French seventeeth-century statesman, Cardinal Richelieu, is contending with a plot against France and himself. He sends his young page, François, on a mission to get possession of a letter exposing the plot. If he does this successfully fortune will smile on him. 'And if I fail?' François asks, and he is given the quoted reply. However, he does fail, for the letter is wrenched from his grasp in the dark by an armed man. When he reports this disaster Richelieu merely sends him back to discover and retrieve the letter, repeating, 'There's no such word as "fail".'

'There is only one genuinely scientific treatment for all diseases, and that is to stimulate the phagocytes'
George Bernard Shaw, *The Doctor's Dilemma*, Act I (1906)

The play is said to have been sparked off by a challenge to Shaw to deal (if he could) with death on the stage. Shaw therefore labelled his play 'A Tragedy', though it is primarily an amusing and not too farcical satire on the medical profession, with five or six brilliantly constrasted sketches of doctors and their weaknesses. Shaw (a sufferer from regular headaches) knew and studied many doctors. Sir Ralph Bloomfield Bonnington is one of his richest creations, a distinguished, complacent consultant with a most convincing bedside manner. His particular foible is a belief in the power of phagocytes (white blood corpuscles) to cure disease.

'There lived a wife at Usher's Well And a wealthy wife was she'
Ballad, *The Wife of Usher's Well*

In this typically grim ballad of the Scottish border country a well-to-do lady sends her three sons to sea. News reaches her that they have been drowned. None the less she utters a wish to see them, and on one of the long nights of Martinmas their ghosts return. The lady is so deceived that she prepares a feast for them and makes up a big bed for them to sleep in. Then she sits contentedly at their bedside. But as soon as the cock crows, the youngest brother says to the eldest, 'Brother, we must awa', and at once the apparitions vanish.

'There lives more faith in honest doubt, Believe me, than in half the creeds'
Alfred Tennyson, *In Memoriam*, xcvi (1850)

Refuting a sweet but rather simple woman who believes religious doubt to be inspired by the Devil, the poet refers to his dead friend Arthur Hallam, whom the poem commemorates. Upright in his life, he was equally honest in his thoughts and was not afraid to examine his doubts and uncertainties. 'He would not make .his judgment blind.' At length he laid his doubts, and his faith was all the stronger for having been frankly tested.

'There never can have been a man who enjoyed his profession more than Mr Creakle did'
Charles Dickens, *David Copperfield*, ch. 7 (1849–50)

Mr Creakle was the master at Salem House, the private boarding school in London to which David was sent by his stepfather. He was an ignorant brute, quite unqualified, and had taken to schoolmastering after being an unsuccessful hop dealer. His enjoyment came from the opportunities his position gave him to bully and thrash the boys under his care – especially the chubby ones. The character was based on a real teacher – Mr Jones, proprietor and headmaster of Wellington House Academy, Camden Town, the school Dickens attended as a day boy. Like Mr Creakle, Mr Jones was more notable for brute force than for his intellectual attainments.

'There's not a joy the world can give like that it takes away'
Lord Byron, *Stanzas for Music* (1815)

The Fourth Duke of Dorset died in 1815 after a fall from his horse. He had been a schoolfriend of Byron at Harrow, and a poem addressed to him had been included in the poet's early volume, *Hours of Idleness* (1807). Byron was now rather shocked to find how little emotion he felt at the death of his friend. This inspired him to write some verses expressing sadness at his inability to feel the emotions that he would have felt when younger. These lines, he declared, were 'the *truest*, though the most melancholy, I ever wrote'.

'There's nothing half so sweet in life
As love's young dream'
Thomas Moore, *Irish Melodies* (1811)

Moore looks back in nostalgic mood to the days when love filled his life.
When my dream of life, from morn till night,
    Was love, still love.
Although there may be milder, calmer days to come, and new and different hopes may arise, they will never equal the dreams of young love. Although Moore was recognized as Ireland's national poet, there is very little distinctively national in most of his work. The only thing Irish about most of his *Irish Melodies* (written to a publisher's order) is that they have been popular with Irish tenors.

'There's the wind on the heath, brother'
George Borrow, *Lavengro*, ch. 25 (1851)

These are the words of Jasper Petulengro, chief of the band of gipsies. Borrow first met him when they were boys. Now a chance encounter on an open heath has brought them together once more. They talk about death, which Jasper views with more reluctance than Borrow does. Why, Jasper asks, should any man want to die? There are the sun and the stars, and even to a blind man there is the wind on the heath. 'Life is sweet, brother.' In this half-fictional autobiography, Jasper is based on a real Norfolk gipsy named Ambrose Smith. It was he who applied to Borrow the term 'Lavengro', meaning 'word-master'.

'There will be too much of me
In the coming by and by'
W. S. Gilbert, *Patience*, Act II (1881)

Gilbert often revealed a rather unchivalrous attitude towards ladies of uncertain age. Lady Jane is one of these, and Gilbert shows her soliloquizing on the disappearance of her former charms, and compelled to "make up" for lost time as best she may' with rouge and lipstick. Her hair is going grey, her gait is less eager, her eyes are spectacled. Even worse is the loss of her figure.
    Stouter than I used to be,
    Still more corpulent grow I.
Such parts were always taken by the leading contralto. Did Gilbert have a grudge against contraltos?

'These reasons made his mouth to water'
Samuel Butler, *Hudibras*, Pt I, c. 3 (1663)

It is sexual desire, not food, which activates the salivary glands of Sir Hudibras, the hypocritical Puritan in Butler's satire. Having achieved a victory in his puritanical crusade against pleasure, he feels the time is ripe for the conquest of a wealthy widow he has met. Although she has hitherto treated him with disdain,

The vict'ry he achieved so late
Did set his thoughts agog.

He now hopes that the valour he believes himself to have displayed will make her change her mind, and he suffers 'am'rous longings to be at her'.

'They also serve who only stand and wait'
John Milton, *Sonnet XVI* (1652?)

Musing on his blindness, with his life not fully spent, Milton concludes that to bear patiently whatever has to be borne is as worthy in God's sight as to accomplish great things. In fact, Milton's blindness did not cause him merely to stand and wait. His greatest work, *Paradise Lost*, was largely composed after he lost his sight (1652). Moreover, he used his own deprivation of sight as inspiration for his fine dramatic poem about the blinded Samson, *Samson Agonistes* (1671).

'They ha'e sworn a solemn oath
John Barleycorn should die'
Robert Burns, *John Barleycorn* (1787)

This ballad appears on the surface to describe the terrible treatment meted out to its unfortunate hero. He is knocked down and buried, but somehow manages to recover. But later, as his strength begins to fail, his enemies attack him again.

They've taken a weapon long and sharp,
And cut him by the knee.

They then cudgel him, and put him in a 'darksome pit' filled with water. We need not worry, however, for John Barleycorn is just what his name suggests, and the ballad is really describing the process of making malt liquor from barley.

'They have a king and officers of sorts'
William Shakespeare, *Henry V*, I, ii (1599)

The Archbishop of Canterbury delivers a lecture on the habits of bees for the instruction of the King and some of his nobles. Not only do these insects have a king and officers; they have magistrates, merchants, and soldiers, not to mention masons and porters. The Archbishop's entomology is dubious: he may (unwisely) have picked it up from Lyly or Virgil. But the point he is making, in a long-winded way, is that different people do different jobs, and while Henry's army is fighting in France, a Home Guard will protect England from the Scots.

'They have annihilated the old distinction between rich and poor travellers'
J. B. Priestley, *English Journey*, ch. 1 (1934)

Priestley is referring to motor coaches, which offer luxury to all but the poverty stricken. They not only travel at speed but also provide the comfort of an expensive private car. No longer can the wealthy go splashing past in their private conveyances, forcing the poor and humble out of the way. There is now even 'over-done comfort' for every traveller. 'This is how the ancient Persian monarchs would have travelled, had they known the trick of it.' When Priestley wrote this book, private cars, though by no means uncommon, were less common and mostly less comfortable than they are today.

'They'll be safe from books and botany all the rest of their lives'
Aldous Huxley, *Brave New World*, ch. 2 (1932)

This satiric novel gives a horrifying glimpse of a strange future. A batch of babies, all belonging to the Delta class (next to lowest) were being given the appropriate treatment to make them hate books and flowers. (Such low-class creatures as Deltas could not be allowed to waste time on refined pleasures.) Each child was allowed to reach for a picture-book and some flower petals. As he started to handle them violent noises sounded, followed by electric shocks. Thus the children were early conditioned to associate flowers and books with unpleasant experiences.

'They say that when good Americans die they go to Paris'
Oscar Wilde, *A Woman of No Importance*, Act I (1893)

The speaker is Mrs Allonby, the witty female counterpart of Lord Illingworth, the witty and cynical nobleman who in some respects bore a strong resemblance to Wilde himself. Wilde, who had visited America some years earlier, took pleasure in making mild fun of Americans, and the saying may be taken as a satirical comment on American dress. But it is not Wilde's own *bon mot*. Mrs Allonby has obviously been reading O. W. Holmes's *The Autocrat at the Breakfast Table* (1858), where the saying is attributed to Thomas Appleton (1812–84).

'They sway'd about upon a rocking-horse, And thought it Pegasus'
John Keats, *Sleep and Poetry* (1817)

Keats is criticizing the poets of the so-called classical school, whose style of writing, he implies, reduced poetry to uninspired triviality, blind to the beauty of nature, often little more than a mechanical task.
Ye were dead
To things ye knew not of, – were closely wed
To musty laws lined out with wretched rule.
Keats specifically referred to the French critic and poet, Nicholas Boileau (1636–1711), 'the law-giver of Parnassus', who had considerable influence on eighteenth-century English verse, and who, despite his merits, was in many ways a deadening influence on poetic expression.

'They took some honey, and plenty of money,
Wrapped up in a five-pound note'
Edward Lear, *The Owl and the Pussy-Cat* (1871)

This unlikely pair had gone to sea in a beautiful pea-green boat. The Owl sang to the Cat; the Cat complimented the Owl and suggested marriage. Unfortunately they had no ring, and it was a year and a day before they found one. It was on the end of a pig's nose, but the pig agreed to sell it for a shilling, which was pretty reasonable for a wedding ring. They were then married 'by the Turkey who lives on the hill', and after a wedding-feast (eaten with a 'runcible spoon') they spent the night dancing by the light of the moon. This is perhaps the best-known of all Edward Lear's nonsense verses.

'They went and told the sexton
And the sexton toll'd the bell'
Thomas Hood, *Faithless Sally Brown* (1826)

This mock-serious ballad tells the story of Ben the Carpenter whose engagement to the lady's maid, Sally, was disturbed when he was taken away by a press-gang. On his return two years later he found that she had transferred her affections to another. He was so cut up that he died in his berth. Each verse is marked by the humorous play on words typified in the quoted couplet.

'They went to sea in a sieve'
Edward Lear, *The Jumblies* (1871)

This unusual seagoing vessel was employed by the Jumblies, creatures easily recognizable through their green heads and blue hands. Although itwwas winter and a stormy day, they insisted on making the voyage. The water, as threatened, did come in a little, but they kept it at bay by wrapping their feet in pink paper and getting inside a crockery jar. After sailing to the Western Seas, they settled down in a well-wooded land where they bought a variety of articles and animals, including 'forty bottles of Ring-Bo-Ree'. Twenty years later they returned to the land they started from, and were welcomed back with a feast of dumplings. In some quarters Lear's deliberate Nonsense Verse has become a cult, like the Theatre of the Absurd.

'A thing of beauty is a joy for ever'
John Keats, *Endymion* (1818)

In the opening line of his poem Keats indicates the spirit in which he is approaching the task of telling the story of the shepherd Endymion, loved by Cynthia the moon goddess. Keats feels himself inspired by the beauty of nature and by 'all lovely tales that we have heard or read'. He writes modestly in the preface: 'I hope I have not in too late a day touched the beautiful mythology of Greece, and dulled its brightness.'

'Thinking is to me the greatest fatigue in the world'
John Vanbrugh, *The Relapse*, II, i (1696)

Lord Foppington, an outrageous coxcomb but with a certain style and even a certain wit, affects surprise that an attractive woman has been able to endure living for a while 'under the fatigue of a country life'. Foppington hates quiet, for it leads, he says, to the fatigue of thinking, and thought is a bore. Even when he reads, he never thinks about what he is reading. Far better to enjoy the pleasures of the town – dressing, eating, drinking, going to the play, strolling in the park, and the rest.

'This is the hour when forth he goes,
The Dong with a luminous nose'
Edward Lear, *The Dong with the Luminous Nose* (1871)

A Dong fell in love with a Jumbly Girl – both creatures known only to Nonsense Verse. When she sailed away the Dong was heartbroken, and resolved to search the world for her. Because he could not see at night he made himself an enormous false nose, painted red, and fitted with a lamp inside, with holes to allow the light to pass through. This was tied to his head with cords. Now every night he can be seen wandering about in search of his Jumbly Girl.

'This is the most astonishing thing of all: this is the high and heroic state of man'
William Hazlitt, *The New Monthly* (1822)

Hazlitt is describing a famous fight between two pugilists of the period – the Gasman (Tom Hickman) and 'great, heavy, clumsy long-armed' Bill Neate. What particularly drew Hazlitt's admiration was their amazing power of recovery after an interval of only half a minute between the rounds. 'To see two men smashed to the ground, smeared with gore, stunned, senseless, the breath beaten out of their bodies; and then . . . to see them rise up with new strength and courage' ready to attack each other again, 'this is the most astonishing . . . man.' Bill Neate was the ultimate winner in the seventeenth round.

'This is the song of the sword of Alan'
R. L. Stevenson, *Kidnapped*, ch. 10 (1886)

The brig *Covenant*, in which David Balfour had been kidnapped, accidentally ran down a small boat in the darkness. The only survivor was Alan Breck, a bold Jacobite carrying money to the Scottish king exiled in France. He bargains with the captain to set him ashore, but the captain treacherously gets the brig's crew to attack him. With David's help, Alan, a fine swordsman, scatters them like frightened sheep. Then he makes up a Gaelic song to celebrate his triumph.

The smith made it,
The fire set it;
Now it shines in the hands of Alan Breck.

'This is the way the world ends
Not with a bang but with a whimper'
T. S. Eliot, *The Hollow Men* (1925)

The quoted lines, which close the poem, seem to echo a children's game ('This is the way we clap our hands'), and are presumably a commentary on the feebleness of society in the years following the First World War. A spirit of disillusionment runs through the verses: the sub-title is *A penny for the Old Guy*. *The Hollow Men* was not written as a single whole but was built up from separate poems, individually published. The phrase 'not with a bang' was probably suggested by an expressive comment on Dante made by a professor (George Santayana) when Eliot was at Harvard.

'This world is a comedy to those that think, a tragedy to those that feel'
Horace Walpole, *Letter to the Countess of Ossory* (16 August 1776)

This was a favourite saying of Horace Walpole, Fourth Earl of Orford, author and politician. Usually it was said fairly lightheartedly, but the particular occasion which drew him to repeat the saying in a letter to the Countess of Ossory was a tragic one. A wealthy friend had committed suicide the previous day. Yet all his riches, Walpole laments, 'are insufficient for happiness, and cannot check a pistol'.

'Those behind cried "Forward!"
And those before cried "Back!"'
T. B. Macaulay, *Lays of Ancient Rome – Horatius* (1842)

According to Roman legend, the Etruscan King, Lars Porsena, led an attack on the city of Rome in the sixth century B.C. He was kept back only by the bravery of Horatius Cocles, who (with two supporters) held a bridgehead against the Etruscans while the bridge itself was demolished behind him by the Romans. His courageous resistance led to a state of confusion in the Etruscan ranks, somewhat similar to that which occurs when excited crowds endeavour to get into a football ground after the gates are closed.

'Those who grow cotton are merciful taskmasters in comparison with those who manufacture it'
Robert Southey, *Letter to Lord Ashley* (13 January 1833)

Southey was a wild republican in his youth but sobered up as he grew older. He was always deeply conscious of genuine distress and oppression, and the factories of the growing industrial society brought too many instances of this. Here he is stressing to one of the great reformers of the nineteenth-century (later Lord Shaftesbury) the abominable conditions in some of the cotton mills, and the callousness of one of the mill owners regarding the working conditions and ill-health of his youthful employees. Slavery in the colonies was rightly on the point of being abolished, but Southey suggests that the often-well-treated negro slaves in the cotton plantations were in fact better off than the neglected slaves of the English cotton mills.

'Those who would make us feel, must feel themselves'
Charles Churchill, *The Rosciad* (1761)

This is a smack at James Quin (c 1692–1766), the stately actor who dominated the stage during the early eighteenth century, until a smaller but greater performer, David Garrick, edged him into the wings. Quin had a fine voice and a good memory, but little gift for entering into the spirit of the character he was playing. He tended to declaim all parts in the same manner, 'too proud for Tenderness, too dull for Rage'. His best parts were those which required least expression of emotion, and Churchill's generalization has enough truth in it to show up Quin's limitations.

'Though I could not get them to stand by me against the enemy, I could not get rid of them now I had a mind to it.'
Charles II, *An Account of His Majesty's Escape from Worcester dictated to Mr Pepys* (1680)

After the defeat of the Royalists at Worcester in 1651, the young Charles II (twenty-one years of age) was anxious to escape unnoticed. But the band of beaten horsemen who hung around him gave conflicting advice, and were a nuisance to a King trying to travel through hostile country without attracting notice. However, they were loyal enough to ask him *not* to let them know what he intended to do, lest they should be captured and forced to confess what they knew. In the end the young King slipped away disguised as a country fellow 'with a pair of ordinary gray-cloth breeches, a leathern doublet, and a green jerkin', and after many adventures succeeded in escaping to France.

'Though Justice be blind she is not deaf'
John Tobin, *The Honeymoon*, III, ii (1804)

A classic reproof to a loud-voiced complainant. In this instance the complaint, however loudly expressed, is not unreasonable. Juliana is protesting to the Duke of Aranza that her husband deceived her into marrying him by pretending to be the Duke. She has been cheated, and demands a divorce. She appears to have some justice on her side, but appearances are deceptive. Her husband really *is* the Duke (pretending not to be to teach her a lesson), and the seeming Duke to whom she is appealing is merely one of her husband's employees playing a part.

*'Three men alive on Flannan Isle,
Who thought on three men dead'*
W. W. Gibson, *Flannan Isle* (1912)

Three men set out to discover why the lighthouse on Flannan Isle remained unlit. A strange sight met their eyes. A table was set ready for a meal, but untouched, and with one of the three chairs overturned. Of the three men who manned the lighthouse there was no sign. Flannan was a lighthouse with a bad reputation.
Six had come to a sudden end,
And three had gone stark mad.
The present affair remained a mystery unsolved. The Flannan Isles are uninhabited rock islands beyond the Outer Hebrides.

'Thrift was only a virtue so long as it paid, which it has ceased to do'
E. M. Forster, *The Second Darkness* (1939)

This essay was written not long before the Second World War began. The shadow of the coming conflict hung over Europe. There seemed little point in saving money. Forster advised spending freely on art and books, for apart from the pleasure gained 'it does maintain an artistic framework which may come in useful in the future'. The attitude was at least a hopeful one, making the assumption that a civilized way of life would not be permanently banished by war. Now that inflation has made money values almost meaningless, perhaps Forster's precept is again valid.

'Thy dawn, O Master of the World, thy dawn'
J. Elroy Flecker, *Hassan*, II, ii (1922)

Ishak the poet was often the companion of the cruel, all-powerful Caliph of Baghdad. One night with two other companions they wandered through the streets, dressed as merchants, seeking entertainment. Ishak slipped away, and the other three found adventure in a house where they were imprisoned. They were rescued early next morning, the Caliph, meeting Ishak, proposes to execute him for his desertion. All too aware of the Caliph's unpredictable moods, Ishak is prepared to die, and recites a poem to the dawn:

The hour that dreams are brighter and winds colder . . .

O Master of the World, the Persian Dawn.

The unpredictable Caliph turns to the executioner and tells him to sheathe his sword.

'Thy necessity is yet greater than mine'
Philip Sidney, quoted in Fulke Greville's biography (1652)

Sidney was commander of an English force assisting the Dutch against the Spanish. At the Battle of Zutphen (1586) he was badly injured. He called for water, but as the bottle was handed to him he noticed a common soldier eagerly watching him. At once he passed the water bottle to the wounded man without himself stopping to drink. His famous words are nowadays often rendered as 'Your need is greater than mine'. His death, shortly afterwards, deprived Elizabethan England of one of its finest and most talented gentlemen.

'Tide after tide by night and day
The breakers battle with the land'
John Betjeman, *Greenaway* (1954)

Greenaway is a Cornish shingle beach between Trebetherick and Polzeath, where Betjeman spent much of his childhood, and it always has large waves at high tide. He is familiar with the area, and loves to watch the great Atlantic breakers pounding on the shingle, leaving a line of small shells behind. A row of rocks acts as protection. But they could not protect him from a dream of engulfing waves plunging 'their weight of water over me'. In the dream he felt himself being sucked by the backwash into a terrifying water-world.

> *'Tiger! Tiger! burning bright*
> *In the forests of the night,*
> *What immortal hand or eye*
> *Dare frame thy dreadful symmetry?'*
> William Blake, *The Tiger* (1794)

This is a contrasting companion piece, from *Songs of Experience*, to *The Lamb* in *Songs of Innocence*. The obvious theme of this poem is amazement that God could create such a wonderful but terrible creature as the tiger and also such a gentle animal as the lamb. ('Did he who made the lamb make thee?') But there are many other interpretations, ranging from the subtle to the ridiculous. Hidden references to the Book of Job, to Icarus, and to Prometheus have been discovered.

> *'Time for a little something'*
> A. A. Milne, *Winnie the Pooh*, ch. 6 (1926)

Learning that it was the birthday of Eeyore the donkey, and that this unhappy animal had received no presents, Winnie-the-Pooh (the good-natured bear of little brain) went home to fetch a pot of honey to give to him. On the way to Eeyore, however, a strange hungry feeling came over Pooh. Deciding that it was lucky he had brought a pot of honey with him, he proceeded to satisfy his appetite. Not till he had finished did he realize that he had eaten Eeyore's present, which now would have to be just an empty pot. However, Pooh has encouraged thousands of people, when they feel peckish, to utter his famous words: 'Time for a little something!'

> *'"The time has come," the Walrus said,*
> *"To talk of many things"'*
> Lewis Carroll, *Through the Looking-Glass*, ch. 4 (1871)

Tweedledee is reciting to Alice the longest poem he knows, which is *The Walrus and the Carpenter*. These two characters have invited young oysters to take a walk with them along the seashore – preparatory to eating them. But the Walrus hesitates to introduce the delicate topic of oyster-eating, and hypocritically suggests holding a conversation on almost any other topic, choosing subjects at random:

> Of shoes – and ships – and sealing-wax –
> Of cabbages – and kings –

Alliteration has made the topics hard to forget, and 'cabbages and kings' has become a common synonym for 'anything and everything'.

> *'Time they could not keep back'*
> Andrew Young, *The Roman Wall* (1929)

The famous wall on the wild Northumbrian moors was built by the Roman emperor Hadrian about A.D. 122 to keep out the unruly Picts and Scots. It did its work well enough until the Romans departed. But the solid square-set stones could not keep Time away, and moss and lichen now crawl over them. The bleat of a lamb – a sound doubtless familiar enough to the Romans – inspires Young to see in imagination a Roman sentry on guard as he would have been nearly two thousand years ago.

'Tis better to have loved and lost
Than never to have loved at all'
Alfred Tennyson, *In Memoriam*, xxvii (1850)

The sudden death (1833) of his college friend, Arthur Hallam, at the age of twenty-two left Tennyson with a great sense of loss. None the less, he does not regret that he is able to experience such a feeling. He would rather have the troubles arising from sensitivity than be like an animal that has no finer feelings, or a person without emotions. Better endure the pangs caused by loss than have no affection to lose. Tennyson began writing *In Memoriam* in 1833, though it was not completed and published until 1850.

'Tis distance lends enchantment to the view'
Thomas Campbell, *The Pleasures of Hope*, Pt I (1799)

A faraway range of mountains always appears more enticing than a nearby hill. Similarly, the future is more delightful to contemplate than the present. Hope helps us to picture a future that is much finer than that brought about by reality. Campbell, a Scot, was living in Edinburgh when he composed the *Pleasures*, and it was sold to a Scottish publisher. There must have been a great many optimists in Scotland, for the poem went through four editions in a year and secured for Campbell (aged twenty-one) a lasting reputation.

'Tis Hobson's choice: take that or none'
Thomas Ward, *England's Reformation*, c. IV (1710)

Hobson was a sixteenth- to seventeenth-century Cambridge innkeeper who hired out horses. He kept a fine selection, but whoever came to the stables to choose one found himself compelled to take the one nearest the door, as Hobson wished his horses to be used in rotation. Thus 'Hobson's choice' came to mean no choice at all. Ward is using the phrase in connection with the selection, by the Dean and Chapter, of Matthew Parker as Protestant Archbishop of Canterbury (1559). As an enthusiastic Catholic, Ward disapproved of the choice, virtually made by Queen Elizabeth, and did his best to denigrate it.

'Tis not in Mortals to Command Success,
But we'll do more, Sempronius, we'll Deserve it'
Joseph Addison, *Cato*, I, ii (1713)

The republican Marcus Cato and his friends may indeed deserve success in defending Rome's freedom, but they do not get it. The ambition of Julius Caesar is too much for them. In the end Cato falls on his sword and dies rather than be taken prisoner, while his son Portius (who utters the quoted lines) flees to safety with a senator's daughter as bride. Addison's play, though rather lacking in action, was quite a success, partly because members of both British political parties imagined that Cato's virtues applied particularly to themselves, and applauded accordingly.

'Tis not the dying for a faith that's so hard ...
'tis the living up to it that is difficult'
W. M. Thackeray, *The History of Henry Esmond, Esquire*, Bk I,
ch. 6 (1852)

The words are put into the mouth of Richard Steele, the
essayist, who figures in Thackeray's novel as a trooper
(which he was in life for a time). Young Harry Esmond
has been brought up as a Catholic. Steele is a Protestant.
When a band of soldiers is billeted in the great house
where Harry lives, the trooper and the boy sometimes
engage in friendly argument. Steele considers that too
many persecutions have occurred on both sides, and
adds that it is harder to live righteously than to die for a
religion. He speaks feelingly, for he is something of a
rake as well as a good man.

'Tis now six months since Lady Teazle made me the happiest
of men – and I've been the most miserable dog ever since'
R. B. Sheridan, *The School for Scandal*, I, ii (1777)

Sir Peter Teazle, in what was then considered old age,
unwisely married a young country girl. But instead of
bringing him the happiness and consolation he had
expected, she caused him endless irritation by her
frivolity, extravagance, and perversity. Nor does he help
the situation, for he tends to nag her incessantly for her
behaviour, constantly reminding her of her inferior
situation before their marriage. In spite of everything,
however, he still loves her, and by the end of Act V it
looks as though his hope of happiness may be met after
all.

'Tis strange the mind, that very fiery particle,
Should let itself be snuff'd out by an article'
Lord Byron, *Don Juan*, XI, lx (1823)

Indulging in one of his long digressions in the story of
Don Juan, the poet is dealing with various contemporary
writers, mainly to their disadvantage. In the quoted
couplet he refers, not unkindly, to John Keats, whose
death had been attributed to an attack in the *Quarterly
Review*. There was no basis for the belief, however.
Keats, one of the sanest and most clear-headed of poets,
was killed not by criticism but by consumption.

'Tis the last rose of summer
Left blooming alone'
Thomas Moore, *Irish Melodies* (1808)

Moore feels such sorrow for the lovely blossom that he
plucks it and scatters the petals with the dead ones on
the ground. This well-intentioned act hardly adds to the
tidiness of the garden, but it is prompted by the sad
reflection that the poet himself does not want to be left
alone when his friends are all dead. The air of this lyric
was taken from an earlier Irish song, adapted by Moore,
but there is nothing very Irish about it. Later it was used
by the German composer Flotow in his opera *Martha*
(1847).

'Tis the sport to have the enginer
Hoist with his own petar'
William Shakespeare, *Hamlet*, III, iv (*c* 1601)

In other words, it is fun to have the bomb-maker blown up by his own bomb. Hamlet is being sent by his uncle (King Claudius) to England, escorted by his two school-fellows, Rosencrantz and Guildenstern, who bear sealed letters asking for Hamlet to be murdered. Though he has not yet had an opportunity to unseal and read the letters, Hamlet suspects his schoolfellows' intentions and pro-poses to doctor the letters in such a way that Rosencrantz and Guildenstern will become the victims instead of himself.

'"'Tis the voice of the lobster"; I heard him declare
"You have baked me too brown, I must sugar my hair"'
Lewis Carroll, *Alice's Adventures in Wonderland*, ch. 10 (1865)

Alice is ordered by the Gryphon to repeat Isaac Watts's well-known children's poem, ''Tis the voice of the sluggard'. She does her best, but Wonderland has the curious effect of turning well-known poems into Carrol-lian parodies. With her mind full of the Lobster Quadril-le, which the Mock Turtle has just been singing to her, Alice finds that the sluggard has become a lobster, and that the rest of the verse has become sheer nonsense. She herself is as puzzled as anybody.

'"'Tis the voice of the sluggard"; I heard him complain,
"You have waked me too soon: I must slumber again"'
Isaac Watts, *Moral Songs – The Sluggard* (1715)

This moral poem indicates that the sluggard not only wastes hours in unnecessary sleep but also wastes his time when he *is* up. Instead of getting on with useful work he just saunters about. Meanwhile his garden becomes overgrown, and his clothes grow shabbier and shabbier. He thinks of nothing but dreaming, eating, and drinking, and never reads or sits and thinks. Watts regards him as a lesson on what to avoid, and adds rather complacently:

> Thanks to my friends for their care in my
> breeding,
> Who taught me betimes to love working and
> reading.

'To beard the lion in his den'
Sir Walter Scott, *Marmion*, VI, 14 (1808)

In days when England and Scotland were constantly at war, Marmion, an English lord, visits the Scottish King for negotiations, under a safe-conduct. The King asks old Douglas, Earl of Angus, to act as Marmion's host during his stay in Scotland. When Marmion leaves he offers his hand to the Earl, who refuses it. Marmion thereupon speaks some angry words, which arouse the fury of the aged Earl. 'Dar'st thou then / To beard the lion in his den, / The Douglas in his hall?' He orders the portcullis to be dropped, and Marmion escapes by the skin of his teeth – or rather, the tail of his horse. Douglas was a very real person, but Marmion is a fictitious character.

*'To be born, or at any rate bred, in a handbag . . . seems to me
to display a contempt for the ordinary decencies of
family life'*
Oscar Wilde, *The Importance of Being Earnest*, Act I (1895)

Jack Worthing is anxious to marry Gwendolen Fairfax,
who approves, but her mother, the formidable Lady
Bracknell, is by no means in favour. She is even more
antagonistic when she discovers that he does not know
who his parents were, and that as a baby he was
discovered by his wealthy benefactor in a handbag at
Victoria Station. A stickler for the proprieties of society,
she expresses utter disgust at the very idea that she and
Lord Bracknell would even consider allowing their only
daughter 'to marry into a cloakroom'.

*'To bend with apples the moss'd cottage-trees,
And fill all fruit with ripeness to the core'*
John Keats, *Ode to Autumn* (1819)

This is the achievement of Autumn, 'close bosom-friend
of the maturing sun'. Not only does the season bend the
boughs of the apple trees with ripe fruit; it also develops
'the vines that round the thatch-eaves run', and swells
the gourds and the hazelnuts. The image of apple trees
lowering their laden branches owes something to the
tragic young poet, Thomas Chatterton (1752–70), who
wrote: 'When the fair apple, red as even sky, / Do bend
the tree unto the fruitful ground'. Keats himself once
said that he always associated Chatterton with Autumn.

*'To be wroth with one we love,
Doth work like madness in the brain'*
S. T. Coleridge, *Christabel*, Pt 2 (1800)

In youth Sir Leoline and Sir Roland de Vaux had been
bosom friends. False rumours had led to misunderstandings, and they parted angrily. Years later Sir Leoline's
daughter, Christabel, met a lovely lady named Geraldine, who told Sir Leoline that Sir Roland de Vaux was
her father.

> And now the tears were on his face,
> And fondly in his arms he took
> Fair Geraldine.

Here was a splendid opportunity for reconciliation with
Sir Roland, it might seem; but alas, the lovely lady was
not Sir Roland's daughter but a malignant supernatural
creature. And what happened in the end nobody knows,
for Coleridge finished only two parts of the poem instead
of five.

'To die in the last ditch'
Remark attributed to William of Orange (1672)

William of Orange, ruler of the Netherlands, was being
urged by the Duke of Buckingham to give up his
country, flooded by the rains and dykes and almost
overrun by the French. 'Do you not see it is lost?' he was
asked. The Prince (later William III of England) replied
that although his country was certainly in danger there
was one way never to *see* it lost, and that was to die in the
last ditch. The saying is recorded in the *History of his Own
Times* by Bishop Burnet (1643–1715).

'To gild refined gold, to paint the lily'
William Shakespeare, *King John*, IV, ii (*c* 1594)

King John has had himself crowned a second time. Some of his nobles question the necessity of such repetition. The Earl of Salisbury suggests that thus to protect a king's title that was not in question 'is wasteful and ridiculous excess', which may be likened to adding gilt to an article that is already gold, or daubing a lovely flower with paint. Many people of a later age accept Salisbury's reasoning but distort his argument by misquotation, and speak of 'gilding the lily'.

'To live a life half dead, a living death'
John Milton, *Samson Agonistes* (1671)

Samson, a captive of the Philistines, is complaining of his blindness.

The sun to me is dark
And silent as the Moon,
When she deserts the night.

Light, he goes on, is necessary to life, light that was the Creator's first decree. Why, then, can it be perceived only by so easily affected a part as the eye. Why not through the skin, so that a man could see through every pore of his body. Blind, he becomes his own sepulchre, 'a moving grave'. Milton himself, of course, was blind, and wrote with feeling about a state to which he never became resigned.

'To marry be like jumping into a river because you're thirsty'
Eden Philpotts, *The Farmer's Wife* (1916)

Churdles Ash, the sardonic old bachelor farm-worker at Applegarth Farm, is not in favour of love, and is still less in favour of marriage. 'Holy matrimony's a proper steam-roller for flattening the hope out of man and the joy out of woman.' He hates to see men chasing after women in the hope of marrying them. To satisfy your sexual desires by marrying is (as the quotation suggests) carrying matters too far. 'Them what skim the cream off women keep bachelors.' None the less, the end of this very successful comedy shows three weddings about to take place.

'Tomorrow let us do or die'
Thomas Campbell, *Gertrude of Wyoming*, Pt III, 37 (1809)

Wyoming was a colonial settlement in Pennsylvania, and reputed to be an idyllic place. Unhappily it became involved in the American Revolution of 1775. Three years later it was devastated by a combination of British troops and Red Indian tribes, and most of its inhabitants were killed. The hero of the poem weeps over the body of Gertrude, his young bride, but a Red Indian friend, whose traditions do not allow him to weep, contemplates revenge.

219

'Tomorrow to fresh Woods, and Pastures new'
John Milton, *Lycidas* (1638)

Too often misquoted as 'fresh fields', which adds nothing to 'Pastures new'. The poem is an elegy in pastoral form on the death of Milton's friend Edward King, who had been a fellow student (though four years younger) at Christ's College, Cambridge, and who was drowned in the Irish Sea at the age of twenty-five. The quoted line concludes the poem, as the speaker of the elegy gathers his cloak about him and moves away.

'To play billiards well is a sign of an ill-spent youth'
(attributed wrongly to Herbert Spencer)

Though billiards has gone out of fashion as a popular pastime, the saying remains familiar. It can be, and has been, transferred to snooker, bridge, or any other amateur game, and there is an underlying truth in it: the earlier you take up a sport the more likely you are to become good at it. But the saying was not really Spencer's: he was merely repeating a comment that had once been made to him (possibly light-heartedly), and he was not at all pleased when it kept appearing in newspapers as a Spencer aphorism. Before he died he dictated a denial to David Duncan, who edited his *Life and Letters* (1908).

'To set a candle in the sun'
Robert Burton, *The Anatomy of Melancholy*, Pt III, 2 (1621)

To hold the feeble light of a candle to the great light of the sun is to perform an act that is useless and unnecessary – a complete waste of time. The useless act that Burton is discussing here is to go into details about the terrible effects of passionate love. These effects, he suggests, are so well-known that there is little point in dwelling on them. Nevertheless, this very respectable celibate Church of England clergyman proceeds to give a mass of examples and illustrations of the power of physical love.

'To strive, to seek, to find, and not to yield'
Alfred Tennyson, *Ulysses* (1842)

This dramatic monologue uses the story of the last years of Ulysses, the restless traveller, to illustrate the need (as Tennyson himself later wrote) for 'going forward and braving the struggle of life'. The well-known closing line here quoted, sums up the spirit in which he feels life must be faced. The poem is one of those inspired by Tennyson's sense of loss after the death of his friend, Arthur Hallam. Dante (*Inferno*, xxvi) rather than Homer is his literary inspiration.

*'To talk of honour in the mysteries of love is like talking of
Heaven or the Deity in the operation of witchcraft'*
William Wycherley, *The Country Wife*, IV, iii (1672)

Horner, the rakish hero of the play, is persuading the
sexy Lady Fidget that there is no truth in the reports that
he has become impotent. She is eager to test his
statement, but coyly affects a concern for her honour. He
tells her that to talk too much of honour to a man eager to
make love has a fatal effect on his physical capacity.
Wycherley's humorous simile showed that he was equat-
ing witchcraft with devil-worship, an attitude common
in the seventeenth century, though later many witchcraft
and magic rites did invoke religious names.

'To the pure all things are pure'
S. T. Coleridge, quoted in letter from Charles Lamb to Robert
Southey (July 1798)

It comes as something of a surprise to discover that such
a pillar of rectitude as Coleridge uttered the quoted
sentiment when talking bawdily to a lady. He was
quoting from the Bible, but Paul's 'unto the pure all
things are pure' (Titus, i, 15) was concerned with
religious faith. It was left to modern society, following
Coleridge, to find the saying more useful as an excuse for
telling bawdy stories.

*'The true use of speech is not so much to express our wants as
to conceal them'*
Oliver Goldsmith, *The Bee, No. 3 – On the Use of Language* (20
October 1759)

In this number of Goldsmith's short-lived weekly periodical he is disputing the conventional view that the
principal use of language is to express our wants with a
view to receiving speedy redress. On the contrary, he
asserts, men who know the world are aware that to
conceal your necessity is the best way of obtaining what
you want. People who are least in need are those who
receive most favours. 'To have much, or to seem to have
it, is the only way to have more.' A wealthy man will
have no difficulty in borrowing a large sum; a poor man
will have difficulty in borrowing twopence.

*'True! very, very dreadfully nervous I had been and am; but
why will you say that I am mad?'*
E. A. Poe, *Tales of Mystery and Imagination – The Tell-Tale Heart*

The narrator's madness becomes more and more evident
as the tale proceeds. It is a horrifying murder story, with
the victim a harmless old man whose only offence was
that his pale, filmy blue eye worried the narrator. After
insanely cautious preliminaries, he enters the old man's
room one night very, very slowly, in order to murder
him, and he seems to hear the victim's heartbeats
sounding like the beating of a drum. He carries out the
murder, but he ultimately gives himself away through
imagining he hears the old man's heartbeats still, and
madly tearing at the floorboards where the body is
skilfully hidden.

'The truth is rarely pure and never simple'
Oscar Wilde, *The Importance of Being Earnest*, Act I (1895)

Jack Worthing has just explained to his friend, Algy, that
he has a country house where his young ward, Cicely,
lives. To avoid having to maintain the high moral tone
suitable to a guardian, he has told her that he has a
young brother named Ernest living in London, and that
he (Jack) has sometimes to go up there to keep an eye on
him. That, Jack insists, 'is the whole truth, pure and
simple'. Algy, who has a passion for epigrams, immediately counters with an aphorism which may perhaps be
true, though, one suspects, more by chance than by
careful thought.

'Twas Catherine Douglas sprang to the door,
But I fell back Kate Barlass'
D. G. Rossetti, *The King's Tragedy* (1881)

In 1437 King James I of Scotland was attacked by a band
of traitors. The door of the room in which he was sitting
was without bars. They had been secretly removed by
disloyal servants. The Queen and her ladies tried hurriedly to hide him beneath the floorboards as his enemies
thundered up the stairs. The men were already at the
door before the floor had been smoothed down. One of
the ladies-in-waiting, Catherine Douglas (the narrator of
the tale), in sheer desperation thrust her arm through the
door staples. The arm was smashed, but the King was
saved. Afterwards she was popularly known as Kate
Barlass.

'The undiscover'd country, from whose bourn no traveller
returns'
William Shakespeare, *Hamlet*, III, i (c 1601)

In his famous soliloquy 'To be or not to be' Hamlet
ponders on the idea of suicide as a way of escape from
his discontent with life. But he is deterred by the
reflection that whatever happens after death is uncertain. Death is a country whose boundaries have never
been crossed in a return journey, and thus we prefer to
bear the ills we have rather than risk unknown terrors.
However, Hamlet must have been suffering from a
curious lapse of memory when he spoke of a boundary
from which 'no traveller returns', for he has recently
been talking with a traveller who *has* returned – his own
father.

'Universal darkness buries all'
Alexander Pope, *The Dunciad*, Bk IV (1743)

The closing line of Pope's satire against Dulness in
general, and anyone who had offended him in particular. At the end of his long poem Pope ironically portrays
Dulness reigning supreme at last, with Truth fleeing in
dismay, and Chaos restored to a leading position.
Despite Pope's wit and skilful versification, it must be
admitted that to write at considerable length about
Dulness is to grasp a two-edged weapon.

'Unlooked for sudden deaths from heaven are sent'
Beaumont and Fletcher, *The Maid's Tragedy*, V, iv (1611)

There is an air of unreality about this famous romantic tragedy. Amintor, the hero engaged to Aspatia, is suddenly commanded by the King to marry Evadne instead. On the wedding night she tells him that she will never share his bed for she is the King's mistress, and was married to Amintor only as a cover for any children she might bear the King. Unlooked for sudden deaths now begin to pile up. Evadne stabs the King, and then herself. Aspatia (the tragic maid) dressed in male attire, picks a quarrel with Amintor to make him slay her; and Amintor, realizing whom he has killed, stabs himself. However, the King's brother brings the play to a close with the quoted line before any more deaths can occur.

'The unspeakable in full pursuit of the uneatable'
Oscar Wilde, *A Woman of No Importance*, Act I (1893)

An epigrammatic description of 'the English country gentleman galloping after a fox', given by Lord Illingworth, a witty and cynical man about town. The epigram is rather forced into the conversation, ostensibly as an example of the popular idea of health. Wilde asserted that the character of Illingworth was based on himself and that the somewhat sentimental plot of the play was taken from *The Family Herald*, a popular journal of the day not usually esteemed for its literary quality.

'Unwept, unhonour'd, and unsung'
Sir Walter Scott, *The Lay of the Last Minstrel*, VI, i (1805)

The wretch thus described by the patriotic Scottish minstrel is the man who has no feeling for his country (especially if this is Scotland), and thus deserves to suffer an ignominious obscurity when he dies. However important his name and titles may be, however boundless his wealth, he merits contempt while he lives, and when he is dead shall go down
> To the vile dust, from whence he sprung,
> Unwept, unhonour'd, and unsung.

'Variety's the spice of life,
That gives it all its flavour'
William Cowper, *The Task*, Bk II (1785)

Most people would agree with Cowper's statement, thinking of pleasant changes of activity in their daily lives. The poet, however, was writing ironically with particular reference to the strange world of fashion. He was satirizing the passion for constant changes of dress according to the whim of 'the sycophant who waits to dress us' and who 'with our expenditure defrays his own'. Fashion designers, it seems, were as arbitrary and extravagant then as they appear to be today, and Cowper gently but firmly condemns people's folly in sacrificing necessities such as food and warmth for 'monstrous novelty and strange disguise'.

'A verray parfit gentil knight'
Geoffrey Chaucer, *The Canterbury Tales – Prologue* (c 1387)

The Knight was one of a company of thirty-one pilgrims who told each other stories on the journey from London to Canterbury. He was a soldier of great experience and distinction in the Crusades and other wars, but in civil life was a man of modest demeanour, more concerned with decent behaviour than with smart appearance – truly an ideal and courteous knight. The shrine of Thomas à Becket in Canterbury Cathedral was freely visited by pilgrims for several centuries after his death (1170).

'The very pink of perfection'
Oliver Goldsmith, *She Stoops to Conquer*, I, i (1774)

Tony Lumpkin, according to one view, was 'an awkward booby, reared up and spoiled at his mother's apron-string'. According to his mother he was 'the very pink of perfection'. The mother is anxious for her son to marry his cousin Constance (who has a nice little fortune in jewels), but his taste is for buxom country wenches rather than fashionable young ladies. Constance, in any case, is in love with somebody else. In the end Tony good-naturedly helps to bring together Constance and her lover – and thus the sub-plot of this famous comedy reaches a happy conclusion.

'Victory, victory at all costs, victory in spite of all terror'
Winston Churchill, speech to the House of Commons (13 May 1940)

When he was appointed Prime Minister in place of Neville Chamberlain, Churchill, at the head of a new Government, wished to make the position absolutely clear to the House of Commons. An all-out effort was needed from people of all political parties. No matter what difficulties and dangers arose, the constant aim must be to defeat Nazi Germany. 'Without victory, there is no survival.'

'A wandering minstrel I'
W. S. Gilbert, *The Mikado*, Act I (1885)

But he is not really a wandering minstrel; he is the heir to the Japanese throne in disguise. Nanki-Poo (as he calls himself) has fled the Court to avoid being forced to marry an elderly spinster. He had fallen in love with Yum-Yum, the prettiest maiden in the town of Titipu. To support his disguise he offers to sing love ditties, patriotic ballads, or sea shanties – whatever is required. He gives an excellent specimen of each, but nobody asks for any more. Either Titipu was indifferent to vocal music or Gilbert forgot to write another solo for his principal tenor.

'War's annals will cloud into night
Ere their story die'
Thomas Hardy, *In Time of 'The Breaking of Nations'* (1915)

'The Breaking of Nations' is war (Jeremiah, li, 20); the poem was written a few months after the outbreak of the First World War (1914–18). In this short but impressive piece Hardy suggests that some of the basic things in life – farming the land, and lovers' meetings – will outlast the sound and fury of wars.

'Was ever such a fool that would not have his wife dumb'
Henry Fielding, *The Mock Doctor*, vii (1732)

In Fielding's version of Molière's *Le Médecin Malgré Lui*, a woodcutter is prevailed upon to pretend he is a doctor in order to cure a gentleman's daughter who has lost her voice. On learning that her suitor would not marry her till she was cured, the worldly wise woodcutter, whose wife was far from dumb, expressed surprise that the suitor was so lacking in sense as to want his wife to be vocal. However, he agreed to cure the young lady, which was easier than he expected, for her dumbness was feigned to avoid a distasteful marriage.

'Was this the face that launch'd a thousand ships,
And burnt the topless towers of Ilium?'
Christopher Marlowe, *Doctor Faustus*, V, i (c 1588)

Faustus, having sold his soul to the Devil in return for twenty-four years of absolute power, makes remarkably little use of the Devil's gift. Towards the end of his time he endeavours to seek oblivion in sexual enjoyment by conjuring up the spirit of Helen of Troy, the loveliest of women. Her beauty (and unfaithfulness) started the ten-year Trojan War in which countless ships took part, and which also led to the destruction of Troy (Ilium). Faustus fondly hopes that Helen's kisses will give him an immortality that he has unfortunately already bequeathed to Lucifer.

'Watch the wall, my darling, while the Gentlemen go by!'
Rudyard Kipling, *A Smuggler's Song* (1906)

The Gentlemen were the local smugglers trotting through the dark on their horses with contraband – brandy, tobacco, and finery. When these men were engaged in their illegal activities, wise inhabitants of the village kept out of the way and encouraged their children to look in the other direction. It was safest to be unable to identify the Gentlemen.

'Water, water, everywhere,
Nor any drop to drink'
S. T. Coleridge, *The Rime of the Ancient Mariner* (1798)

The ship in which the old mariner was sailing into
Antarctic waters was followed by an albatross, a great
seabird. It was regarded as a good omen until the
mariner shot it. The spirits of the region then plague the
ship by making it becalmed in the intense heat of the
sun. All the seamen suffer miserably from thirst. This
part of the poem was Wordsworth's idea. He had
recently been reading about albatrosses seen in the Cape
Horn area, and suggested that it would make a good
story if one of them was killed, thus bringing ill-fortune
on the expedition. Coleridge agreed.

'Wax to receive, and marble to retain'
Lord Byron, *Beppo*, xxxiv (1817)

Beppo was a Venetian merchant who often travelled
abroad. On one occasion he was away so long that his
wife, Laura, feared he must be lost. Being an attractive
Italian lady, she obviously needed a protector, and so an
Italian Count took on the role of 'vice-husband'. He was
a very accomplished man, a dancer, an authority at the
opera, 'wrote rhymes, sang songs, could also tell a
story'. But most important, he was an excellent lover,
whose heart was as easily impressed as wax and whose
love was as constant as marble. Thus they were a happy
pair, 'as happy as unlawful love could make them'.

'Wealth, Sir John, was made to wander'
Samuel Johnson, *Short Song of Congratulation* (1780)

Sir John Lade, nephew of Johnson's friend, Mr Thrale,
had just inherited his father's fortune. He was a foolish,
dissolute young man, and Johnson wrote this satirical
lyric (rather out of his usual vein) to amuse Mrs Thrale. It
sardonically invites the young man to 'bid the Slaves of
Thrift farewell'.

> Wealth, Sir John, was made to wander,
> Let it wander as it will:
> See the Jockey, see the Pander,
> Bid them come and take their fill.

Which they duly did, and Sir John proceeded to waste
his large inheritance in racing, wenching, gambling, and
other dubious pursuits.

'We are a nest of singing birds'
Samuel Johnson, in Boswell's *Life of Johnson* (1791)

It is difficult to picture the unwieldy doctor as a singing
bird, and one suspects that the metaphorical nest was
coloured by nostalgic sentiment. Johnson looked back for
the most part with affection to his time at Pembroke
College, Oxford, even though it was affected to some
extent by the poverty which ultimately led him to
withdraw without a degree. Like all good ex-students, he
was always ready to praise his old college, and on one
occasion maintained that it was 'a nest of singing birds',
owing to the number of poets it turned out. Very few are
remembered today except Shenstone and Johnson
himself.

'We are as near to Heaven by sea as by land'
Humphrey Gilbert, In *Hakluyt's Voyages* (1589)

In 1583 Sir Humphrey Gilbert led an expedition to discover lands north of Cape Florida and to settle Christian inhabitants there. Five ships of varying sizes set out. After founding the first British colony in New-foundland, Gilbert himself went aboard the smallest vessel, the *Squirrel*, a ship of only ten tons, mainly because she was the most convenient for exploring the coast. On the return journey, during a storm, Edward Hayes, captain of a companion ship, saw Gilbert 'sitting abaft with a book in his hand'. When the two ships were near enough Sir Humphrey called out his well-known last words. That same night the *Squirrel*'s lights suddenly went out, and no sign of ship or Gilbert was ever seen again.

'We are they who ride faster than fate'
J. Elroy Flecker, *War Song of the Saracens* (1909)

The Saracens were the Mohammedans, especially from Syria, who fought against the Crusaders in the Middle Ages, and won many battles against the European Christians. They often regarded themselves as tougher and hardier than their European enemies. 'Not on silk nor in samet we lie' but 'we sleep by the ropes of the camp'. They travelled 'with the sun or the moon for a lamp, and the spray of the wind in our hair', and they brought fear wherever they went. The song was later used (chanted by soldiers) in Flecker's play *Hassan*, III, iii (1922).

'A weary lot is thine, fair maid'
Sir Walter Scott, *Rokeby*, c. III (1813)

The first line of a rather sad song sung by the young minstrel of a robber band. It has no relevance to the story, which is based in Yorkshire at the time of the Civil War (1642–9). The brief song tells of a maid wooed by a dashing soldier in uniform, who then gallops away, crying 'Adieu for evermore!' That is all there is to the song. The story continues, in rather humdrum verse, for another three cantos. Soon afterwards Scott tired of verse narrative and turned to prose novels, with immense success.

'A week! – why I shall be an old woman by that time!'
John Vanbrugh, *The Relapse*, IV, i (1696)

Hoyden is a young rustic heiress who has been kept away from men by her father for fear she should be seduced by some money-seeking fellow. The frustrated girl has become man-crazy, ready to marry any male at a moment's notice. Young Fashion, poor but lively, courts her in the guise of his wealthier brother, Lord Foppington. Afraid of exposure before the wedding takes place, he tells her that a week (her father's wish) is too long to wait for the pleasures of the marriage-bed, and she is sex-mad enough to agree.

'We have changed all that'
Henry Fielding, *The Mock Doctor*, viii (1732)

A woodcutter forced to act as a doctor, owing to a prank
played on him by his wife, does his best to assume the
role, pretending to explain the patient's symptoms in a
farrago of nonsensical Latin. He also talks confidently
about the liver and the heart, but unfortunately mis-
places these organs. When it is pointed out that the liver
is in fact on the right and the heart on the left, he airily
replies that all that has been changed by the College of
Physicians! And such is his assurance that he is believed.
The play is adapted from Molière's *Le Médecin Malgré Lui*.

'Weighed in the balances, and found wanting'
Bible, Daniel, v, 27 (*c* 240 B.C.)

Belshazzar, King of Babylon, was somewhat disturbed
when a cheerful but profane feast was interrupted by the
sight of a bodiless hand writing a strange message on the
wall of the palace. No one could interpret it except
Daniel, a Jewish captive, long recognized as a master
magician. The writing – MENE, MENE, TEKEL, UP-
HARSIN – meant, briefly, that the King's time was up.
TEKEL indicated, 'Thou art weighed in the balances, and
found wanting'. According to the Bible story, Belshazzar
was slain that very night. According to other authorities,
however, the writing on the wall, though splendidly
dramatic, was legendary.

'A well-written Life is almost as rare as a well-spent one'
Thomas Carlyle, *Critical and Miscellaneous Essays – Richter*
(1827)

In an early essay for the *Edinburgh Review* Carlyle, a
serious student of German literature, reviews the life of
one German writer written by another. He has a pretty
low opinion of the book and says so with unusual
directness. 'This thing of shreds and patches has been
vamped together for sale only.' Having dismissed Hein-
rich Doring's *Life of Richter* with ignominy, Carlyle
proceeded to remedy the deficiency by assessing Jean
Paul Richter's work in a way that is both crisp and
readable.

'We made an expedition;
We met a host, and quelled it'
T. L. Peacock, *The War-Song of Dinas Vawr* (1829)

This boastful war-song is from the novel *The Misfortunes
of Elphin*, a parody of Arthurian legends. The verse, in
Peacock's own words, is 'the quintessence of all war-
songs that ever were written'. In 'Dyfed's richest valley'
King Melvas has captured the castle of Dinas Vawr, on
the River Towy. He and his followers have seized cattle,
sacked houses and cellars, slaughtered opposing soldiers, and cut off the head of their King. They are now
celebrating their exploits in braggart song.

    His wine and beasts supplied our feasts,
    And his overthrow our chorus.

'We must take things rough and smooth, as they come'
Samuel Foote, *The Mayor of Garrat*, Act I (1764)

An apothecary named Lint has been trying to persuade
the squire of the manor, Sir Jacob Jollup, to pay him extra
for treating injuries which are likely to follow the riotous
proceedings of a mock election, held each year at the
village of Garratt (at that time a village on the outskirts of
South London). Lint complains that the price of drugs
has gone up, and the number of patients gone down. Sir
Jacob replies tritely that a bad year may be followed by a
good one, and that it is necessary to take the rough with
the smooth.

'We take the Golden Road to Samarkand'
J. Elroy Flecker, *Hassan*, V, ii (1922)

The pilgrimage from Arabia to Samarkand, now in
Russia near the Afghanistan border, was an important
Mohammedan occasion. In Flecker's poem *The Golden
Journey to Samarkand* an Epilogue shows various mer-
chants and pilgrims chanting in chorus, 'We make the
Golden Journey to Samarkand.' Flecker adapted this
Epilogue to form an Epilogue for his play, *Hassan*. For the
sake of smoothness and dramatic emphasis the chorus
line was altered to 'We take the Golden Road to
Samarkand'. It made a most effective climax to a play
which, though put together in very much a piecemeal
way, had tremendous dramatic effect.

'We wear no swords here, but you understand me'
R. B. Sheridan, *The Rivals*, III, iv (1775)

The duel-loving Irishman, Sir Lucius O'Trigger, is offering bad advice to the peace-loving countryman, Bob
Acres. To discourage duelling, swords were not allowed
to be worn in Bath; but men with a taste for sword or
pistol could always sneak outside the city for their illicit
activity. Sir Lucius wants Acres to issue a challenge to a
rival in love. He succeeds at last – but the rival turns out
to be Bob's closest friend, and the challenge is hastily and
eagerly withdrawn.

*'We were not fairly beaten, my lord. No Englishman is ever
fairly beaten'*
George Bernard Shaw, *Saint Joan*, IV (1924)

A fervent English chaplain is present when the Earl of
Warwick and the Bishop of Beauvais are discussing the
possible capture and fate of Joan of Arc. She has recently
led a French army to defeat an English force, and the
indignant chaplain cannot bear to think that the English
lost the battle by fair means. He insists that the Maid
secured victory by using witchcraft and sorcery. Shaw,
like J. M. Barrie, knew that English audiences love to
hear jokes against themselves.

'What a dreadful thing 'twould be to be hurried back to Hampshire'
George Etherege, *The Man of Mode*, III, i (1676)

Harriet, daughter of Lady Woodvil, has been brought to fashionable London from their home at Hartley (Wintney) in Hampshire. She is no country miss, however, but a lively, intelligent, and witty young woman who loves London and has no desire to spend her time in 'a great rambling lone house that looks as if it were not inhabited, the family's so small'. I can vouch for the fact that living in Hampshire is not really so terrible a fate as Etherege supposed. But in the seventeenth century, no doubt, the forty miles between Hartley and the Court seemed a dark and bottomless pit.

'What can I do to drive away Remembrance from my eyes?'
John Keats, *To —* (1819)

Though not published until after his death, this poem was almost certainly addressed to Fanny Brawne, the girl Keats loved and would probably have married if he had lived. It was written soon after a meeting with her, and is an assertion of his great passion. He longs (purely rhetorically) for his old liberty, when no woman, however attractive, had any real hold on his mind. Now he is so deeply in love that the thought of her dominates his whole being. But these ideas are merely the stepping-stones to his final acceptance of the position. 'It is enough for me / To dream of thee.'

'What is past my help is past my care'
Beaumont and Fletcher, *The Double Marriage*, I, i (1647)

This philosophic attitude is shown by Virolet, a noble gentleman of Naples, who is plotting with some companions to rid the State of a tyrant King, Ferrand. The companions introduce a new member to the conspiracy. Virolet is not impressed, for the newcomer, Ronvere, has been one of the tyrant's chief officers. He now assures the conspirators that he has changed sides because of Ferrand's ill usage of him, but Virolet remains suspicious. But it seems that other doubtful people have also been let into the secret. Virolet therefore shrugs his shoulders and accepts the situation.

'What is the use of a book without pictures or conversations?'
Lewis Carroll, *Alice's Adventures in Wonderland* (1865)

Alice peeped into the book her sister was reading and saw that it was not illustrated and had no dialogue. She could think of no use for such a book, and had half a mind to get up and make a daisy chain. But it was a hot day and she was sleepy; so sleepy, indeed, that when a white rabbit ran by her, talking to itself, she was not a bit surprised. Luckily she was not too sleepy to follow it down the rabbit-hole to experience those delightful adventures that make up *Alice in Wonderland*.

'What I tell you three times is true'
Lewis Carroll, *The Hunting of the Snark* (1876)

The Bellman, leader of the crew who set out to catch a Snark, had assured his followers that the spot where their boat had landed was 'just the place for a snark'. By repeating it three times he made sure (to his own satisfaction) that it must be true. Not a few politicians have followed the same principle. As the place where they had landed consisted of 'chasms and crags', the crew were not too happy, despite the jokes that he retailed. However, after he had served them grog with a liberal hand, 'they drank to his health and they gave him three cheers'.

'What millions died – that Caesar might be great'
Thomas Campbell, *The Pleasures of Hope*, Pt II (1799)

The wars of Julius Caesar have been estimated to have cost two million lives. That Caesar was a great general and a clever administrator can hardly be gainsaid, but to what extent he was humanity's benefactor is another matter. Though personally inclined to clemency, he was a natural dictator, and it has been said that by destroying liberty he crushed the sense of dignity in mankind. Campbell is here picturing an earnest reader poring over a pile of books – narrative verse, dramatic tragedy, and (as here) 'Truth's historic page.' But whether Truth and History are really synonymous the reader must decide for himself.

'What passing-bells for those who die as cattle?'
Wilfred Owen, *Anthem for Doomed Youth* (1917)

Helpless anger, indignation, and anguish mark the short elegy by this fine young poet, who sadly was killed at the very end of the First World War. He contrasts in imagination the conventional peacetime burial service with the grim rites received by the soldiers slaughtered on the battlefield. In place of bells there was rifle fire; in place of burial hymns there was only the wailing of shells and the bugler's Last Post.

'What's lost upon the roundabouts we pulls up on the swings'
Patrick Chalmers, *Roundabouts and Swings* (1912)

In other words, good and bad events balance out in the long run. The propounder of this comforting precept is the owner of a travelling show. Accosted in his painted caravan near Framlingham, Essex, he is asked how things are going. He replies with this homely piece of philosophy.

'What was he doing, the great god Pan?'
Elizabeth Barrett Browning, *A Musical Instrument* (1862)

What he was doing was making a shepherd's pipe from a reed plucked near the river. He hacked off the leaves, cut the stem short, drew the pith, and finally notched holes, maintaining that this was the only way to make sweet music. He was no mean musician, for his simple instrument was so effective that

> The sun on the hill forgot to die.
> And the lilies revived, and the dragon-fly
> Came back to dream on the river.

Pan was the god of shepherds and huntsmen, usually depicted with horns on his head, and the legs of a goat.

'What will Mrs Grundy say?'
Thomas Morton, *Speed the Plough*, I, i (1800)

Mrs Grundy has gained an undeserved reputation as guardian of the proprieties. The original Mrs Grundy was merely a neighbour of Farmer Ashfield and his wife, both important characters in Morton's melodramatic sentimental comedy. Mrs Ashfield envied her neighbour (who does not appear in the play), and was constantly referring to her, to the irritation of Farmer Ashfield: 'Always ding dinging Dame Grundy into my ears! What will Mrs Grundy say? What will Mrs Grundy think?'

'What your real bully likes in tossing is when the boys kick and struggle'
Thomas Hughes, *Tom Brown's Schooldays*, ch. 6 (1856)

Tossing younger boys in a blanket was not uncommon in nineteenth-century public schools. Sometimes it was done with the consent of the victim. On Tom Brown's first night at Rugby, following the example of his new-found friend East, he agreed to be tossed. He found it not too bad an experience, except when he met the ceiling and his inside seemed to stay sticking to it before the descent. But bullies such as Flashman preferred to toss unwilling boys, who struggled, or tried to grasp the blanket and so got pitched on to the floor. Better still, if two boys were tossed together they would struggle in the air to be the top one.

'When a man is tired of London, he is tired of life'
Samuel Johnson, in Boswell's *Life of Johnson* (1791)

Boswell had expressed a fear that if he were to reside permanently in London he would lose the extreme pleasure that he received from visists to the city, and might grow tired of it. Johnson maintained that no man of intellect could tire of London 'for there is in London all that life can afford'. He encouraged Boswell, however, in the idea that he should spend part of his time at his ancestral home in Scotland. To Johnson, the great attraction of London was the immense variety of company that it afforded.

'When Britain really ruled the waves'
W. S. Gilbert, *Iolanthe*, Act II (1882)

This rousing, patriotic, satiric song contrasts delightfully with Sullivan's splendid tune. Gilbert is making fun of the peerage, which a hundred years ago 'made no pretence to intellectual eminence'. His lyric cheekily asserts that Britain's renown in the days of Elizabeth I and George IV was due largely to the distinct inactivity of the nobility.

> The House of Peers, throughout the war,
> Did nothing in particular
> And did it very well!

Although one peer, at any rate, played a not inconsiderable part in the Napoleonic Wars, the lines remain a classic piece of satire.

'Whenever a man dies without any property of his own, he always seems to think he has a right to dispose of other people's'
Charles Dickens, *Nicholas Nickleby*, ch. 3 (1838–9)

The complaint comes from Mr Ralph Nickleby, whose brother has died penniless after some injudicious speculation, with a dying wish that Ralph will look after his family. Ralph Nickleby is the chief villain of the novel, and quite an unpleasant character. But one cannot help feeling that in this instance he has some right on his side, for he is being asked to use his own property (money) for the benefit of a financially reckless brother whom he has not seen for years.

'Whenever he met a great man he grovelled before him and my-lorded him as only a free-born Briton can'
W. M. Thackeray, *Vanity Fair*, ch. 13 (1848)

Mr Osborne was a self-made man whose business had prospered. But although he was proud of his wealth ('My guineas are as good as theirs') he had a great respect for the nobility and was eager for his son, George, to mix with titled people. Against his father's desire, George married a girl whose father had lost money, and although Mr Osborne himself had originally instigated the match, the old man spitefully obliterated his son's name from his will, and even from the family Bible.

'Whenever I see you kissing a very young lady, I shall know it's an elderly relative'
W. S. Gilbert, *Iolanthe*, Act II (1882)

Phyllis, the charming heroine of the play, finds her lover (aged twenty-five) embracing a young woman (apparently aged about seventeen). She is naturally unconvinced by his explanation that the lady is his mother. However, in due course it appears that the young man's mother is a fairy, and consequently retains a youthful appearance indefinitely. As Phyllis would rather have a man she loves, even if he is only half mortal, than half a dozen men she does not love, she has to accept the daunting fact that his grandmother and his numerous aunts all look as young as his mother.

'When everyone is somebody,
Then no one's anybody'
W. S. Gilbert, *The Gondoliers*, Act II (1889)

Two gondoliers reigning jointly (but temporarily) as
Kings of Barataria, introduced a system of social levelling
up into their court. Every member of it, even the
humblest, was given high office. The result was that the
Kings had to do most of the work themselves. In one of
Gilbert's best-known songs an experienced Court
official, the Grand Inquisitor, points out the dangers of
trying to make everybody equal. It merely reduces the
best to a lower status.

When every blessed thing you hold
Is made of silver or of gold,
You long for simple pewter.

'When from the cradle to the grave I look,
Mine I conceive a melancholy book'
George Crabbe, *The Parish Register – Burials* (1807)

Melancholy indeed is the note sounded as Crabbe turns
the pages of his parish register. It covers both Baptisms
and Burials, but almost twice as much space is devoted to
Deaths as to Births. Even the births do not always bring
joy, by any means; and as the poet notes the names of
those who have died, and briefly tells their story, he
dwells on the blacker side more often than on the greyer.

We are going all;
Like flowers we wither, and like leaves we fall.

'When Greeks joined Greeks, then was the tug of war'
Nathaniel Lee, *The Rival Queens*, IV, ii (1677)

The speaker is Clytus, a blunt old soldier at the court of
Alexander the Great. Alexander has been asking his
courtiers to name the bravest general ever to have led an
army. Naturally they hasten to offer the expected tribute
to Alexander himself – all except old Clytus, who boldly
(and drunkenly) asserts that Alexander's father, Philip of
Macedon, was a better leader. He goes on to add that the
fiercest fighting he had known was when the Greek
states were warring among themselves. 'Joined' is, of
course, used in the sense of 'engaged in conflict with'.
The common saying 'when Greek meets Greek' is a
misquotation.

'When he (a writer) sets out on his travels the one person he
must leave behind is himself'
Somerset Maugham, *The Gentleman in the Parlour – Preface*
(1935)

Maugham is writing a travel book covering his journeys
in the East. He points out that if a writer takes with him
his English interests and prejudices, he is liable to return
very much the same as he set out. If his experiences are
to effect any change in him he must see them with fresh
eyes; only thus can he really profit from his journey. 'I do
not bring back from a journey quite the same self that I
took.' This was the spirit in which Maugham set out on
his rather casual journey 'through Burma, the Shan
States, Siam, and Indo-China'.

'When I go into a bank I get rattled'
Stephen Leacock, *Literary Lapses* (1910)

Inasmuch as Leacock (1869–1944) was a university professor of economics, it is most unlikely that his approach to the banking world was a timid one. But perhaps his sketch *My Financial Career* was suggested by a youthful experience. In any case it is a hilarious account of a young man's timid attempt to open a bank account, written in days when banks were indeed somewhat austere and unapproachable. The young man, after unnecessarily summoning the manager, pokes his fifty-six dollars at the bank clerk. Then he writes his first cheque, intending to draw out six dollars, but finds he has unwittingly written 'fifty-six' and drawn all his money out again.

'When I say an ill-natured thing 'tis out of pure good humour'
R. B. Sheridan, *The School for Scandal*, II, i (1777)

Sir Peter Teazle's young country wife had joined the scandal-mongering circle that flourished in eighteenth-century fashionable society. She had a lively mind and was well able to hold her own among the waspish tongues of her companions. Unlike most of them, however, she had no malice towards those whose reputations she attacked, as she lightheartedly tells Sir Peter.

'When lovely woman stoops to folly, And finds too late that men betray, What charm can soothe her melancholy, What art can wash her guilt away?'
Oliver Goldsmith, *The Vicar of Wakefield*, ch., 24 (1766)

Olivia, the Vicar's elder daughter, sings this 'melancholy air' (rather strangely) to cheer up her father after the vicarage has been gutted. The song was at any rate apt, for she herself was in the unfortunate position of having been seduced and deserted. The second verse concludes that death is the only solution to the deserted woman's situation. Happily Olivia does not find this extremity necessary, and when it turns out that Olivia was after all (without his knowledge) legally married to her rascally betrayer, everyone accepts this as a happy ending to the affair. Luckily she was awarded part of his fortune, and his reform seemed likely to follow.

'When our toes are turned up to the daisies'
R. H. Barham, *The Ingoldsby Legends – The Babes in the Wood* (1843)

In this humorous version of the legend the parents of the two children are dying through having eaten too many plums. The mother begs their uncle to look after them.

Now think, 'tis your sister invokes

Your aid, and the last word she says is,

Be kind to those dear little folks

When our toes are turned up to the daisies.'

The toes, of course, are in a grave, and the daisies in a graveyard. Alas, the uncle villainously fails to keep his promise, but in due course he falls under a curse that brings about his downfall and suicide.

> *'When the Rock was hid by the surge's swell,*
> *The mariners heard the warning bell'*
> Robert Southey, *The Inchcape Rock* (1802)

This poem was based on an old traditional tale. Twelve miles from land in the North Sea the Inchcape Rock (now Bell Rock) shows its head in calm weather. To protect mariners the Abbot of Aberbrothok (Arbroath) had a bell fastened to the rock, so that when it was hidden by stormy seas its presence would be indicated by the sound. But one still day a pirate captain thought of annoying the Abbot by cutting the rope holding the bell. 'Down sank the bell with a gurgling sound.' As poetic justice demanded, the next ship to sail near the Rock was the pirate ship itself, which met its appropriate fate.

> *'When they reach the scene of crime – Macavity's not there!'*
> T. S. Eliot, *Old Possum's Book of Practical Cats* (1939)

In this diverting book of cat poems for children Eliot invents a mystery cat based obviously on Professor Moriarty, the clever villain of the Sherlock Holmes saga. Like Moriarty, Macavity 'sways his head from side to side'. Like Moriarty, he organizes international intrigues. Like Moriarty, he works behind the scenes, and is so subtle that it is impossible to pin him down.

> 'At whatever hour the deed took place –
> MACAVITY WASN'T THERE!'

Some readers of Eliot's usual work have been surprised to find him capable of such straightforwardness and humour.

> *'When will the bell ring, and end this weariness?'*
> D. H. Lawrence, *Last Lesson in the Afternoon*

Many a schoolmaster has felt as Lawrence did at the end of a day's teaching. What is the point of it all? Why should I go on trying to force knowledge into this mob of boys? What does it matter whether they can write a description of a dog? Lawrence shuts his mind, refuses to beat his head against the wall, and just waits for the bell. He also took an early opportunity to escape from a job that brought him no satisfaction, and became a full-time writer instead. A few have followed his example, and many more have wished that they dared.

> *'When you have eliminated the impossible, whatever*
> *remains, however improbable, must be the truth'*
> A. Conan Doyle, *The Sign of Four*, ch. 6 (1890)

This logical axiom was the basis of Sherlock Holmes's method, and very convincing too – though it failed to explain how one could reliably distinguish between the impossible and the improbable. What might seem to be the one might well turn out to be the other. In this instance the impossibility was for anyone to enter a room by door or window when these were securely fastened on the inside. This left entry via the roof and ceiling, which, however unlikely, was the way (as Holmes demonstrated) in which the murderer of Bartholomew Sholto gained access to the premises.

*'When you're a married man, Samivel, you'll understand a
good many things as you don't understand now'*
Charles Dickens, *The Pickwick Papers*, ch. 27 (1837)

Mr Weller is talking to his son, Sam, the lively and keen-witted servant of Mr Pickwick. Mr Weller has married a widow (landlady of the Marquis of Granby tavern) who has turned out to be less amiable than he had hoped. Among her other faults, Mrs Weller is greatly attached to Mr Stiggins, a phony religious minister who spends most of his time drinking pineapple rum at the Wellers' home. Sam asks his father why he allows Stiggins to 'show his red nose in the Markis o' Granby'. Mr Weller replies, 'Cause I'm a married man', and goes on to suggest that Sam will understand better when he is married himself.

'Where are the songs of Spring? Aye, where are they?'
John Keats, *Ode to Autumn* (1819)

The poet is praising the beauty of Autumn, putting aside the merits of the earlier season. 'Think not of them, thou hast thy music too.' In a letter written shortly after composing this ode to Autumn, Keats said to a friend: 'I never liked stubble fields so much as now – Aye better than the chilly green of the Spring. Somehow a stubble plain looks warm.' This ode is imbued with warmth and plenty:

To set budding more
And still more later flowers for the bees,
Until they think warm days will never cease.

'Where are you going to, all you Big Steamers?'
Rudyard Kipling, *Big Steamers* (1910)

The Big Steamers are going to fetch bread, butter, beef, eggs, and other food items from places such as Melbourne, Quebec, and Vancouver. The narrator undertakes to pray for fine weather and to build a new lighthouse, but is told that Big Steamers do not worry about the weather, and that there are already plenty of lighthouses and pilots. The needful thing to do is to insist that there are enough warships to protect the merchant vessels, 'That no one may stop us from bringing you food.' This children's poem may be thought prophetic, as it was written four years before the start of the First World War.

*'Where ignorance is bliss
'Tis folly to be wise'*
Thomas Gray, *Ode on a Distant Prospect of Eton College* (1742)

At the ripe age of twenty-five Gray put on his rose-tinted glasses and became convinced that children were happy creatures, free from the many miseries of adult life. It may have been true of Gray himself; his Eton schooldays seem to have been free from the traditional bullying and violence. As he grew older, however, he began to suffer from fits of depression, accentuated by the death of his friend Richard West in 1742. The Ode was written at Stoke Poges (three or four miles from Eton) in that year, though not published till 1747.

> *'Where is the woman that would scruple to be a wife if she had it in her power to be a widow whenever she pleased'*
> John Gay, *The Beggar's Opera*, Act I (1728)

Peacham, the rascally receiver to a gang of highwaymen, is a living disproof of the adage that there is honour among thieves. When his daughter falls in love with the leader of the gang, Captain Macheath, and marries him, Peacham is at first furious. 'Macheath may hang his father and mother-in-law in hopes to get into their daughter's fortune.' But he soon sees a way out of the trouble. 'Secure what he hath got, have him peached at the next sessions, and then at once you are made a rich widow!' Polly, however, proves a disobedient daughter, and refuses to murder her husband.

> *'Where there is a necessity, a Christian is bound to help his neighbour'*
> John Vanbrugh, *The Relapse* (1696)

The neighbourliness that Mr Worthy is mischievously proposing, however, is corrupt rather than Christian. He is inviting his former mistress, Berinthia, to help him in his efforts to seduce her friend, Amanda. This in turn, he suggests, will make it easier for Berinthia to carry on her existing intrigue with Amanda's husband. In the event, Berinthia's affair is more successful than Worthy's, for the latter is ultimately disarmed by Amanda's persistent virtue. Even before the end of the century hints of morality were beginning to seep into Restoration comedy.

> *'Where youth grows pale, and spectre-thin, and dies'*
> John Keats, *Ode to a Nightingale* (1819)

Listening to the lovely song of the nightingale, Keats wishes he could drink deep of some rich wine that would help him to lose his senses and fade into the forest with the nightingale, forgetting the troubles of the world – 'the weariness, the fever, and the fret'. The quoted line is particularly poignant, for not long before he had been sadly nursing his brother Tom, who died of consumption that year.

> *'While I would reward the deserving, I would dismiss those utterly unqualified for their employment'*
> Oliver Goldsmith, *The Bee*, no. 6 – *On Education* (10 November 1759)

Goldsmith is writing of schoolmasters in this short-lived periodical. Unlike some dogmatic writers on education, he was not without personal experience. For a while he was usher at a school in Peckham, South London. He almost certainly hated the work, and was among 'those utterly unqualified for their employment'. He is here insisting on the importance of the schoolmaster in society, and protesting at the low regard in which he is generally held. The remedy, he claims, is to increase schoolmasters' salaries and admit to the profession 'only men of proper abilities'. The same view is often heard more than a couple of hundred years later.

'Whistle and she'll come to you'
Beaumont and Fletcher, *Wit Without Money*, IV, iv (1639)

Isabella, a wealthy young woman, has fallen in love with penniless Francisco and sends him money anonymously. When he discovers who has helped him he goes to thank her. She is unwilling to admit her feelings openly and tends to slight him, but to retain his interest in her she presents him with an expensive ring which she pretends he has dropped. After he has left, Francisco's servant, an old falconer, assures him in the language of falconry that she must be truly in love with him. Burns used the expression in his song, 'O whistle, and I'll come to you, my lad.'

'The white flower of a blameless life'
Alfred Tennyson, *Idylls of the King – Dedication* (1862)

The wearer of this figurative floral decoration was Albert, the Prince Consort, to whom the *Idylls* were posthumously dedicated soon after his sudden death in 1861. He had very much admired those parts that had been published while he lived. The dedication, just over fifty lines in length, paid tribute to a man who was greatly respected for his character and abilities – 'a Prince indeed ... Albert the Good'. The lines closed with sympathy for Queen Victoria, now left with 'the crown a lonely splendour'.

'Whoever loved that loved not at first sight?'
Christopher Marlowe, *Hero and Leander*, I (1598)

Hero was a lovely priestess of Aphrodite (Venus) on one side of the Hellespont. On the other side, at Abydos, lived Leander, a brave and handsome youth. He went one day to the temple of Venus, where he saw Hero engaged in the (to us) somewhat repulsive act of sacrificing a turtle-dove to her goddess. More concerned with feminine beauty than with cruelty to animals, he fell instantly in love with her and she with him. As she opened her eyes and saw him gazing amorously at her, Hero's 'gentle heart was strook'. Love at first sight is the only real love, Marlowe asserts, with more enthusiasm than psychological insight.

'Who left scarcely any kind of writing untouched, and touched nothing that he did not adorn'
Samuel Johnson, *Inscription on monument in Westminster Abbey* (1776)

This inscription, in Latin, was placed in the Abbey after the death of Oliver Goldsmith (1731–74). A good many members of Johnson's Literary Club would have liked the epitaph written in English, but Johnson firmly refused to lower the dignity of the Abbey (as he thought) by an English inscription. Johnson's admiration for Goldsmith's writing was considerable, though incomplete. The inscription pays tribute to him as 'Poet, Naturalist, Historian'. To posterity, however, these are not the most significant of Goldsmith's claims to fame. Literary history regards him preeminently as 'Dramatist, Essayist, and Novelist'.

'Whom the gods love die young'
Lord Byron, *Don Juan*, IV, xii (1821)

The familiar aphorism is given as a quotation by Byron, though his is probably the first use of it in English. It comes originally from the Greek historian Herodotus. In *Don Juan* it is used in connection with Haidee, a pirate's daughter who falls in love with Juan. When he is taken away and shipped aboard a slave-ship, she dies giving birth to his child.

'Who shall decide when doctors disagree?'
Alexander Pope, *Moral Essays*, Epistle III (1731–5)

This essay on 'The Use of Riches' was, according to his own account, the most laboured of Pope's writings. This was a pity, for he got off to a good start with the quoted sentence. The point in dispute was whether riches were or were not a benefit to mankind. In the essay the matter was argued, as a dialogue, by Pope himself and Lord Bathurst (with Pope giving himself the lion's share). No conclusion was reached. It should be noted that the doctors of the quotation, whom we probably picture arguing in hushed whispers at the bedside of an invalid, are not physicians but Doctors of Philosophy disputing moral issues.

'Why do they call me a witch?'
Christopher Fry, *The Lady's Not for Burning*, Act II (1949)

The reason was that the playwright had set his comedy (lightheartedly) in the year 1400 'more or less exactly', and in those times almost anybody could be called a witch for almost any reason. Jennet Jourdemayne, the attractive 'witch' of this play, received the angry attentions of both villagers and officials because her late father was an alchemist, and because Jennet herself followed the antisocial practice of living alone. Moreover, she spoke to her pet poodle in French. Consequently, when a villager disappeared, it seemed obvious to everyone that she had murdered him by witchcraft. The play is not strictly historical; nor was the burning of witches the practice in England, and witch persecution was less common in the fifteenth than in the next two centuries. But the play, though wordy, is an appealing one, with an agreeable ending.

'Why do you walk through the fields in gloves, Missing so much and so much?'
Frances Cornford, *To a Lady Seen From a Train* (1910)

The offender was 'a fat white woman whom nobody loves', whose gloved appearance seemed incongruous in a field of soft grasses sweetly inviting to the touch. One can understand the poet's feeling. Yet it is really a one-sided impression, and it was G. K. Chesterton who sprang to the lady's defence with a poem that gave *her* point of view.

Why do you rush through the field in trains,
Guessing so much and so much?

And the fat white lady suggests (through her champion) that, for all the poet knows, she is on her way to meet someone who loves both her and her nice white gloves!

'Why is a raven like a writing-desk?'
Lewis Carroll, *Alice's Adventures in Wonderland*, ch. 7 (1865)

This riddle, put forward by the Mad Hatter at his tea party, has puzzled innumerable people. Alice, indeed, at first thought she could guess it, but she was sidetracked into a discussion on other matters. In fact, this was almost certainly meant to be a riddle without any answer, invented as a typically meaningless remark for the Mad Hatter to make. But the unanswered riddle produced so much frustrated conjecture among readers that thirty years later Carroll published a not very convincing solution: 'Because it can produce a few notes'. No doubt it was the best he could do, and no one else has done any better.

'Why so pale and wan, fond lover?'
John Suckling, *Aglaura*, IV, i (1694)

A song sung by a young lord to some companions to pass the time, offering sensible advice to any love-sick swain. Briefly, the singer points out that if a lover cannot win his mistress when he is hale and hearty, he is even less likely to do so if he looks pale and sickly. There is only one thing to be done – give her up!

> If of herself she will not love,
> Nothing will make her,
> The Devil take her!

The song has nothing to do with the plot of the play and was probably written independently of it, but, like the songs in Shakespeare's plays, it serves a purpose.

' "Will you walk into my parlour?" said the Spider to the Fly'
Mary Howitt, *The Spider and the Fly* (1821)

The Spider's efforts to entrap the Fly are at first unsuccessful. 'Oh no, no,' said the little Fly, 'to ask me is in vain.' But when at last he uses flattery the Fly falls for it. After being praised for her prettiness she enters the web. Her fate is sealed.

> He dragged her up his winding stair, into his dismal den
> Within his little parlour – but she ne'er came out again!

Mary and her husband William, both separately and together, were prolific writers of all kinds of books.

'Will you, won't you, will you, won't you, will you join the dance?'
Lewis Carroll, *Alice's Adventures in Wonderland*, ch. 10 (1865)

The chorus line of the *Lobster Quadrille*, sung to Alice by the Mock Turtle. A whiting is inviting a snail to join the dance, but the snail is reluctant to accept the invitation. The dance involves being thrown out to sea, and the snail is afraid of the distance. He is reminded by the whiting that 'the further off from England the nearer is to France', but being (no doubt) a very English snail and aware of French eating habits, he prefers to stay in England.

> 'Wilt thou forgive that sin where I begun
> Which was my sin, though it was done before?'

John Donne, *A Hymn to God the Father* (1633)

Donne is indicating his belief in 'original sin' – the idea that Adam's transgression was passed on to his successors, making everybody guilty. The second stanza of the poem asks forgiveness for his own sins. The third reveals what he believes to be the sin of Doubt – the fear that death means annihilation. But he seems to find comfort in the thought of Christ's resurrection, and is even able to make a typical Donne pun on the subject.

> Swear by thyself that at my death thy Son
> Shall shine as He shines now.

> 'Wistfully watching, with wonderful liquid eyes'

D. H. Lawrence, *Kangaroo* (1923)

Lawrence depicts a mother kangaroo, with the paw of her tiny offspring protruding from the pouch, watching sadly, as if waiting for something new to arrive in her chosen land, 'that silent lost land of the South' – a land of small creatures only. Her eyes, he thinks, are like those of the Australian black boy, 'lost for so many centuries on the margins of existence'.

> 'A witch has been a-walking in the fields in front of me'

Walter de la Mare, *As Lucy Went A-Walking* (1902)

It was Christmas Day when Lucy went walking and saw certains signs that indicated witchcraft. There were three crows on a bough, and seven shadows cast by seven poplar trees. Moreover, in a little pool of water, iced over, she hears the sound of fairy bells. Presently she sees some witches – 'a witch and witches, one and nine'. Nine, three, and seven are all magic numbers. Mysterious effects appear: flowers floating like singing-birds, precious jewels hanging in the trees like fruit. But when she mentions the word 'Christmas' it breaks the spell. 'Like a dream which vanishes, so vanished were they all.' The poem comes from De La Mare's delightful *Songs of Childhood*.

> 'With all our faults, we love our Queen'

W. S. Gilbert, *The Pirates of Penzance*, Act III (1880)

The very inoffensive pirates of Penzance have battled with a force of policemen, and have won the day. The police lie prostrate, the pirates standing over them with drawn swords. But the police sergeant suddenly defeats them by charging them to yield in the Queen's name! A rapid change of situation occurs. At the mention of the Queen the pirates at once drop to their knees, and the police then get the upper hand. Whether or not Queen Victoria was amused by this typically Gilbertian volte-face, audiences have continued to laugh for over a hundred years.

'With ... a profound bow to his patrons, the Manager retires, and the curtain rises'
W. M. Thackeray, *Vanity Fair – Before the Curtain* (1848)

Vanity Fair first appeared in serial form. When it was published as a book the author presented it as a puppet show at a fair, with the dolls playing the characters. He added that he is proud to think that the puppets have given satisfaction to all kinds of people. At the close of the novel he repeats his theme: 'let us shut up the box and the puppets, for our play is played out'. Whether it is wise for an author to emphasize the unreality of his characters is a point often discussed.

'With clinging dainty catlike tread'
Walter de la Mare, *Blondin* (1950)

The poem describes the skill of Jean Gravelet, one of the most famous acrobats of all time, who performed under the name Blondin. The feat which made his reputation was the first tightrope crossing of Niagara Falls (1859) on a rope high above the water. Later he repeated the feat in various ways – blindfold, or pushing a wheelbarrow, or on stilts, or carrying a man on his back. He performed the feat, the poem says, with an eye as serene as that of a person sitting quietly at his fireside. He makes his way above the Falls with 'each inch-long toe precisely pat'.

'Within certain limits it is actually true that the less money you have, the less you worry'
George Orwell, *Down and Out in Paris and London*, ch. 3 (1933)

The point about extreme poverty, Orwell argues, is that it annihilates the future. With a hundred francs, you worry about how to spend it to the best advantage. With only three francs, you know that it will just about feed you tomorrow, and there is no point in thinking further than that. Moreover, when you have really reached rock bottom you know there is no further to fall. Orwell was not spinning fanciful theories about poverty. Though an old Etonian, he actually experienced the poverty and discomfort about which he wrote so honestly. One is tempted to think that he rather enjoyed it.

'Within that awful volume lies The mystery of mysteries'
Sir Walter Scott, *The Monastery*, ch. 12 (1820)

The mysterious volume is, in fact, the Bible, which in the sixteenth century was thought by Catholic clergy to be a dangerous book to be allowed to fall into the hands of the laity. The monks of Melrose Abbey had confiscated it from the hands of a dying woman. In those days most respectable houses had a family ghost, and a spirit known as the White Lady of Avenel promptly snatched the volume back. A friend of the family begs her to let him see and read the book. She warns him of the dreadful secrets it may contain, and of the fearful fate that will fall upon anyone who reads it in the wrong spirit.

'A woman dipt in blood, and talk of modesty!'
Thomas Middleton and William Rowley, *The Changeling*, III, 4
(1623)

Beatrice wickedly commissions her father's servant, De
Flores, whom she finds repulsive, to murder her future
husband so that she can marry another man. The crime is
committed, but De Flores is not content with a purse of
gold. He blackmails Beatrice into sharing his bed, and
when at first she shrinks with anger and disgust from the
mere suggestion – 'I cannot see what way I can forgive it
with any modesty' – he cynically points out that a
murderess is in no position to raise objections. Her noble
birth no longer avails, for crime has made them equals.

'The woman had a bottom of good sense'
Samuel Johnson, in Boswell's *Life of Johnson* (1791)

The great man meant that the lady was fundamentally
sensible, but his choice of words invited merriment,
particularly as his manner of speech was so earnest.
'Most of us,' Boswell commented, 'could not forbear
tittering and laughing,' while Hannah More hid her
smiling face behind someone else's back. Only a bishop
kept his countenance. Johnson was not amused.
'Where's the merriment?' he demanded. Nobody told
him, but his forceful personality triumphed. When he
repeated his statement in a slightly different form 'we all
sat composed as at a funeral'.

'A woman's preaching is like a dog's walking on its hind legs. It is not well done, but you are surprised to find it done at all'
Samuel Johnson, in Boswell's *Life of Johnson* (1791)

One Sunday in 1763 (3 July) Boswell told Johnson that he
had been that morning 'at a meeting of the people called
Quakers, where I had heard a woman preach'. Boswell
doubtless hoped to provoke his tame bear into some
characteristic utterance, and he succeeded. Johnson's
quoted comment has become one of his best-known
observations. It would obviously be wrong to regard it as
anything more than an off-the-cuff bon mot. It may well
have been literally true, however, for eighteenth-century
women had few opportunities to practise sermonizing.

'Women, however personally vain they may be themselves, despise personal vanity in men'
William Cobbett, *Advice to Young Men – Letter 1* (1829)

Cobbett assures his young readers that this piece of
information is worth half a fortune to them. So it may
have been for, as he points out, if fine clothes do bring
you a wife they are not likely to bring you a frugal and
sensible one. He is stressing the folly of extravagance in
dress, and in the early nineteenth century his words were
probably justified. In our own day, of course, they
hardly apply, for some pop stars have little to commend
them except their plumage.

'Woodman, spare that tree'
G. P. Morris, *The Deserted Bride* (1838)

The author of this verse, dear to the hearts of conservationists, demands that the oak tree planted by his father shall be left untouched. Beneath its branches he had spent many happy hours in his childhood along with his sisters and parents.

Then, woodman, leave the spot;

While I've a hand to save,

The axe shall harm it not.

George Pope Morris (1802–64) was a versatile American journalist and poet, for many years editor of *The New York Mirror*.

'The word "horrible" in connection with goodness was a novelty that commended itself'
Saki, *The Story-Teller*

The clever humorist (Hector H. Munro 1870–1916), who wrote under the name Saki, is here relating the sad tale of an aunt trying to keep three irritating small children quiet on a railway journey. The aunt had invented a tedious story of a good little girl saved from death by reason of her goodness. They are bored stiff – and say so. A fellow traveller undertakes to show her how the task really should be done. He tells the story (full of ingenious embellishments) of a little girl who is 'horribly good', and who meets a sticky end *because* of her goodness. The children love it.

'Work expands so as to fill the time available for its completion'
C. Northcote Parkinson, *Parkinson's Law* (1958)

Professor Parkinson is adept at making serious fun of bureaucracy and other forms of public administration. His law indicates that there is no relation between the work to be done, the time available, and the size of the staff to which the work is assigned. If the size of the staff is increased, the work is not completed more quickly. Draft reports are drawn up, checked, and revised by several people instead of by one person – the final result often being exactly what would have been achieved in the first place by one person. The author gives some illuminating statistics to show that (for instance) the number of Admiralty officials almost doubled in fourteen years while the number of ships and men greatly decreased.

'The world forgetting, by the world forgot'
Alexander Pope, *Eloïsa to Abelard* (1717)

This is the situation of the virgin who enters a convent before she has experienced any physical passion, and consequently (it is assumed) enjoys a tranquil existence without longing or regrets. How different from the woman who is forced into a nunnery after having experienced sexual enjoyment with a lover. The comparison is made by Eloïsa, the poem being based on the story of Héloise and Abelard, victims in the Middle Ages of the cruel ecclesiastical rules of the time. After a passionate love affair they were incarcerated in convent and monastery, and induced to look on their natural love as a crime.

> *'The world has had great heroes,*
> *As history books have showed;*
> *But never a name to go down to fame*
> *Compared with that of Toad'*
> A. A. Milne, *Toad of Toad Hall*, II, iii (1929)

This is the song (composed by himself) of the conceited but likeable Mr Toad, in the popular play which Milne based on Kenneth Grahame's *The Wind in the Willows* (1908). For his own good, Toad is being kept in confinement by his friends Badger, Rat, and Mole, in an attempt to cure him of his crazy passion for motoring. After getting away by tricking Rat, he sings his song triumphantly. Captured by the police and sentenced to imprisonment, he sings it again defiantly. His good nature makes it difficult to take offence at his conceit.

> *'The world is mine!'*
> Oliver Goldsmith, *The Traveller* (1764)

Though not published until 1764, parts of *The Traveller* were written much earlier, when Goldsmith was a penurious traveller on the continent, playing for his suppers with his flute. The poem begins by congratulating his brother Henry on having a happy home. He then passes to his own situation, seated on an Alpine peak and gazing at the variety of scene beneath him – towns, fields, lakes, labouring peasants. The abundance of it all overwhelms him, and he is carried away by a mood of joyful appreciation: 'Creation's heir, the world, the world is mine!'

> *'The world must be safe for democracy'*
> Woodrow Wilson, *Address to Congress* (2 April 1917)

In the third year of the First World War the U.S.A., hitherto neutral, felt impelled to enter the conflict because of attacks on its shipping by German submarines endeavouring to blockade Britain. War on Germany was officially declared by America on 6 April 1917. Addressing Congress four days earlier, Wilson made his purpose clear. America could not allow the violation of her right to use her ships as she required, or her seamen and passengers to be wantonly sacrificed. The German government was a natural foe to liberty, and the U.S.A. must fight for the liberation of nations and the ultimate peace of the world.

> *'The worst sin towards our fellow creatures is not to hate them, but to be indifferent to them'*
> George Bernard Shaw, *The Devil's Disciple*, Act II (1897)

Anthony Anderson, Presbyterian minister of Websterbridge, New Hampshire, in the year 1777, is talking to his wife. She has just confessed to feeling hatred towards Richard Dudgeon, who prides himself on his wickedness and liking for the Devil. The minister, good-humoured and broad-minded, suggests that hatred, unlike indifference, is a genuine emotion and therefore not so different, after all, from love. His wife, Judith, is startled at the idea. But in due course her hatred does change to something very close to love when Richard is prepared to sacrifice himself to save the minister.

'Would you have me give my secret for his?'
George Farquhar, *The Beaux' Stratagem*, I, i (1707)

The two heroes of the play, travelling as master and servant, have put up at a tavern whose rascally innkeeper wrongly suspects that they may be highwaymen. Since they do not belong to his own gang he would like to betray them to the authorities and gain the reward. But proof is needed. He proposes to his pretty young daughter that she shall let the servant seduce her, to wheedle information out of him. She protests at such a suggestion. In fact, when the 'servant' makes himself agreeable, it is not she who does the wheedling.

'Would you your son should be a sot or dunce?'
William Cowper, *Tirocinium* (1784)

Cowper's question is answered by his own ironic advice to send the lad to a public school. There, the poet suggests, he will learn a variety of vices, including drunkenness, window-breaking, hooliganism, and the art of picking up prostitutes. The sensitive poet's criticism was largely inspired by his own education at Westminster School (1741–9), where he was far from happy. Early-nineteenth-century education was not notable for excellence; boys were often left uncontrolled after school hours. However, a good classical education was sometimes received.

'The wretched have no friends'
John Dryden, *All for Love*, III, i (1678)

In this version of the story of Antony and Cleopatra the hero is being persuaded by his general, Ventidius, to abandon Cleopatra and make peace with his wife, Octavia, and his brother-in-law, Octavius Caesar. Ventidius stresses the support Caesar can obtain from other countries, whereas Antony's only source of help is Cleopatra's Egypt. Pressed by such blunt, though prejudiced, advice, Antony is driven into a mood of morbid self-pity, complaining in effect that nobody loves him. A friend helps him to recover his more manly spirit, but also enables Ventidius to gain his point and bring Antony and Octavius together.

'Write me as one who loves his fellow men'
Leigh Hunt, *Abou Ben Adhem* (1838)

This brief story poem relates that Abou awoke one night to see an angel busily writing in a golden book the names of those who loved the Lord. Abou's name was not among these, so he good-humouredly asked to be put down as a lover of his fellow men. The next night the angel appeared again, and this time 'Ben Adhem's name led all the rest'. The moral of the tale is that good deeds are more important than professions of faith.

> *'The writer, when he sits down to commence his novel,*
> *should do so, not because he has to tell a story, but because*
> *he has a story to tell'*
> Anthony Trollope, *An Autobiography*, ch. 12 (1883)

Trollope is giving a few rules for novelists in this chapter of his posthumous autobiography. Although he himself sometimes wrote novels because he had to, he nevertheless tried to have a story to tell. The secret, in his view, was to live with the fictitious characters he was creating. 'He must learn to hate them and to love them. He must argue with them, quarrel with them, forgive them, and even submit to them.' Just as people change with time, so must the characters in a novel.

> *'Years steal fire from the mind'*
> Lord Byron, *Childe Harold's Pilgrimage*, III, viii (1816)

The expression would seem to be that of an elderly man looking back in tranquillity upon the fervour of his youth. In fact, however, Byron at the age of twenty-eight is regarding himself as he was no more than four years before. In 1812 he had published the first two cantos of *Childe Harold* with immense success. It was followed by some lively personal activities, which included real or supposed affairs with various women (among them the reckless Lady Caroline Lamb), marriage with Anne Milbanke, the birth of a daughter, legal separation from his wife, and a reputed affair with his half-sister. Society was scandalized, and Byron exiled himself.

> *'Ye may break the body, but ye cannot break the spirit'*
> John Galsworthy, *Strife*, Act III (1909)

David Roberts, the passionately intense leader of the strike at the Trenartha Tin Plate Works, is addressing the equally stubborn Chairman, Mr Anthony. However, he discovers that events have overtaken him. The men have voted to abandon the strike, while the company directors have just over-thrown their dominating chairman and agreed to a compromise. Ironically, the compromise which was reached in this very powerful drama is precisely that which was proposed by a union official and the company secretary before the strike began. The intransigence of Roberts and Anthony has achieved nothing.

> *'Yes, I remember Adlestrop'*
> Edward Thomas, *Adlestrop* (1915)

Few people would have heard of Adlestrop but for Thomas's poem. The village lies close to Stow on the Wold in the Cotswolds. A train in which Thomas was travelling stopped at Adlestrop station. No one got in or out, and the casual peace of the place seemed to him symbolic of the eternal peace of the countryside. He recorded it for ever in a short lyric which has wonderfully captured, in easy, natural language, the atmosphere of a quiet country station on a calm summer's day. The station, alas, is now closed, though the sign bearing the name was rescued and placed in a bus shelter.

'Yet men will murder upon holy days'
John Keats, *The Eve of St Agnes* (1819)

There was a legend in medieval times that on St Agnes's Eve (20 January) a girl would dream vividly of her lover if she went supperless to bed. Madeline, lovely and innocent, has carried out this simple rite. Meanwhile the eager young lover himself has ventured into her castle, despite the enmity between his family and Madeline's. The girl's ancient serving-woman, Angela, warns him that the bloodthirsty male members of the family will kill him if they find him, even though it is a saint's day. No doubt they would have done, but he makes his way safely to Madeline's room, making her dream come true; and they then elope together.

'Yet portion of that unknown plain
Will Hodge for ever be'
Thomas Hardy, *Drummer Hodge* (1901)

The poem is concerned with the fate of a young country lad killed in the Boer War. He was buried without a coffin in a rough grave on a little hill. Hardy muses on the strangeness of the fact that the intensely English lad, who knew nothing of the country he was fighting in, will henceforth, in the nourishment he gives to the tree beneath which he is buried, become part of an alien landscape. The theme is almost the opposite of Rupert Brooke's later *The Soldier* (1915).

'You are no better than you should be'
Beaumont and Fletcher, *The Coxcomb*, IV, i (1647)

The illogical sentence usually has a sexual implication, but here the suspected vice appears to be picking pockets rather than harlotry. Viola had run from home from an unkind father with all her jewellery, but was robbed by rogues. Two milkmaids find her and take her to their mistress to seek work. The good but sharp-tongued woman looks at Viola's hands and knows at once that she is no working-girl. For reasons that are perhaps clearer to her than to us, she at once assumes that Viola is 'no better than she should be'.

'You can't make people good by Act of Parliament'
Oscar Wilde, *A Woman of No Importance*, Act I (1893)

The comment is made by Lord Illingworth, and has been repeated a good many times by a good many people. Usually the thought is uttered regretfully. Lord Illingworth, however, had a reputation for cynical wit – like Wilde himself, on whom the character was based – and his observations were therefore apt to run counter to popular opinion. He is here expressing satisfaction that goodness cannot be achieved by law, for goodness is allied to earnestness and then 'the human being becomes a bore'.

> *'You don't suppose any serious-minded person imagines a revolution is going to bring liberty, do you?'*
> Aldous Huxley, *Antic Hay*, ch. 3 (1923)

Mr Bojanus's eccentric reason for favouring revolution was that it would make a change. 'I was always one for change and a little excitement.' He is a tailor with a certain resentment towards the classy customers he obsequiously serves. But he is realistic enough to doubt whether the cause of liberty is ever advanced by any political movement, and he cites the French Revolution, the Reform Bill, the Franchise Acts, and Votes for Women – more and more political liberty, without meaningful result.

> *'You know my method. It is founded upon the observation of trifles'*
> A. Conan Doyle, *The Adventures of Sherlock Holmes* (1892)

This observation (from *The Boscombe Valley Mystery*) typifies the most famous of all fictional detectives. The character was based on Dr Joseph Bell (1837–1911), under whom Doyle studied medicine, and who seems to have had the gift of making astute deductions from simple facts. In this story Holmes deduced the identity of the murderer from a few footprints and some cigar ash, finding him to be a tall, left-handed man who limped with the right foot, wore thick-soled shooting-boots, smoked Indian cigars, and carried a blunt penknife.

> *'You may scold a carpenter who has made you a bad table, though you cannot make a table'*
> Samuel Johnson, in Boswell's *Life of Johnson* (1791)

Johnson is arguing the right of a critic to condemn a play even though he cannot write one himself. On the general principle the great man was undoubtedly correct, though the particular instance invites less certainty. Boswell and two others were combining to write a pamphlet against a recent tragedy, *Elvira* (1763) by David Mallet. To launch a special attack on it seems unduly harsh. *Elvira* was far from the worst of its psuedo-classical type. Moreover, it had been made the victim of a totally unjustified demonstration by an irresponsible mob incensed because Garrick had raised prices to an economic level.

> *'You must wake and call me early, call me early, mother dear'*
> Alfred Tennyson, *The May Queen* (1832)

In the first poem of this trilogy a young girl, carefree and light-hearted, is eagerly waiting for the morrow, when the old rural Mayday ceremonies will be carried out, with herself as Queen of the May, crowned with flowers. The second poem, *New Year's Eve*, faintly echoes the first but on a pathetic note: 'If you're waking, call me early.' But now the girl is seriously ill, hoping just to live to see the first flowers of Spring. *Conclusion* (added 1842) finds her still alive but completely resigned to the peace of death, when 'the wicked cease from troubling and the weary are at rest' – a sentiment which Tennyson borrowed from the Bible (Job, iii, 17).

'You're a better man than I am, Gunga Din'
Rudyard Kipling, *Barrack-Room Ballads* (1892)

Gunga Din is a Hindu water-bearer attached to a British regiment in India, and notable for his fearless devotion to duty. The narrator of the poem tells how when he himself was wounded, Gunga Din first brought him a drink and then carried him to safety. Immediately afterwards the Indian was shot dead. The narrator fancifully pictures the gallant water-bearer carrying drinks 'to poor damned souls' in Hell. The poem concludes with the well-known quoted sentence.

'You're about to become my gateway to eternal rest'
Christopher Fry, *The Lady's Not for Burning*, Act I (1949)

Thomas Mendip, discharged from the army after seven years of warfare, returns to England sickened with disgust of life. He makes his way to the local Mayor's office, very slightly drunk, demanding to be hanged. When the Mayor appears, Thomas addresses him as the gateway through which he will reach everlasting peace. The Mayor indignantly refuses his request for hanging. 'It's a most immodest suggestion!' Thomas himself finally withdraws the plea when he falls in love with a girl who is being pursued as a witch by the mob. This stylish if wordy verse-comedy is set in the year 1400.

'Your muse has hitherto been independent – do not put her into harness'
Duchess of Buccleuch, *Letter to Walter Scott* (1813)

Scott had been offered the title of Poet Laureate and had asked the Duchess's opinion. She was strongly against acceptance, and believed it would injure his reputation. No doubt she had a point, especially as all the preceding Poets Laureate, after Dryden, had been notable only for their insignificance as poets. There was no kudos to be gained from joining them. Moreover, Scott was just beginning to turn his attention from poetry to novel-writing. He recommended Robert Southey for the Laureateship, and thenceforth the post achieved literary respectability. Wordsworth and Tennyson followed Southey, and Bridges, Masefield, and Betjeman have covered most of this century.

'Youth on the prow, and Pleasure at the helm'
Thomas Gray, *The Bard* (1758)

A Welsh tradition held that Edward I, in conquering Wales, had all the existing bards hanged, so that they could not stir up trouble with provocative songs. Gray, a gentle soul, felt that this was not the right way to treat poets, and in this ode he portrays an old bard who had escaped the slaughter singing a curse against Edward and his successors. In the quoted line he is dealing with the early magnificence of Richard II, in order to contrast it with his miserable death. Richard's youthful kingship is symbolically presented as a 'gilded vessel', ignorant of the 'sweeping whirlwind' awaiting it.

Author Index

Keyword Index